S.S. GREAT BRITAIN
THE MODEL SHIP

WILLIAM MOWLL

S.S. GREAT BRITAIN

THE MODEL SHIP

This book is published and distributed
in the United States by the
NAVAL INSTITUTE PRESS
Annapolis, Maryland 21402

Dedicated to the memory of my father,
WILFRED RUTLEY MOWLL 1910–1979
who shared with me his love of ships and
steam power, and to my wife and family,
Sue, Benjamin and Joshua, who have had
to live with the consequences ever since.

"I have been making half a dozen boats lately,
till I've worn my hands to pieces".
Isambard Kingdom Brunel, as a schoolboy
at Hove. (L.T.C. Rolt).

Model and Allied Publications
Argus Books Ltd
14 St James Road
Watford, Herts, England

© Argus Books Ltd 1982
© William Mowll 1982

ISBN 0 85242 767 0

First published 1982

Printed and bound by
Morrison & Gibb Ltd, London and Edinburgh
Origination by Tenreck Ltd

Composition in Photina by
Filmtype Services Ltd.
Scarborough, North Yorkshire

Designed by Kaye Bellman

FOREWORD

The whole of shipbuilding can be divided into pre-metal and metal ships and into the pre-mechanically propelled and mechanically propelled eras. The climactic point at which the changes took place and shipping history branched into modern ships occurred around 1840. It is a stroke of almost incredible good fortune that the only really early metal and screw propelled ship that has survived is the most important of them all, the S.S. *Great Britian.* Six or more generations of her descendants have come and gone and she is still with us.

The ship has always exercised a fascination on the minds of men, not only when built as the world's largest ship, but even now when she is no larger than an ordinary Cross-Channel ferry. This fascination led to many people banding together to mount a salvage operation and to bring the ship back from the Falkland Islands to her birthplace to restore her and show her for what she was, an achievement par excellence of the early Victorians. The salvage from a far off and isolated grave and the subsequent restoration are themselves both romantic and one of the most ambitious of such efforts ever undertaken.

The author of this book, The Reverend William Mowll, has succumbed to the fascination of the *Great Britain,* becoming one of many over the last 140 years. He has done the old ship proud. We who are restoring her, one might say modelling at 1:1 scale, share his enthusiasm and admire the splendid model he has constructed on 1:48 scale and described so entertainingly.

Throughout its pages one is repeatedly impressed by William Mowll's sheer zest both for ship modelling and for the *Great Britain.* In this spirit and in his confidence of purpose he is in good company with Brunel and his Building Committee who created this great ship, and with those who salved and are now restoring the ship.

By the end of this decade, the *Great Britain* should look externally and, to a considerable extent internally, just as she did when completed in December, 1844. The ship and the models of her will serve as a reminder, then, to coming generations of the days when Britain gave to the world steam, screw propelled, metal ships to parallel her gift of railways on land.

Ewan Corlett

ACKNOWLEDGEMENTS

The invaluable help given to me by:

The S.S. Great Britain Project Committee
Richard Goold-Adams C.B.E., Chairman of the Project.
Ewan C. B. Corlett, M.A., Ph.D., F.Eng., F.R.I.N.A., F.I. Mar.E., Hon. Naval Architect of the Project.
Commander Joe Blake, Project Director.
Commander James D. Richard, M.A., C.Eng., M.I.Mech. E., M.Inst.P.I., 'Replica' Engine Committee.

I owe various debts of gratitude to the following people, who have been loosely bracketed into the different skills which they have taught me:

ART
Mary Gifford Meades   Canterbury
Jillian McDougall   Edinburgh
George Maynard   Canterbury
Elizabeth Fox   London

WOODWORK
David Pratt (the late)   Ireland
Alan Mileson   Taunton
Tadeusz Filip   Ashford, Kent
Brian Higenbotham   Canterbury
Leonard Dickson   Salisbury
Roger Dawson   Newton-le-Willows
Barry Kirby   Bromsgrove

METALWORK
Geoffrey Sheppard   Bristol
Bill Priest   Worcester

PHOTOGRAPHY
John Cundell   Leighton Buzzard
John Johnston   Worcester

MODEL SHIPBUILDING
Tony Lench   Bossingham, Kent
Michael Pope   Patrixbourne, Kent
Mike Taylor   London

AUTHORSHIP
Bernard C. Cooper   Guild of Master Craftsmen
John Cundell   Editor, 'Model Boats', Hemel Hempstead
John Bowen   Editor, 'Model Shipwright', London

My grateful thanks to Phyllis Hislop for making the full wardrobe of miniature sails with such meticulous care, enabling this ship to sail as well as steam.

A final debt of gratitude to Helen Carslake for her untiring work in the correction, typing and indexing of the manuscript against the background of being a mother of four fine children.

ACKNOWLEDGEMENTS

The School of Technical Illustration, Bournemouth and Poole College of Art and Design, Dorset.

Full colour illustrations for display in the Museum alongside the ship at Bristol are indicated by an asterisk (*). All have been specially drawn for this book under the direction and design of Senior Lecturers Michael E. Leek, MISTC, MSAI and Stanley Paine, ARCA.

T. L. Alner	Ship's Capstan.	pp. 129	line ill.
,,	Model Capstan.	pp. 129	line ill.
Michael Barton &			
K. MacStocker	1845 Profile.	pp. 146	line ill.
,,	1846 Profile.	pp. 147	line ill.
,,	1852 Profile.	pp. 153	line ill.
,,	1857 Profile.	pp. 158	line ill.
,,	1882 Profile.	pp. 159	line ill.
Stephen M. Carter	1845 Ship's Engines.	pp. 37	colour ill.
Jeremy C. Cave, ASAI	Body Plan.	pp. 27	line ill.
,,	Lines Plan.	pp. 26	line ill.
,,	The Ship at the Falkland Islands.	pp. 136	wash drwg.
,,	The Crack.	pp. 120	wash drwg.
,,	The Ship being brought back home.	pp. 136	wash drwg.
Keith Clayson	The Ship's Windlass.	pp. 101	line ill.
,,	The 'Compressor Stoppers'.	pp. 103	line ill.
,, after			
Peter J. Jarvis,			
MISTC, MSAI	Model Power Plant.	pp. 53	line ill.
David Ditcher &			
Joan-Marie Abley	1845 Longitudinal Elevation.*	pp. 112-113	colour ill.
Timothy Davis	1845 Profile.*	pp. 40	colour ill.
Tanya Dixon	Schematic of Model Power Plant.	pp. 57	colour ill.
,,	Schematic of Model Steam Engine	pp. 49	colour ill.
Paul Glaister	The Ship's Wheel.	pp. 96	line ill.
,, after			
Michael Harvey,			
FSDC, MSIAD	Title Lettering.		
Lynn Gregory	Ship's Profile on End Papers.		line ill.
,,	Ship's Decoration.	pp. 45	colour ill.
,,	1846 Profile.	pp. 41	colour ill.
Ian Henley	Crew's Companionway.	pp. 92	line ill.
,,	Forward Passenger Companionway.	pp. 91	line ill.
Ian Henley	Square Skylight.	pp. 93	line ill.
,,	Circular Skylight.	pp. 92	line ill.
Peter J. Jarvis,			
MISTC, MSAI	Model Power Plant.	pp. 56	colour ill.
Peter Jarvis	19th Century Ropemaking	pp. 141	line ill.
Kevin P. Jones	Ship's Funnel and Bridge.	pp. 87	line ill.
,,	Engine Room Skylight.	pp. 84	line ill.
,,	Aft Companionway.	pp. 90	line ill.
,,	Aft Companionway. Perspective.	pp. 90	line ill.
Anita Lawrence	Falkland Islands Profile, 1970.*	pp. 117	colour ill.
Gillian M. Lever	Passengers of the 1840's.	pp. 105	colour ill.
D. Light	Map of Bristol	pp. 29	line ill.
,,	The Dock where the Ship was built.	pp. 107	line ill.
Steven Mace	Six-bladed Propeller.	pp. 66	line ill.
,,	Six-bladed Propeller Perspective.	pp. 67	line ill.
Steven Mace	Four-bladed Propeller.	pp. 67	line ill.
,,	Four-bladed Propeller Pers.	pp. 67	line ill.
S. R. Martin	The Ship's Steering Gear.	pp. 73	line ill.
Timothy A. Maunder	The Ship's Binnacle.	pp. 100	line ill.
,,	The Ship's Pumps.	pp. 103	line ill.
Stefano Mazzeo	Trotman Anchor.	pp. 97	line ill.
Stephen Palfrey	Weather Deck.*	pp. 104	colour ill.
,,	1st Class Dining Saloon.*	pp. 104	colour ill.
,,	Crew Brawling.	pp. 105	colour ill.
Medwyn Parry	The Ship's sails	pp. 140	line ill.
Nick Phillips, BEd	1846 General. Arrangement Plan.	pp. 151	line ill.
,,	1846 Perspective.	pp. 152	line ill.
A. C. Ridgway	Ship Model Construction I.	pp. 30	line ill.
,,	Ship Model Construction II.	pp. 31	line ill.
Paul Rodgers	The Iron Lifeboats.	pp. 64	line ill.
,,	Model Lifeboat Construction.	pp. 62	line ill.
Gavin A. Taylor	The 1845 Ship's Boiler.	pp. 82	line ill.
,,	Rigging Details I.	pp. 145	line ill.
,,	Rigging Details II.	pp. 150	line ill.
John A. Unwin &			
Peter J. Jarvis	The Ship's Construction.	pp. 33	colour ill.
Martin Wale	Model Ropemaking Machine	pp. 141	line ill.

CONTENTS

Contents Continued

INTRODUCTION

There is no doubt that the S.S. *Great Britain* is a unique ship. She represents the transition from sail to steam power, paddle to screw propulsion, and wood to iron for the structure and plating of the hull. Her various historical roles as a luxury liner, a stranded vessel on Dundrum Bay, an emigrant ship, a troopship, a cargo ship, a storage hulk and finally a crown wreck in the Falkland Islands, demonstrate her will to survive against all the odds. Her final triumphant return to the place of her birth in Bristol for restoration is a response to, and a recognition of, her importance, and a salute to her designer, Isambard Kingdom Brunel.

A number of books about her life and restoration have been written, and there are works describing the construction of other models, but with the exception of Nepean Longridge's classic treatise on the "*Victory*", a volume such as this, majoring on the model whilst interweaving the history and social comment surrounding the vessel is, if not unique, certainly not an everyday occurrence.

The author first came to my notice in 1977 when he submitted an article to Model Boats magazine describing the construction of the paddle steamer, "*Sirius*", of transatlantic fame. His obsession with this fascinating period of hybrid ship development led to a number of ideas for his next project, which after long deliberation, culminated in "S.S. *Great Britain*".

Such a decision cannot be taken lightly. At the scale of one quarter of an inch to the foot, and the early consideration to produce a working model, steam powered and under radio control, he was committing at least three years valuable leisure time to a project where turning back the clock would be impossible.

My suggestion to the author that we should follow the construction through by means of a monthly series of articles, profusely illustrated, met with an enthusiastic response. The series started in early 1979 and ran until mid 1981, during which period overwhelming praise was received from readers.

The author's humorous, sometimes even mischievous style, belies his almost hypnotic method of imparting a well researched knowledge of practical ship modelling. Although a relative newcomer, his thorough and inquisitive approach leads him to adopt, or if necessary, to adapt existing techniques and where these are not readily available, to develop his own.

The modeller will find a wealth of practical information throughout this book, all well illustrated, in many cases with step by step photographs: for example, thermoplastic moulding, etching, embossing, engraving, sandcasting, silver soldering, boilermaking and so forth.

Together with the excellent drawings by the Bournemouth and Poole College of Art's Technical Illustration School, this book must be as unique as its subject: "S.S. *Great Britain* – The Model Ship".

I look forward to the author's next project with considerable interest, excitement and enthusiasm.

John Cundell,
Editor, Model Boats

PREFACE

Why Scale Model Ships?

The small carved and painted ship, found in the pyramid tomb of the boy pharaoh, Tutenkhamun, was placed there by his relatives so that his soul would have a vehicle in which to travel from his pyramid grave on the long and difficult journey to immortality.

A strange introduction perhaps, to a book on building a miniature working scale model of an historic Victorian liner, but it may indicate some kind of answer as to why someone should spend a sizeable amount of time making a replica of a ship, which, when it is finished, will be of no practical use. In a life which is full of untied ends and intangibles, I find it increasingly necessary to have an enthusiasm over which I can exercise some kind of authority and control. That there is an 'end product' which is neat and tidy and finally finished, is important in itself. That it should also provide a fourth dimension, acting as a vehicle which allows me to journey from reality into fantasy, is an added bonus. Like Tutenkhamun, I need the vehicle to go on the trip.

As far as I can tell, in no other hobby does history rub shoulders so closely with a basic knowledge of plumbing, electronics, sewing, chemistry, ropemaking, physics, engineering, techniques of carving, moulding and casting, coupled with plain old-fashioned whittling of wood. I make no pretence to being an expert in any of these fields, but in order to produce a working scale model ship, with live steam propulsion, each of the above skills has to be fairly and squarely faced.

For me, ship-modelling is finely balanced between Art and Science. The counterpoise is often difficult to keep, because there is a constant battle being fought within the eternal triangle of correct scale, artistic consideration and working practicality. Perhaps a simple illustration of this is with working doors. Everyone likes to see that doors will open and close. In fact, it is important that they should, as it gives depth to the model and creates the illusion that there are people aboard. This requires the making of hinges which are tough enough to withstand the relatively clumsy movement of a hand a thousand times its size and yet small enough not to look absurdly out of scale. Similar problems and issues will recur time and time again.

Scale modellers are in the illusion business. In the final analysis therefore, mood and atmosphere must take precedence over measurement and mathematics. A ship-model fails if it gives no hint of the age in which the prototype was launched and no smell of the sea. The hope is always that the replica will have the ability to convince the onlooker by its inherent authenticity and to deliver, in the most direct way possible, its own secret message to the viewer's mind.

William Mowll

HISTORIC BEGINNINGS 1818

Smoke signals from the New World.
The P.S. Savannah.

The very first transatlantic steamship was built in 1818 by Messrs. Crocker and Fickett, in the American state of Georgia and named after her home port of Savannah. Life began innocently enough for this three masted windjammer, on the stocks of the local shipyard, but was destined for a conversion which would ultimately change the face of the world's shipping forever.

Early in the year of 1818, Captain Moses Rogers was scouting around for the embryo shipping company of Messrs. Scarborough and Isaacs, looking for a ship which would be strong enough and suitably proportioned to house a 90 nhp single cylinder steam engine in conjunction with a pair of handsome copper boilers. The idea in the mind of the two entrepreneurs, Scarborough and Isaacs, was that the selected vessel could be suitably converted to demonstrate to Europe, the wonder and effectiveness of auxiliary steam propulsion.

The shipyard's "elegant" solution to this proposal resulted in perhaps the most comical looking vessel in maritime history. Her elbow-jointed funnel and collapsible, canvas paddlewheels provided an easy target for those who wanted a good belly-laugh at the whole idea of transatlantic travel by steamboat, and the wonder is that she was ever promoted as a luxury vessel at all, in the midst of a financial depression which had hit America in the early part of the last century.

At the time when "Francis Fickett's Steam Coffin" was launched, the public acceptance was that no steamboat could manage to make the crossing from the New World to the Old World, without the use of sails for the greater part of the journey.

The 110 ft. *Savannah* did nothing to disprove this, nor anything to dislodge the old saying that it would take a coalmine to propel a ship by steam alone across so great a distance. Even I.K. Brunel's father, Sir Marc, believed firmly that steam power was unsuitable for ocean navigation despite his close involvement with the development of the marine engine and automatic stoking apparatus. It was the pure genius of his son, Isambard, who would finally dispose of the old myth, in the design and construction of his first ship, the P.S. *Great Western*, nineteen years after the maiden voyage of the *Savannah*.

There was nothing wrong with the concept of converting the strongly constructed sailing vessel to auxiliary steam power. The *Savannah* was carvel built, with a raked, curved stem and a plain square transom. She was a sturdily built vessel which her owners had every reason to think would bring them favourable publicity for being the trailblazers of transatlantic steam. Luckily for the newly formed Savannah Ship Company, President Monroe happened to be on tour in the Southern States at the time of the steaming trials, and the opportunity for a prestigious visit was seized upon by the infant Company. The President and the President's men were impressed by their short trip, and foresaw certain military possibilities, which was hardly surprising, as President Monroe had arrived in the company of two judges and five generals.

Despite the national and local publicity this gave to the pioneer steamship, the advertised sailing date approached

The P. S. Savannah 1818. The first transatlantic steamboat. (Courtesy of the Science Museum, London).

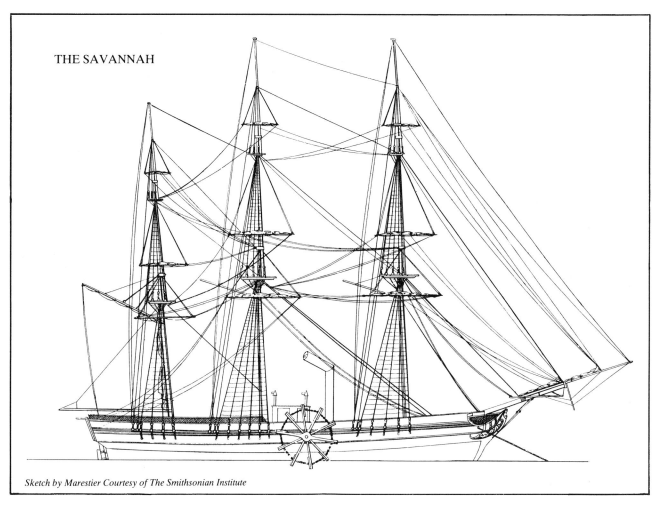

THE SAVANNAH

Sketch by Marestier Courtesy of The Smithsonian Institute

with an ominously thin enquiry list from prospective travellers. Two days after they should have departed, Captain Rogers set sail for England in ballast alone, with 75 tons of coal and 25 bundles of cordwood aboard, to supply the necessary energy for firing up the Morristown engine made by Stephen Vial of New Jersey. None of the advertisements detailing the elegant furnishings in the two staterooms, or the promise of oriental carpets and the well appointed 32 berths available on the ship, had brought forth a single soul for this historic voyage.

If the Americans lacked a certain interest in boarding the vessel, the Irish did not. The *Savannah* had put to sea on May 24th 1819, and was sighted off the West Coast of Ireland some 24 days later. To the astonishment of the coastguard at Cape Clear, they saw a ship moving at approximately 6 knots under bare poles with a blazing inferno amidships. Quite properly, they telegraphed the naval squadron in the Cove of Cork, and the revenue cutter *Kite* with Lt. John Bowie in command, hurried to her assistance, to save such souls as might be left alive. To his certain dismay, Lt. Bowie found that he could not catch up with the fiery little monster and, this time to the amazement of the Yankee captain, the *Kite* started to fire cannon shot across the *Savannah's* bows, in the name of King George. Captain Moses Rogers gave orders for the engines to be shut off and his rescuers to be welcomed aboard. No doubt laughing from his socks to his sleeves he proudly showed off his engine room and boilers and the

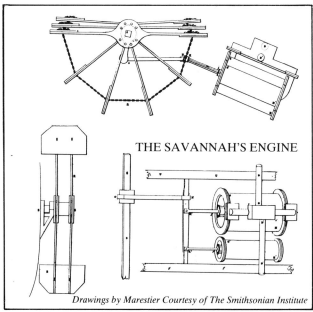

THE SAVANNAH'S ENGINE

Drawings by Marestier Courtesy of The Smithsonian Institute

way in which the swivelling elbow-jointed funnel improved the draught up the riveted flues.

The ship's arrival in the Mersey on June 20th met with a mixed response. Some observers were obviously impressed by her ability to move without sails, whilst others felt that the *Savannah's* Atlantic crossing was "the most

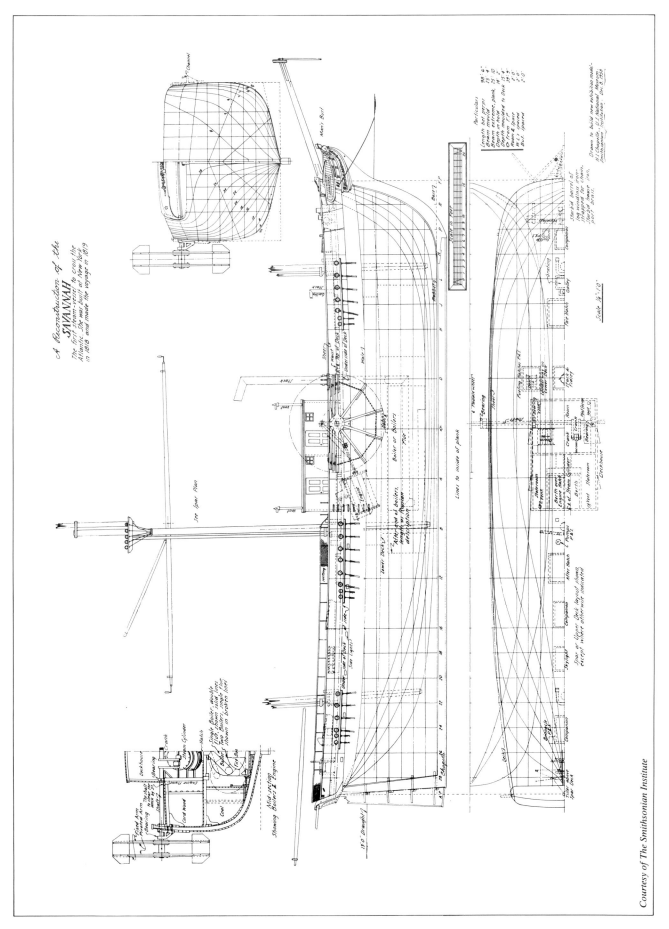

(Above) Author's model of the P. S. Sirius, nearing completion in 1977 as a fully working steam powered model. (Right) Overhead shot of the foc's'le.

dangerous thing which has occurred in the history of British Shipping.''

The most important visitor to the docked ship, from an historical point of view, was an ex-patriot American called Junius Smith. He was a barrister who was later to become a successful businessman, with a rightful place in the honours list of the transatlantic steam story. Had *he* been offered a trip in the *Savannah*, I have no doubt that he would have relished the experience, such was his dislike of the time wasted by sailing vessels on the Atlantic run. He yearned for the day when a regular and reliable steam-packet service would set sail and arrive on time, and 19 years after his very thorough inspection of the *Savannah*, he was responsible for setting up his own steam-ship company called the British and American Steam Navigation Co., which successfully sponsored the run made by the P.S. *Sirius* in 1838 against the mighty *Great Western*, where the story of the transatlantic race really begins.

The future of the *Savannah* was blighted by her inability to find a buyer with ready cash, which was what Capt. Rogers had in mind. The King of Norway and Sweden wanted to swop her for some iron and hemp and the Czar of Russia wanted to keep her for patrolling the Black Sea with an option on the Baltic, but no one offered to purchase her for money. After this European flirtation was over, and, having seen that the continental grass was no greener than the plains of Georgia, Capt. Rogers headed for home, the company having lost a total of 30 thousand

(Top) Detail of the P. S. Sirius' bows. Note the figure head of the dog clutching the star which gave the vessel its name. (Above) The engine room using Wilesco horizontal mill engine.

dollars, proving that transatlantic steam navigation was indeed possible, but for the moment at least, premature.

The *P.S. Sirius*

For almost twenty years, nothing very much happened in terms of steamships crossing the Atlantic, despite the enormous strides made with railways in Britain and the increased engineering skill which this employed.

Until 1834, the development of the marine steam engine was stunted by the problem of boilers having to use salt water which hopelessly clogged them. No continuous steaming was therefore possible until the surface condenser was patented by an engineer named Sam Hall, from Nottinghamshire. This ingenious device recycled the steam, making a continuous, economic circuit by condensation, allowing ships to travel as far as their coal would take them.

The scene was therefore poised for a regular Atlantic service which could for the first time, guarantee a passage to travellers between Europe and America, regardless of the weather.

Rising to this challenge, two shipping companies were formed almost simultaneously. The Great Western Steamship Co. and the British & American Steam Navigation Co. of London, and these two rivals were at the focus of the transatlantic race.

The Great Western Steamship Co. had as their champion Isambard K. Brunel, the enormously prestigious engineer whose brainchild, the P.S. *Great Western*, was nearing structural completion in Bristol, by August 1837. She would soon set sail for London where her engines would be fitted and her internal decoration completed.

In the rival offices of the British & American Steamship Co. There was no such smooth plan in operation. The Director, Junius Smith, had fallen victim to a serious delay with the delivery of their ship, The *Royal Victoria*, and it was now obvious that they would have to change their plans.

Realizing that they needed some sort of a dog to run in the race, Junius Smith and his fellow directors cast round for an alternative ship, which might be no more than a flea bite for their rivals, but would at least give their infant company some publicity in the anticipated glory of the *Great Western*'s arrival in New York.

And "dog" it was they found – a little mongrel ship called the *Sirius*, which had as a figurehead a dog holding a star, from whence the ship derived its name. Commissioned in August of 1837, this functional little schooner had been designed for coastal work only, carrying out the normal duties of a steam packet ship. She was built from wood by a Scottish firm, Robert Menzies & Sons, and fitted with side lever engines of 320nhp. Her length was 178.4ft. and she had a top speed of 9 knots.

Hasty changes had to be made for her conversion to long-distance travel. As she consumed about 24 tons of coal a day, increased coal bunkering was needed to accommodate space for 450 tons. Orders were also given to spruce her up and modify her paddle boxes to a round, rather than a rectangular, shape. These orders account for her rather smart appearance, although she always had "rakishly handsome lines" and she was said to be "comely in her proportions".

Meanwhile, in Bristol, the *Great Western* was being floated out before a crowd of 50,000 people, and taken under sail to Brunswick Wharf, in London's dockland to have her engines fitted and the specialised craft work carried out to her saloon, which was a magnificent 71ft. × 21ft. in the neo-gothic style, the like of which had never been seen before aboard a ship. It was such a prestigious undertaking, that the normally grumpy Duke of Wellington deigned to visit the wharf, and to everyone's surprise, gave it his unqualified approval and signed his name in the cabin's guest album.

The alterations to the *Sirius* were in a much lower key, but were finished rather more quickly than her rival's. On March 28th, 1838, the two ships were, quite by chance, steaming down the Thames, abreast of one another, and the inevitable race down-river developed. The *Great Western* was officially out on a cruise to impress yet more dignitaries, whilst the *Sirius* was en route for Cork, where she would fill to capacity with coal and take on 40 passengers. By the time the *Great Western* had reached Gravesend, which is at the mouth of the Thames, the *Sirius*, at full steam ahead and in great earnest, had outdistanced her rival – an omen for the future Atlantic contest.

Three days later, still in the waters of the Thames, disaster struck the *Great Western* and Brunel nearly lost his life in a nasty outbreak of fire. It was a typical piece of teething trouble which nobody would have guessed could happen. The engineers had fixed the insulation round the boilers with red lead paint. When the boilers' temperature reached their peak, oil-gas created spontaneous combustion, which set the ship alight. This tiny unforeseen detail cost Brunel the Atlantic honours and allowed the *Sirius* to assume pride of place by 12 hours. It also caused 50 nervous passengers to cancel their bookings on the maiden voyage.

(The man who rescued Brunel was Capt. Christopher Claxton RN, whose name will recur with great regularity throughout this book. It is noticeable that whenever Brunel needed practical help or advice, it was Claxton to whom he turned.)

Neither ship had an easy crossing. The weather was foul and paddle ships behave badly in high seas, with difficulty of steering doubled by problems of coal haulage. Nearly two-thirds of the total burden of the *Sirius* was accounted for by coal. She ended up with only 15 tons to spare, because of the extra consumption she had used up through the stormy headwinds. It is doubtful whether she could have bunkered any more coal, even if the atrocious weather had been anticipated, and there was an ugly rumour that spars and furniture were burnt in the furnaces, shortly before her arrival, such was the desperate shortage of fuel.

There was a crew of 35 officers and men on board the *Sirius*, captained by Lt. Richard Roberts, RN, a man of determination and resolve. After a week in mountainous seas, there was an air of doubt, some say mutiny, about the wisdom of the whole venture. One report, which is probably envious slander, says that Lt. Roberts threatened members of his crew with a loaded revolver in his resolution to make the crossing. He was certainly determined, and had to overcome not only "a dangerous sea, and a bounteous fall of snow", but also the doubts of those who sailed with him in a steamship of just over 178ft.

The specially designed *Great Western* was also having problems. Both ships had paddle floats which came loose. The *Great Western*'s figurehead of Neptune lost his golden trident, one day out of Bristol. There was awful seasickness on board. The stokers were demanding double time for hauling coal from either end of the ship. Above the deck, the fore-topmast was swept away in a gale. Nine days out, it became difficult to coax the weary stokers to maintain steam, and the practicalities of transatlantic steam navigation both above and below decks were

becoming all too obvious. Less than a week later, all this could be forgotten with the stunning record of the crossing made by the *Great Western*, in 15 days and 5 hours.

It was, however, the *Sirius* which was the first ship to be sighted at 8.00 p.m. on April 22nd, 1838. She was exhausted but triumphant. The New York Port Authorities were caught unawares, and the first ship to reach her was a news schooner (the *Eclipse*) chartered by the

(Below) View across the paddle boxes of the P. S. Sirius. *(Bottom) Rigging detail of the mainmast.*

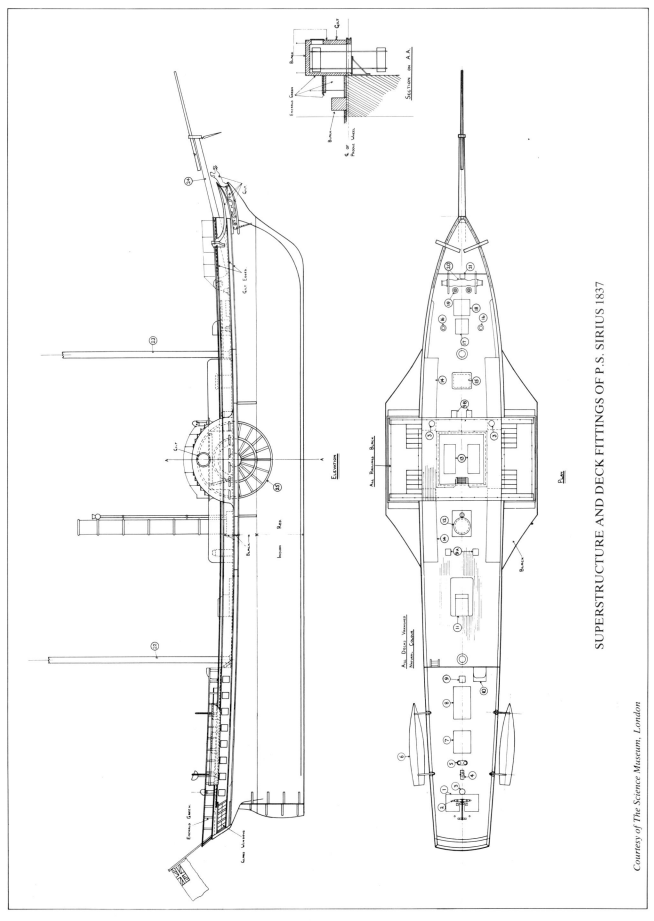

Courtesy of The Science Museum, London

SUPERSTRUCTURE AND DECK FITTINGS OF P.S. SIRIUS 1837

SECTION ON A A.

ELEVATION

PLAN

New York *Courier and Enquirer*, whose reporters boarded her as soon as she stopped engines. Captain Roberts waited for a pilot, but none came before the tide caused the ship's hull to rest gently on a mudbank in Sandy Hook Bay.

There she lay, like a basking alligator, until the following morning, when she staged her triumphal entry accompanied by a blaze of publicity. She stole the thunder of the *Great Western*, the hearts of the people of New York and for a brief 12 hours, wore the Atlantic Crown with mischievous pride,

The reception which the *Sirius* received in New York was phenomenal. All manner of extravagant language was used . . . "The broad Atlantic bridged at last. the annihilation of space and time." The celebrations on both steamers were enormous. There were speeches, brass bands, feasting and finally a banquet on Blackwell's Island for the commanders of both ships.

The people of New York spared nothing in their welcome of the new technology. This is all the more surprising in that it was a British victory in a field where American competition was hot. It shows a generosity which one might not have expected. The feeling was obviously genuine because, at the departure of the *Sirius* on May 1st, 1838, a salute of 17 guns was fired as a mark of respect, seldom or never paid to any merchant vessel before.

The future of the two vessels was very different. The *Great Western* continued to ply between New York and Bristol for eight years, crossing the Atlantic 64 times in all. Thereafter, she provided a further ten years' service to the Royal Mail between Southampton and the West Indies, until ultimately broken up in 1857.

On the return trip, the *Sirius* was nearly wrecked on one of the rocky Scilly Islands, but a clearing in the channel fog came soon enough for her to take avoiding action.

Lt. Roberts returned to a wholly personal triumph. He

The P. S. Great Western arriving in New York on the 23rd April 1838 having crossed the Atlantic in fifteen and a half days. (Copyright Hulton Picture Library).

was given the freedom of the city of Cork and a silver tea service valued at £200. He was also promised a presentation to her Majesty, Queen Victoria, at the next meeting of the Court.

The *Sirius* made one further trip to New York under her old captain, Stephen Mowle. She then, like Cinderella, resumed her intended career as a coaster, until on 16th June, 1847, en route from Glasgow to Cork, she lost her way in the fog and ran onto the rocky shores of Ballycotton Bay. More than 50 years later, deep sea divers, attracted by her legend and salvage possibilities, went to see what might be left. They found a number of relics, including her figurehead of the dog, holding the star between its front paws. This was sent to the Museum of Fisheries & Shipping, in Hull, England.

There was also a bigger salvage attempt in 1910, under a man named Henry Ensor, which revealed the cast iron hubs of the paddle wheels to be in excellent condition, and the insides of the cylinders to be "quite bright and slippy with tallow", in spite of 65 years' immersion in sea water, a tribute to the precise engineering of Thomas Wingate, whose firm in Glasgow had manufactured the heartbeat of this lovable hybrid ship.

Acknowledgement

I am indebted to John Malcom Brinnin, Professor of English at Boston University, for the resource of his magnificent social history of the North Atlantic entitled *The Sway of the Grand Saloon*. Published by MacMillan, ISBN 333 13612 8.

NEW PLANS

Why the S.S. *Great Britain?*

In 1975, I built a working steam model of the P.S. *Sirius*, (1837) and I became very absorbed by both the ship and its history as a transatlantic giantkiller.

I was swept along by the enthusiasm which the vessel had engendered on her arrival in New York.

PADDLE STEAMER SIRIUS—

"Nothing is talked of in New York but about this *Sirius*. She is the first steam vessel that has arrived here from England, and a glorious boat she is. Every merchant in New York went on board her yesterday. Lt. Roberts, RN, is the first man that ever navigated a steamship from Europe to America."

The *New York Courier & Enquirer*, April 23rd, 1838

Quite unfairly, just like the people of Manhattan, I fell in love with the *Sirius* and chose to build a model of her, with her ridiculously thin funnel and figurehead of the dog clutching the star from whence she derived her name. The logical step on the completion of this model, would have been to retire gracefully, but tickled by the success of this model, I started to entertain the idea of tackling the first screw propeller ship, the *Archimedes*, another handsome little topsail schooner, "saucy, rakish and sleek", a mere 107ft in length, with her masts raked at such a steep angle that they looked like porcupine needles.

Sir Thomas Guppy, the man in charge of building the S.S. *Great Britain*, confessed to being "wholly seduced by the performance of the *Archimedes*, seeing that screw propulsion was not only feasible, but inevitable". As a result of a series of trials in the mouth of the River Avon, and a trip to Liverpool, the Great Western Steamship Co. following a lengthy and historic report from Brunel, ordered Francis Humphreys to stop building his paddle engines for the *Great Britain*, and design screw engines instead. The young engineer died soon afterwards of brain fever.

It is still a source of amazement that this virtually untried feature of screw propulsion should be incorporated into this prestige ship, designed for paddles, the box frames of which were already installed by the timely visit of the *Archimedes* in May 1840.

Change of Plan

Not only were Brunel's plans changed by the *Archimedes* but so were mine. I found mayself seduced by the idea of making a 1:48 scale of the *Great Britain* and abandoned the cheeky little *Archimedes*, going instead for another Atlantic First, continuing my growing obsession for the hybrid period of shipping on the North Atlantic sea route. A chance screening on television of an appeal for more money to help with the restoration of this vessel in Bristol acted as the mental "click" that I was making the right choice. I was embarking on an exciting ship which would provide the trio of challenge, courage and beauty, combined with an extremely well documented history which included the Australian Goldrush, the Crimean War, shipwreck and finally rescue and restoration, in the place of her birth in Bristol.

Fig 1. Early Beginnings – The P. S. Sirius 1837. The author's first attempt at a Victorian transatlantic ship.

Fig 2. The lithograph above shows the Great Britain *in rough seas in 1846, following the refit where the mast abaft the funnel was removed. Her length from figure-head to taffrail is 322ft×51ft beam×16ft loaded draught. Displacement is 2984 tons. (Photograph by permission of the Science Museum). Fig 3. (Right) Photographed in October 1977, at Bristol in her original dock, S.S.G.B.'s restoration work makes slow but sure progress, with stepping of the mainmast under way.*

Practicalities

In the Science Museum, the models of the *Sirius* and the *Great Britain* are within a few yards of one another. The precious model which the Museum are lucky enough to possess was presented to them by Thomas Guppy, and at 1:48 scale, is impressively large. She is there shown with the original rig of six masts, progressively raked, and classically beautiful, with her uncluttered deck and tasteful decoration. Despite her undoubted appeal, she is no good to the "live steam" enthusiast, until one discovers that in her remarkable career and history she had as many rigs as she did major new roles as one of Britain's most interesting ships.

There are two lithographs, each dedicated to the proprietors of the Great Western Steamship Co., showing her in gale force winds. They were part of the extensive publicity advertising the new style of transatlantic travel. The original paintings are by the famous artist, Joseph Walter, and as such are very accurate. The first of these shows the original rig of six masts, and the later one depicting the vessel in exactly the same attitude, but in the refitted rig of 1846 with the mast immediately abaft the funnel removed. Thus shown, the ship immediately

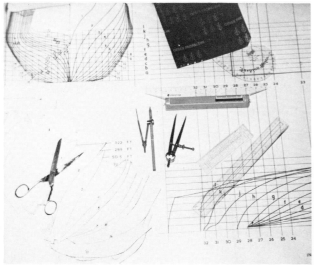

Fig 4. (Above) Just a brief idea of the depth of research work required before embarking on such a mammoth project as this. Fig 5. (Left) Note the use of squared graph paper under the scissors for frame templates and body plan.

becomes a practical proposition for live steam, in that the removed mast at 1:48 scale allows a gap of approximately 2ft into which a muscular steam unit can be fitted and operated.

Information

One of the factors which put me off building the *Archimedes* was a lack of information and the non-availability of any plans. Almost exactly the opposite is the case of the S.S.G.B. about which there is a plethora of hard, factual information. The Science Museum produce dye-line plans of their model and a good deal of back-up material as well; there are four books as well as an informative pamphlet on sale at "The S.S.G.B. Project", and undoubtedly the ace card in the pack is the totally authoritative work by Dr Ewan Corlett, the consultant naval architect for the restoration work now going on in Bristol. In his book, "The Iron Ship", every single process of ship-building in this 'new' material is covered along with a highly detailed narrative and exposition which, for the keenly interested, is like the sighting of land after a long voyage. The usefulness of this book, and a much valued correspondence with its author, who is himself a ship modeller, has urged me on and encouraged me no end, giving me the necessary impetus to undertake this, the largest model I have ever attempted.

Sets of dyeline prints are available at Bristol as is also the coloured wall chart by members of the Bournemouth and Poole College of Art's Technical Illustration School.

Time and Money

Modellers have a natural reluctance to talk about how long it will take and how much it will cost. The *Great Britain* cost £117,295. 6s. 7d., exclusive of the construction of the specially excavated dockyard, which itself cost £53,000. As for the ship, 73% of this was accounted for by the hull, and as late as 1842, the public still did not know "how this prodigious floating mass" was to be propelled.

At the outset of a major model, some kind of schedule

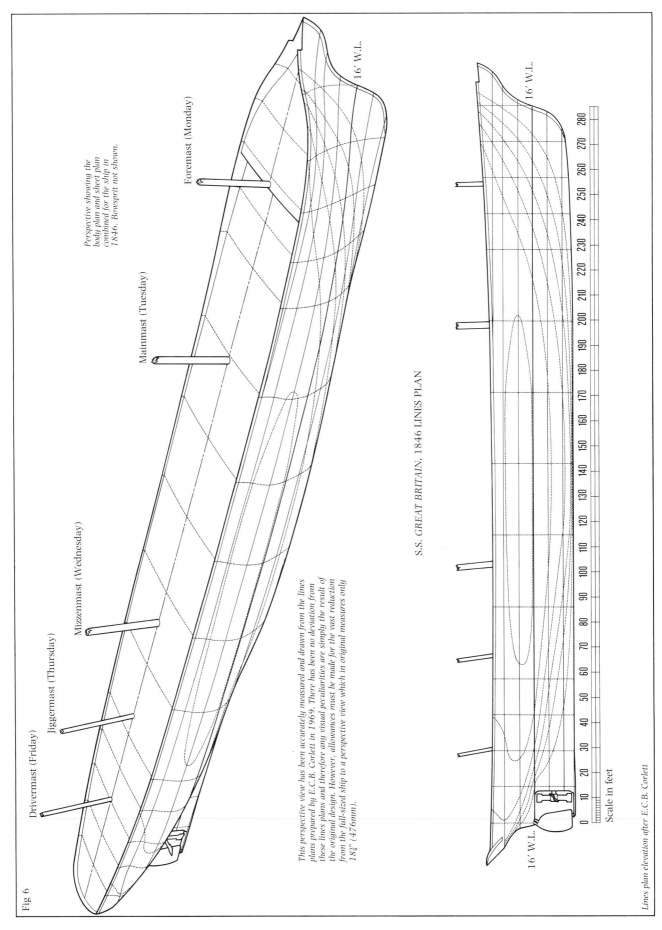

Fig 6

Perspective showing the body plan and sheet plan combined for the ship in 1846. Bowsprit not shown.

Foremast (Monday)

Mainmast (Tuesday)

Mizzenmast (Wednesday)

Jiggermast (Thursday)

Drivermast (Friday)

16′ W.L.

This perspective view has been accurately measured and drawn from the lines plans prepared by E.C.B. Corlett in 1969. There has been no deviation from these lines plans and therefore any visual peculiarities are simply the result of the original design. However, allowances must be made for the vast reduction from the full-sized ship to a perspective view which in original measures only 18¾″ (476mm).

S.S. *GREAT BRITAIN.* 1846 LINES PLAN

16′ W.L.

16′ W.L.

280
270
260
250
240
230
220
210
200
190
180
170
160
150
140
130
120
110
100
90
80
70
60
50
40
30
20
10
0

Scale in feet

Lines plan elevation after E.C.B. Corlett.

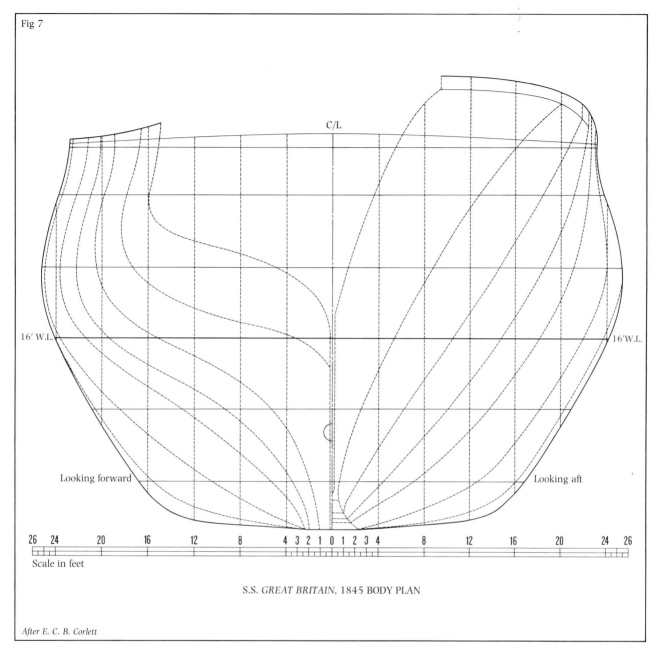

Fig 7

C/L

16′ W.L.   16′W.L.

Looking forward   Looking aft

| 26 | 24 | 20 | 16 | 12 | 8 | 4 3 2 1 0 1 2 3 4 | 8 | 12 | 16 | 20 | 24 26 |

Scale in feet

S.S. *GREAT BRITAIN*, 1845 BODY PLAN

After E. C. B. Corlett

of time and money needs to be worked out. No scratch modeller will ever tell you exactly how long it will take to build a model because it is almost impossible to say what should be included in the estimate, and there is enormous difference between people's capacity for the best use of time as well as its availability. There are those who are apparently swift and accurate and others who, because of their previous experience, spend less time than the novice in necessary experimental work. Machine tools put yet another slant on the time factor, and with the arrival of such wonders as the vibro-saw and the mini-drill, these days the tortoise can quickly change into an electrically driven hare.

What I personally most fear is loss of interest. It is so easy to be diverted by other demands, and there must be a graveyard full of models that fell by the wayside because the kitchen had to be decorated or because a change of house and job meant that Rawlplugs and papering took

over from planking and framing. Yet the successful completion of any model has to allow for all these things because it has to be built around the other pressures of seemingly more important jobs.

Because I need a target, (and I was also moving house) I set my sights on January 1980. This is about half the time it took to build the *Great Britain*, whose keel was laid in December 1839 and the first floating was in July 1843. If it takes longer than my estimate, I am covered by the fact that a model like this is never finished as one can go on adding detail for years.

Costing

Costing a model is almost as difficult as estimating the time factor. The only time I want to build a static model is when I am faced with paying for the engine particularly as I am hooked on steam. Because of the tricky nature of live

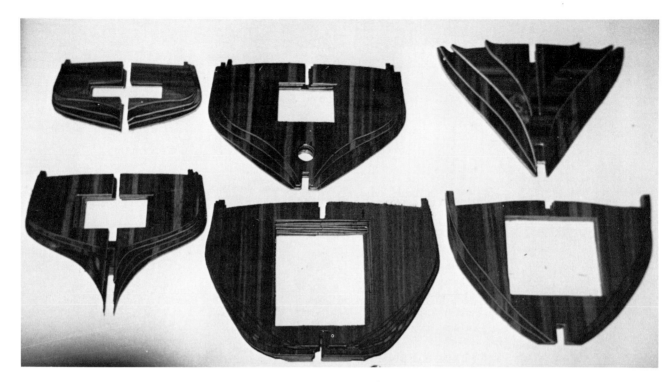

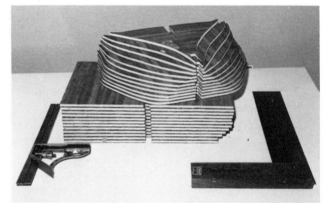

Fig 8. (Above) The prepared frames show effectively the unusual lines, especially the fine entry and excess tumblehome. Fig 9. (Right) Bulkhead frames. Fig 10. (Bottom) Frames laid over plans.

steam units, it is an unsafe policy to begin building a model without first having the unit, so all the money outlay comes at once, with the purchase of both the unit, (in my case, machined castings of a Stuart Double 10) and the raw material to make the keel, ribs, planks, etc. Many model shops now offer credit card facilities, and this is probably the least painful way of going about financing this kind of undertaking. £2.00 per week spread over two years sounds better than an initial outlay of £200. By the time the model is finished even more will have to be sunk, though I hasten to my own defence in saying that the money is not lost, but handsomely invested ... unless of course, she should sink!

Materials

Never mind Brunel's problems with his iron plates, every modeller today who is involved with scratch building knows the hardest part of the undertaking is to get hold of the raw material. It is unusual for a woodyard to stock BS1088 marine plywood these days and I had a round trip of 80 miles to get one sheet of 8ft × 4ft. Prior to this outing, I had worked out on a piece of graph paper that an 8ft × 4ft sheet would just allow the 'spine' of the ship and the 32 bulkheads plus transom to be bandsawn out. The main bulkhead frames are approximately 1ft sq, but carefully placed, this one sheet has sufficed to build up the skeleton of the ship. In passing, the use of graph paper cannot be overemphasised for preliminary work and accurate profile cutting. I note with interest that Brunel always sketched on graph paper, so that engineers could quickly draw up his work and so speed the process of mind into matter.

THE HULL

Sheerline Plans

I had the sheerline plan scaled up to 1:48 by photography. It was at this point that I received a letter from Dr Corlett cautioning me on the use of the Science Museum plans of their model which do not turn out to be very accurate, differing in a number of significant ways from the way the ship was actually built. I had already guessed at this but was interested to have my suspicions confirmed. The accurate hull version is drawn up in the book, "The Iron Ship", and the most noticeable difference as seen from the sheer is the chamfering of the keel towards the stempost rather than the continuous flat as per the museum model. There are a lot of other details which differ, in some cases quite drastically from this much copied model which cannot really be given the title of a 'builder's model' as we would understand it today. Actually, the Science Museum model is shrouded in mystery, and no-one knows who made it.

As can be seen in the photographs, the bulkhead frames are a quite extraordinary mixture. The display of cut-out sections shows the razor sharp entry instead of the traditional bluff-ended bow, which heralded the coming shape for the clipperships in their slicing action of the water. The centre section of frames amidships look as though they belong to a century or so earlier with their highly feminine tulip shape which is nothing if not sensuous, smoothing their way back to the anachronistically decorated mock quarter galleries. This shape has never before or since been repeated as far as I know, and for the hull shape alone, this ship is a celebration of innovation and olde worlde sentiment.

The hull was built like this for two reasons. Firstly, to give the ship maximum width combined with good hydrodynamics, and secondly so that she could be released through the very tight fit dictated by the 'upper lock' gates of the Cumberland Basin, (see map of Bristol Docks.) As we will see later, the ship had a difficult delivery but her eventual appearance from the Bristol Docks into the River Avon on 12th December, 1844 marked a resounding success for the triumphant design team of Patterson, Guppy and Brunel.

Hull Strength

The 'wood versus iron' argument was in full swing at the end of the 1830's. Iron was an unnatural material to use for ship-building and the associated technology in fabrica-

tion was still in its infancy. This ship, called at first *The Mammoth*, was built "against nature" and in the teeth of some fierce criticism, of which the precocious Brunel seems to have taken little notice. The S.S. *Great Western* had proved the point that an increased size of hull did not require an increase of power to drive it through the water at the same ratio. This is because the hull resistance to the water only increases by its square whereas the carrying capacity of the hull may be increased by its cube. Therefore to build a large ship, in which ample coal could be bunkered and still have plenty of space available for cargo and passengers was the economically sound thing to do. But this meant fabricating a ship of such dimensions that the timber would simply collapse under the strain. There is a maximum length for timbered ships, beyond which it is unsafe and unwise to go. The *Great Western*, launched in 1838, was the giant of its day, 236ft long, built of timber, but massively reinforced with iron, to match the excesses of the North Atlantic run. By comparison, the *Great Britain* was a veritable Leviathan – 322ft in length by 51ft in beam by 16ft at the loaded draught. She was approximately 2,000 tons heavier than her elder sister and, whilst sharing the same beam as Nelson's *Victory*, the hull of the S.S.G.B. was 136ft longer than the old First Rater.

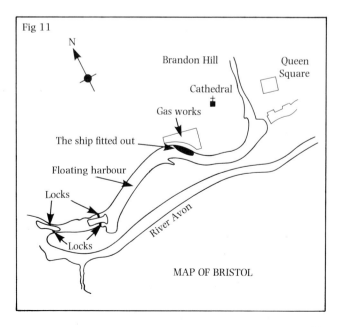

Fig 11

N

Brandon Hill

Queen Square

Cathedral

Gas works

The ship fitted out

Floating harbour

Locks

Locks

River Avon

MAP OF BRISTOL

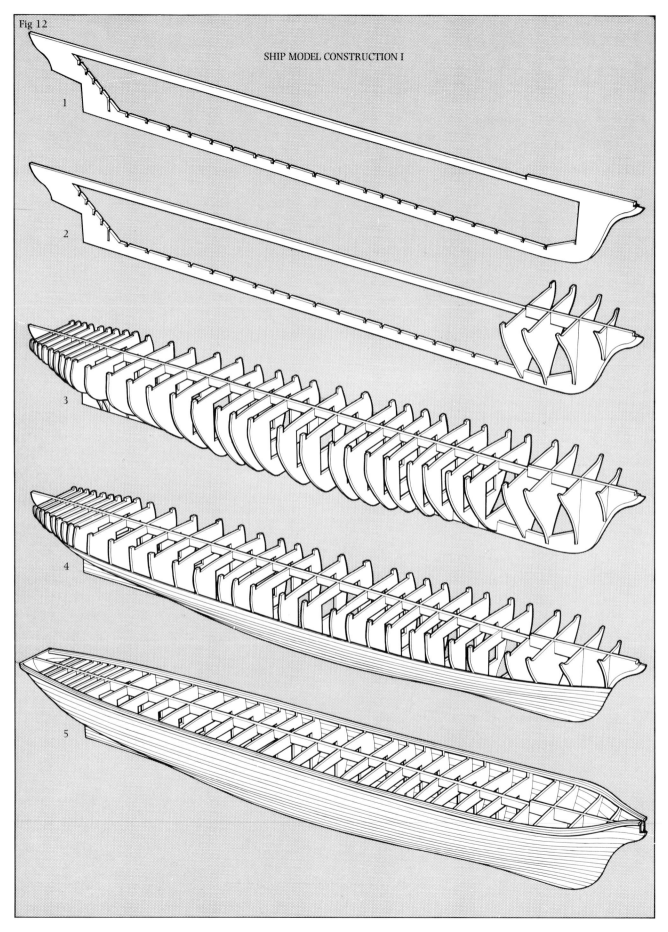

Fig 12

SHIP MODEL CONSTRUCTION I

Fig 13

SHIP MODEL CONSTRUCTION II

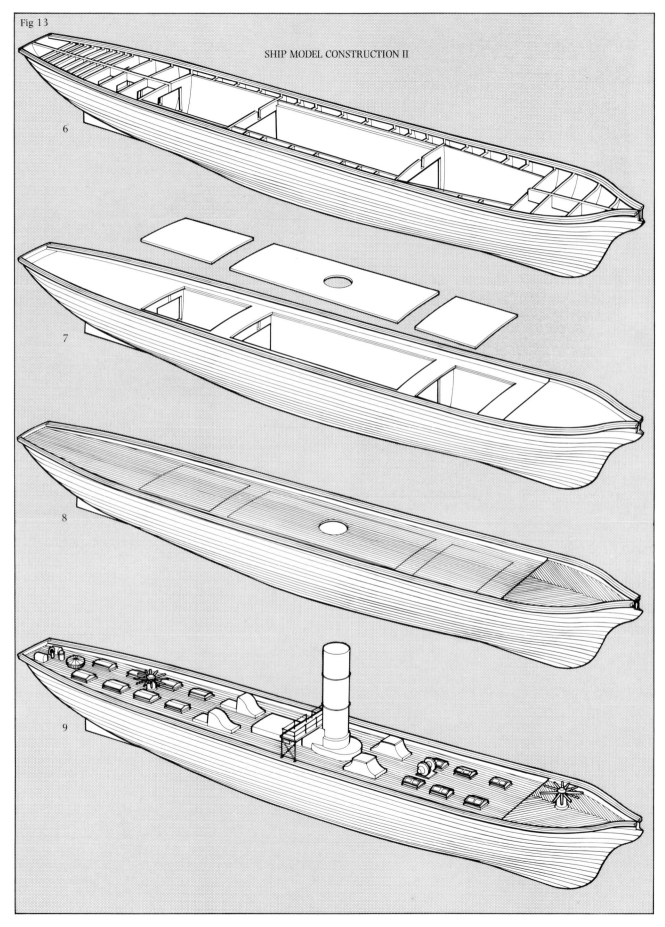

6

7

8

9

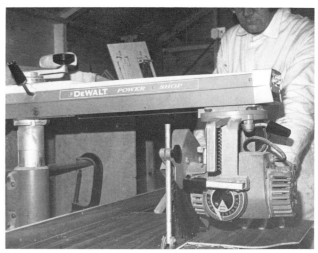

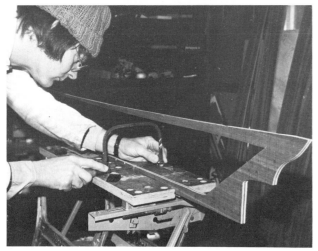

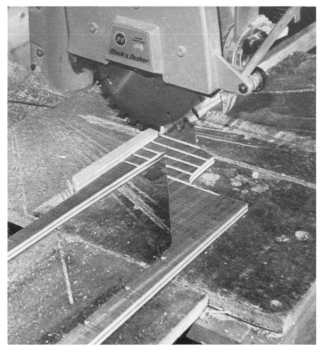

Fig 14. (Top Left) The keel piece jig is laid, and grooved to accept the frames. Fig 15. (Top right) The circular saw mounted on a radial arm makes short work of cutting out the ply spine or backbone of the ship. Fig 16. (Above) The slots for the frames are cut by hand. Note the double lamination for the spine. Fig 17. (Right) The circular saw is used to cut the rebates for the stern frames.

Brunel, with his experience of bridge building, favoured the new material of iron, knowing full well that a ship built of iron would be stronger and roomier than a composite hulled ship, and with so much valuable cargo space given over to engine, fuel and boilers, the extra space would mean the difference between the ship earning money for her owners, or being a very costly pioneering experiment, doomed to financial failure.

Despite the upturned noses of traditional ship builders, and the incredulity of The Admiralty, the keel of the S.S. G.B. was laid in the specially excavated dock in 1839, with the plates fashioned first, and the frames laid to the plates. In her construction, Brunel adopted the thoroughly modern system of shifting butts and double riveted plates. The *Mammoth*, as she was first called, was built particularly well, and enjoyed a good record of watertightness and obvious durability. The filthy stench of decaying and infectious bilge water, which was an accepted nuisance on wooden ships was not to be a feature of the new age of iron.

In my model, I will refer to a 'spine' rather than a keel. This backbone is simply the outline shape of the hull centre to which the bulkheads are attached, and is made in two halves out of the aforementioned ply. It is made like this in order to get round the difficult process of drilling out the propeller shaft and rudder holes and the brass inserts into the stempost. These are all grooved out and joined against the natural bias of the ply. A total spine is really better than just having a keel, as the bulkheads are aligned top and bottom for greater accuracy.

Because it is only a flimsy backbone, it needs artificial strengthening to prevent warping or hogging, an item which has to be continually watched right through the planking process.

At the outset, this was done by grooving out channels in a piece of scrap Contiboard, which exactly matched the bulkhead markings in the spine. This jig was in turn nailed to a flat piece of solid timber and the total provided a rigid basis on which to attach the bulkhead frames. This channelled base meant that the frames were all set square

THE SHIP'S CONSTRUCTION

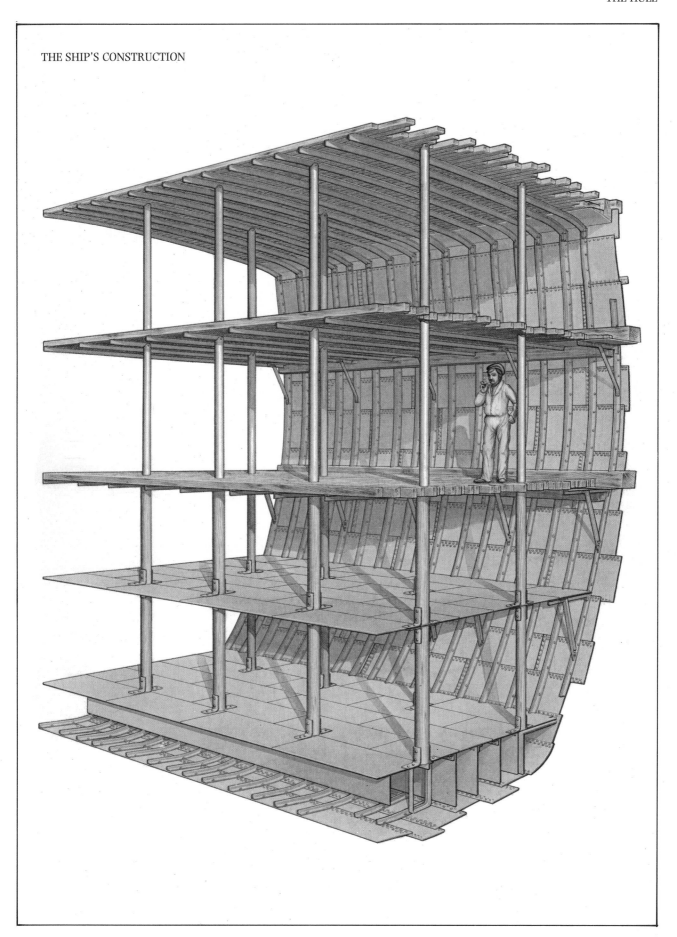

to the spine and obviated that difficult business of lining them all up. The top part of the spine also meant a double check on the vertical plane. When removed from the channelled base, the ship's skeleton was still very flimsy, the bulkhead frames outweighing the backbone to which they were attached.

Clinker Planking

The first bit of real rigidity is built in by a false keel plate. This is a piece of 6mm ply grooved and fitted on the underside of the ship, which has an appreciable flat area on which the ship rests perfectly upright. I have not seen this suggested anywhere but my guess is that one of the reasons the Old Lady survived her time in the Falkland Islands is directly due to her (excuse me) flat bottom, on which she settled for 56 years. Had she had a lesser area to sit upon, or an old fashioned keel protrusion, I believe she would have rolled over and broken up years ago.

Once fixed, my false keel plate was then clinkered over with planking in $\frac{1}{16}$in ply, having first worked out exactly where each plank has to fit. This is done by using masking tape which, having been measured and drawn, is then transferred to the $\frac{1}{16}$in ply, (or at least that's the theory). Unlike lovely old carvel building, where you can joggle bits in and, when all else fails, reach for the fibreglass filler, each of these clinker lines shows, for the length of the whole hull. Worse still, in one way but not in another, $\frac{1}{16}$in ply is well out of scale on its projected edge, and so each

Fig 18. (Below) Spine piece under construction using pegs and clamps to hold laminations together during setting. Fig 19. (Bottom) B&P photo. Interior of ship showing plates.

Fig 20 a, b, c Stages of frames' installation. Note in photo on right the 'chunky' piece of brass epoxied into the stem to act as a sharp entry. Fig 21. (Below right) Shaping of the false keel plate prior to planking.

length has to be grooved out (rebated), and this is on lines which are necessarily curved. The plus factor here though, is that by virtue of the rebate, longitudinal strength is increased phenomenally although the process was only originally developed because of my desire to scale the look of the clinkering.

As you will see from some of the pictures, I am well equipped with a De-Walt radial arm saw, but even with this advantage it was a while before I got the hang of producing these rebates using a floating blade technique. I am somewhat embarrassed by the knowledge that a conventional circular saw is not able to tackle this kind of work which requires the operator to be able to see the saw blade as it is cutting. Although my machine is now obsolete, I saw the latest version was selling well at the last Model Engineering Exhibition, but you'll have to sell the Hi-Fi to get one these days.

Box Girder

Somebody ought of course, to be building a model of this ship out of iron ... or at least brass, but for the time being, I am happy to go on working in the material which Brunel rejected. I have already mentioned graph paper and I used more of the stuff when tracing out the bulkhead frames, transferred from the plan by the use of carbon typing paper, tightly stretched and tacked onto the 6mm ply. These were then bandsawn. At the same time as cutting out the shapes, I used three cardboard templates for the

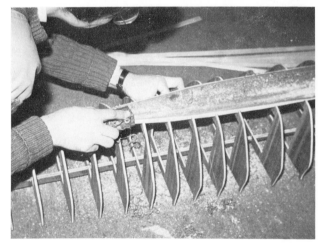

square inner section which will be reinforced on the same principle as a box girder bridge. (I am not sure whether Brunel would approve of my adaptation ...) This central rigid box is the second way in which I hope my construction will have enough built-in strength to combat a displacement of approx. 8 5lb.

Stem

The insert, made of a substantial piece of brass, which acts as the sharp entry has already been referred to and can be seen in several photographs. On the prototype, the entry

Fig 22. (Above) Brunel's original at Bristol, as photographed in late 1977, clearly shows the large number of close frames. Much progress in reconstruction has been made since then. Fig 23. (Right) 'Stem'. Photo of brass insert.

diminishes to only 1½in from a "massive and beautiful forging 18ft high, hammer welded in one piece". On the model, tapering the clinker strips into the brass is done with epoxy resin, which is the first change of adhesive from Cascamite as used throughout the timber joints and planking of the hull. I dare not make this stempost absolutely to scale, or the prow would have literally a blade-sharp edge, which could have interesting consequences if dropping the model on one's left toe! It does reinforce however, the point made earlier about the original design slicing the broad Atlantic apart as opposed to punching it – an axe rather than a sledge-hammer.

The Transom

Before the hull can be completely planked, the transom needs to be attached. This was copied, not from Guppy's model, but from Dr Corlett's book, "The Iron Ship". Much of the decoration is overdone on the Science Museum model, which is a pity, because the trailboards are actually more artistic than the real thing, an over-enthusiasm with which modellers will be able to sympathise with the greatest of ease.

Having taken a tracing, I cut out the transom and the windows which had been drilled and pierced with the 'magic' vibro-saw. Because the transom has a curvature

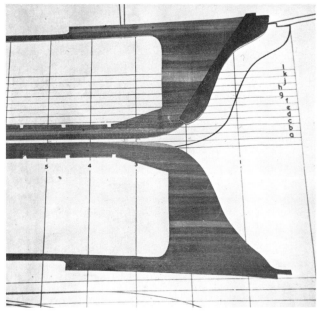

we see the first demonstration of the 'blow-lamp and copper tube trick'.

The plywood is soaked for about half an hour and then pressed round the curvature of the hot tube, which in turn produces a satisfying hiss of steam. The wood will quickly dry out on the exterior of the ply and it should be dunked again once or twice. As it is only a gentle curve that is required, the newly assumed shape remains without the use of further tension.

SHIP'S ENGINE 1845

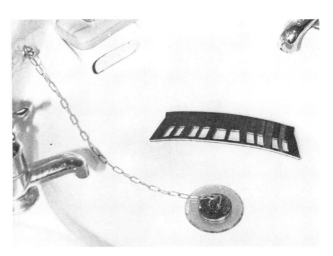

Fig 24. (Above) Using the vibro-saw to cut the windows of the transom piece. Fig 25. (Top right) Soaking the plywood transom piece for 30 minutes. Fig 26. (Right) Shaping the transom piece over a length of hot copper tube.

Stern

The clinkering at the stern, in line with the rest of William Patterson's hull design is distinctive but difficult to fabricate. The 'plates' are radiused out into a fan shape around the stern post. This involves a fairly wicked piece of interpretation as far as handling plywood is concerned, preceded as so often by the prodigious use of card templates.

Up till this point, it has not been necessary to use any soaking and steaming on the planks as $\frac{1}{16}$in ply is obligingly flexible, but the tight turn around what is called the 'counter' really requires the use of hot tube steaming. It looks impressive but is not hard to do with the blow lamp as before, stuck up a piece of thinnish copper tubing. Soaked ply at this thickness will take a turn around a bend no bigger than your little finger and will retain the contour given with comparative willingness and no loss of strength.

The New Material

I enjoy this sort of thing, and how much easier it is to do than the bending of iron plates must have been in Patterson's yard at Bristol. At this relatively early date there were not many firms involved in the production of iron plates, and such as there were, produced plates of variable quality. As a generalisation, thicker plates were used at the base of the hull, and they diminished in thickness as they rose above the waterline. Their main drawback was their small size (6ft × 3ft approximately) which meant that production was a tedious task, especially as double riveting was ordered. There is no record of complaint as far as I know, from the good people of Bristol, but surrounding the dock were machines for shearing and punching the plates, bending machines, paraphernalia for drilling and counter-sinking as well as furnaces for heating the plates and the rivets. Add to this 200 gas lamps so that work could carry on through the night, and you have a formula which would bring forth today the combined

forces of complaint from 'Citizens' Rights' and the 'Noise Abatement Society'. Modellers who will insist on hammering away in the small hours of the night can equally upset a long-suffering family with ever lessening levels of enthusiasm for the project.

Over this poly-hybrid hull, iron plates were manoeuvred and carefully riveted into place. They did not have to be 'fitted' as such and this method saved a good deal of time on the S.S.G.B. but not on my model. You will appreciate that because I have had to rebate all the plystrips, they necessarily need to be made to fit exactly. Had I chosen to work in a thinner material ($\frac{1}{32}$in for instance) which would have allowed the full face edge to show, I would have lost both the natural sweep of the wood and also the necessary strength for which I am looking.

At this level, those who have fibreglass technology under their belts do a better job, possibly, in absolute accuracy; (Dr Corlett has produced just such a hull in 1:48 scale) but for my part, I find working in fibreglass a perfectly hateful pastime and am content to continue in the material which I love. I cannot entirely avoid the use of fibreglass, in that I use the resin filler in a diluted form to seal both the interior and the exterior of the hull and give it at the same time the authentic 'rough' look of a genuine working hull.

I will talk about finishing and painting the hull at a later date, but in passing, there is a world of interest in the

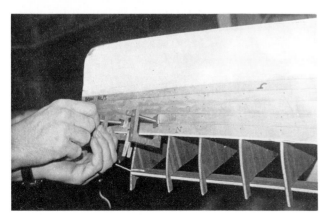

Fig 27. (Above) B&P photo. Prototype plates. Fig 28 a & b (Left) Two shots taken during the earlier planking clearly show the method adopted to obtain accuracy of planking.

problems they had with anti-fouling on iron. It seems that marine growth finds iron a most attractive surface on which to proliferate. Apparently they tried every potion from cow dung to asphalt, and sandwiched between these, "grease from boiled bones, kitchen stuff and butter without salt mixed with poisonous matters". The standard red lead and tallow was applied to the S.S.G.B., but this meant a continually laborious maintenance programme for her and was really one of the only drawbacks of the 'new' material.

The long lengths of plywood timber are in various places, under a good deal of stress, twisting through the curvature of this strange and unique hull. No matter how careful one is in positioning the bulkheads, lows and highs will appear the length of the hull and these have to be dealt with by filling in the dips with layers of resin paste filler.

Initially this has to be dolloped on like suet pudding, much as a plasterer would do with a trowel, and this is not a bad tool to use for the job. The troughs are best marked before the process takes place, as when the hull is upside-down it is possible to miss the subtleties of the way in which the light falls when it is the right way up. A long length of flexible timber will indicate where the dips are and these should be scribbled on. It is wise to overfill and

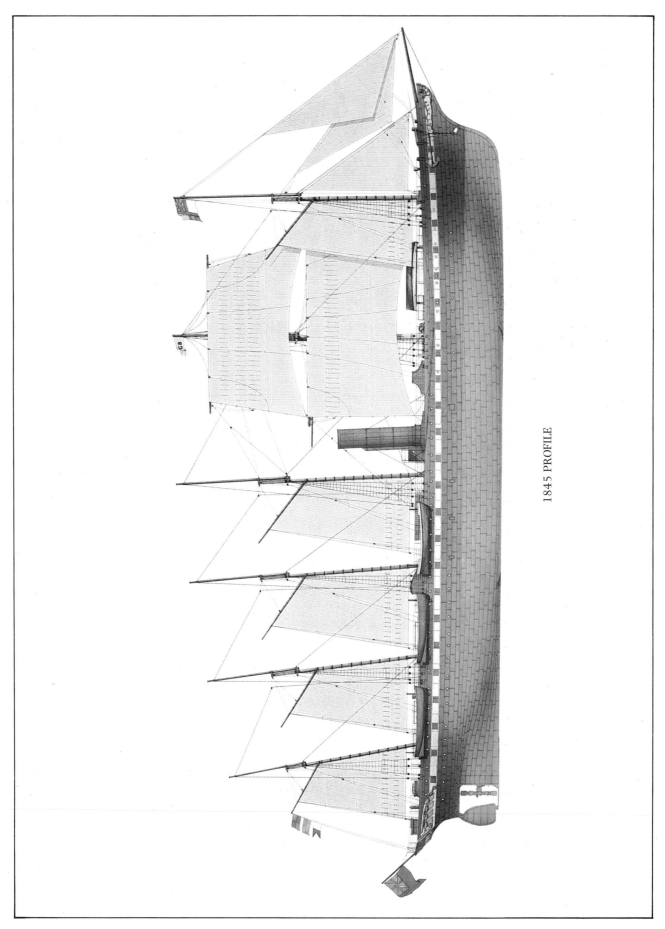

1845 PROFILE

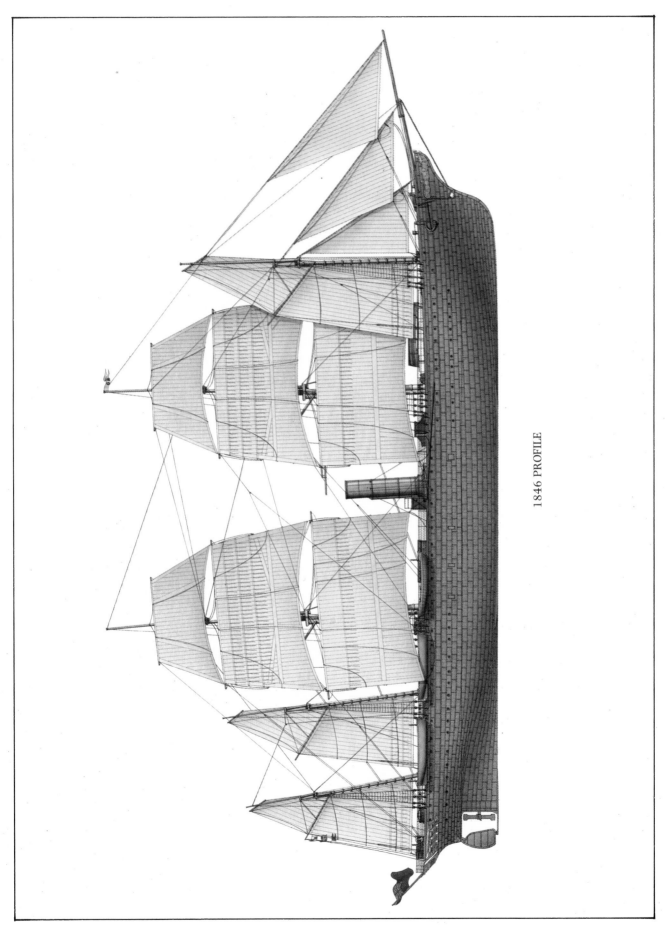

1846 PROFILE

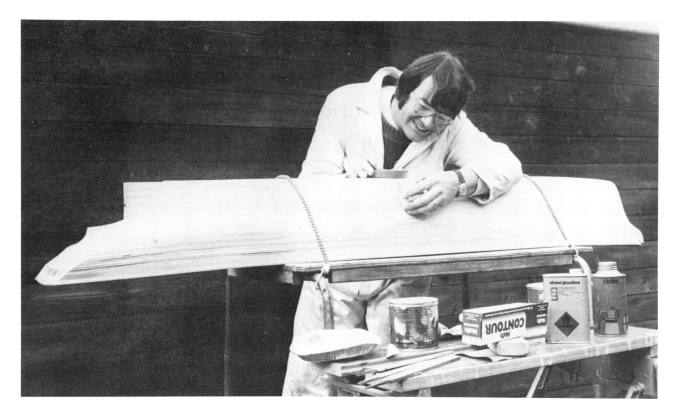

Fig 29. (Above) At last the enormous size of this model is apparent as the author prepares to fill in the gaps and hollows with glassfibre resin paste. Fig 30. (Right) Filling-in at stem and sheer. Fig 31 (Below right) Note the extreme curvature at the counter.

cut back the paste, rather than risk having to make another application, and a spare piece of whippy timber can also be employed in conjunction with the trowel.

Resin paste cures very quickly, but it can be slowed down by using acetone thinners, or just plain cellulose thinners will do the job. The problem then is that you lose some of the body of the paste and it becomes like thin icing on a cake, so you mustn't overdo the thinning process at this stage.

When all the troughs have been filled, then the tedious job of cutting back has to begin; at the moment of writing, I have been doing this for a month off and on, and I am still nowhere near the point of being able to say that it is done. The problem is that the hull is clinkered and the strakes are an absolute give-away on the accuracy of the job through the whole length of the ship's hull. The slightest dip shouts at you and likewise any part which is proud needs attention. It is fairly exasperating work in that one thinks one has it right when the hull is 'sunny side up' but when reversed the light shows up a deficiency which has to be attended to.

The actual cutting back is done with a combination of files, initially fairly coarse. In my travels, I have discovered a file which I suspect is rightly found in a blacksmith's tool kit, for cleaning off the excess hoof nail, when a new shoe has been put on. It has a single half moon cut on a flat edge and is immensely sharp, much more than Surform. It quickly removes unwanted fibreglass and is non-clogging, though the action is fairly brutal. The next stage of cutting

the strakes into the paste has to be done with a double cross-cut file, with a milled edge that cuts the top of the strake in and a flat face which at the same time cuts back the surface. For this, it is necessary to mark the line prior to the filing and to keep a wire brush handy to clear the file constantly. None of this would be necessary normally, and perhaps accounts for the fact that all the models I have seen so far, are not properly clinkered, but simply scored where the overlaps should be. There is however, a great deal of character in the clinkering of this ship, something which hits you when you first glimpse the original and is certainly part of the uniqueness of the ship to which I feel it is important to give proper attention and value.

Reflection on the Reality

Seeing the S.S. *Great Britain* for the first time is an uncanny experience, especially if you are sensitive to the history of her birth. She cannot be rightly understood unless you put her into her historical context, being the Industrial Revolution personified. The massive weight of the structure is at its claustrophobic best when one stands

under the stern and looks upwards to the hugely complicated plating leading down to the counter. It looks experimental – very much a one off job – and I allowed myself a chuckle, having great empathy with the difficulties of executing this in the model. A passing opinion is that it is more fancy than it needs to be, but thankfully the Victorians were not simply pragmatists, but artists as well.

My immediate thoughts are that I am glad to be under way with the hull of this ship, for, seen in the flesh, as it were, the task before me is daunting to say the least. But all the while I keep thinking that I must try to do justice to the prototype, for not only did the great Brunel sweat his heart out over this, but the rescue operation of bringing her back from the Falkland Islands makes a moral demand that she must be as good as I can possibly manage, and the 'Project's' slowness must be my carefulness, such was the courage involved in the salvage operation.

Everything about her impresses me; the illusive lines which no camera can capture, as they appear to change with each step that is taken; at one point the stern looks like a wine goblet whilst the stem looks like a ploughshare with the hook of a scythe. The restoration has been remarkable for those who have seen the pictures of the state in which she arrived. Fibreglass has played a major role in the decorative as well as the structural renovation.

Fig 32 a&b. A photographic 'reflection on reality' between the part finished model hull and the real thing. Note the extreme tumblehome.

Fig 33. (Above) Original carving in Museum. Fig 34. (Right) Restoration work on transom. Fig 35. (Below right) The replica coat of arms is of glass fibre.

At this level at least, we share in this revolution of our own age, and it looks well, if a little 'crisp' as yet. The weather will however take care of that in its own good time. Some of the old traditional carving has been preserved in the Museum alongside the ship, and very lovely it is; I would quite have thought that this would have perished entirely, but not a bit of it – mature English oak, resilient against years and years of almost total neglect, has hoodwinked ship's weevil, deathwatch beetle and our old friend, *Anobium punctatum*, commonly known as woodworm.

A question often asked is whether or not this ship, which floated on her own bottom in July 1970, will ever be able to put to sea again. Such a suggestion is inclined to draw sharp intakes of breath from those concerned with the restoration. Apart from the fact that the Bristol Pilots are reported ("Return of the Great Britain", Richard Goold Adams, p.170) to have sworn an oath amongst themselves never to allow her to be taken out of Bristol again, if the ship had to be moved, much of the restoration work put into her would have to be taken out again, including the funnel and masts. Commander James Richard, in charge of building the engine replica for the restored vessel, dismisses any question of putting the work to the test, saying quite simply that the work is not intended to be seaworthy.

For the super-sensitive there is a feeling of sadness that despite all this creativity she will never again put to sea as a working ship – that she will always be a static vessel,

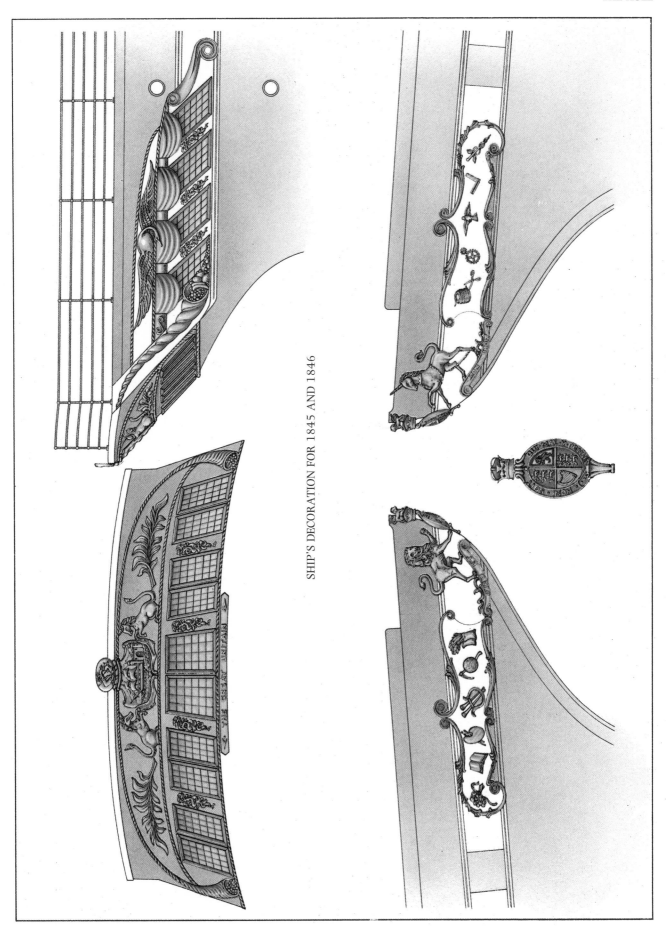

SHIP'S DECORATION FOR 1845 AND 1846

preserved as a museum to keep us all humble when we start to imagine that we invented technology! I have this sadness whenever I see museum models that, in my mind's eye, require only water to complete them and yet will always be kept away from their natural habitat. This is where a working model leaves even a prototype behind, in that eventually there will be a launch and a voyage, and steam raised amidships ... just now, this seems almost as far off as the completion of the restoration programme which stretches I understand into the 1990's.

Mind over Matter

It may appear that ship-building in miniature is one long continuous process which goes at a nice steady pace into the middle distance of time without too much effort or thought. This is of course a travesty of the truth and ship modellers have tried through the years to devise techniques which alleviate the tedium involved in making a decent job of the bits which necessarily come under the heading of "donkey work". On a large model, it is more than likely that the hull will have to be finished out in the open. Part of the reason that this hull has taken me six months to finish is precisely because one is at the behest of the weather, but only outside can one really get a good look at the critical areas, some few paces from the model.

There is something which experienced judges look for in any model and that is "building to a constant and consistent standard". It is no good having superb superstructure and decoration, if the hull is inaccurate or rough, (even though the S.S.G.B. is itself slightly out of true). It is therefore essential not to tire of the spade-work on the hull, but it is possible to ring the changes a bit. Psychologically, this is a critical time when one considers that it has taken longer to finish the exterior of the hull than it took to plank it onto the bulkheads, but this work simply must not be rushed. Much better to remind oneself of modelling and do some of the most delicate work, namely the transom, the figureheads and the trailboards.

Transom Decoration

I have been aching to experiment with these features, in that they involve a development of technique which I have not previously tried. It involves "chasing" sheet pewter – in both senses! During the long months of finishing the hull, I happened to see a lady at a 'Country Fayre' working some of this sheet metal into floral patterns and I was spellbound by the possibilities which this process throws up.

This metal is so ductile and malleable, that one can raise the embossing by a full $\frac{1}{4}$in off the natural surface, without it splitting or distorting. One can also emboss letters through it and although to date I have not tried doing so, one must be able to make mouldings in it and from it. The problem is the usual one – that of finding a supplier, because it is not readily available.

If you have ever smoothed an aluminium milk bottle top with your thumb, then you will begin to appreciate that with ductile metal, the shapes of a unicorn's flanks and the flowing mane of a lion rampant become a possibility. To produce the same by a carving technique would

Fig 36. (Below) The first tasks for any modelling process involve research, and the author used original drawings and information available from the S.S.G.B. Project. Fig 37. (Middle) The model's finished pewter representation of transom. Fig 38. (Bottom) . . . offered up to the model's transom.

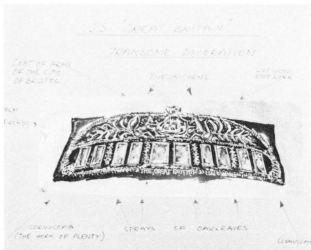

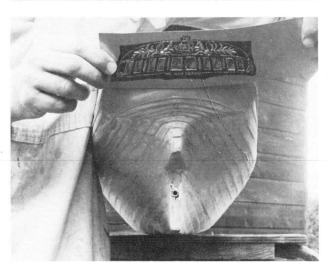

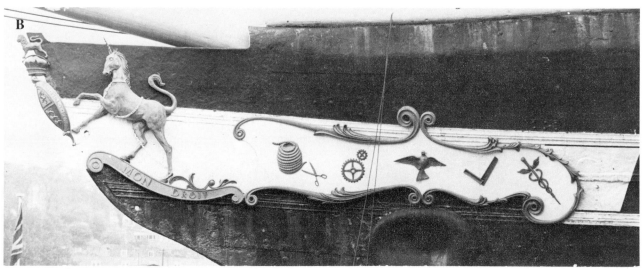

Fig 39. (Top) Pewter representation of trailboards decoration. Fig 40. a&b (Above) The replica trailboards on the rescued S.S. Great Britain are constructed from glassfibre mouldings. From left to right, symbols depicted are: a bouquet of flowers, a book, an artist's palette, lyre and trumpets, a sheaf of corn, Royal Arms of Lion and Unicorn, coil of rope and scissors, gear wheels, a dove of peace, carpenter's square, and Caduceus, (the rod of Hermes – a messenger of the gods) – the rod surmounted with two wings and entwined by two serpents.

require a talent I do not possess.

Initially, the process is to draw on the front side of the sheet pewter, to reverse it and push out the inner shape of the outline. Thus raised, stomachs, legs, heads, etc. stand proud of the flat surface. The metal is then worked several times over using the same method, until you are satisfied with the result. The raised parts have to be filled with plaster or glue in order that they cannot be pressed in from the outer face. This work is very much in the land of "have a go and surprise yourself". After a bit of experimentation, the really lovely decorative effects of this material begin to show – a superb antidote to sanding down resin paste, and a reminder that modelling can be fun.

The Gunwale and Sheerstrake

The fixing of the wooden gunwale and the sheerstrake, like a massive flange encircling the entire ship, poses its own set of problems. As on the prototype, this "stringer" consists of several lay-ups of timber, and because it is strongly glued, adds great strength to the upper shell.

It twists through a series of different contours, particularly at the prow, where it assumes a shape that I will

Fig 41. Techniques used to shape and fit ramin strips to form the wooden gunwale and sheerstrake: a) Kerfing the ramin strip with fine tooth metal hacksaw. b) Bending the kerfed strip. c) Offering up the kerfed strip to the shoulder. d) Increasing the shoulder by the addition of the kerfed strip. e) Trimming off the kerfed strip. f) Planing down the gunwale.

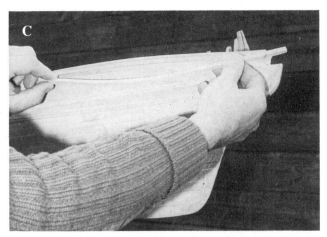

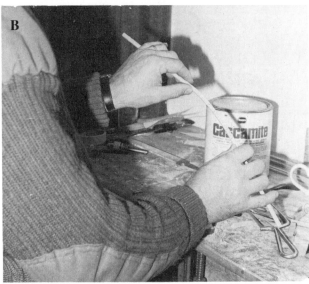

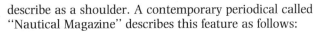

describe as a shoulder. A contemporary periodical called "Nautical Magazine" describes this feature as follows:

"What can I say of this gigantic vessel? I have had but a transient view of her, but sufficient to impress me with the belief that she will prove to be something out of the common build of sea-going craft. There is no other steamer, nay vessel of any class, I believe, with such an extraordinary overhanging bow."

This "extraordinary overhanging bow" included the sheerstrake of iron plates and the shoulder in a double twist action, which required all the skill of the old craftsmen to fabricate. I heard a lecture given recently by one of the "Project Committee" who stated that there are no craftsmen now able to handle iron plates in this way. It had to be restored instead, in glass reinforced plastic.

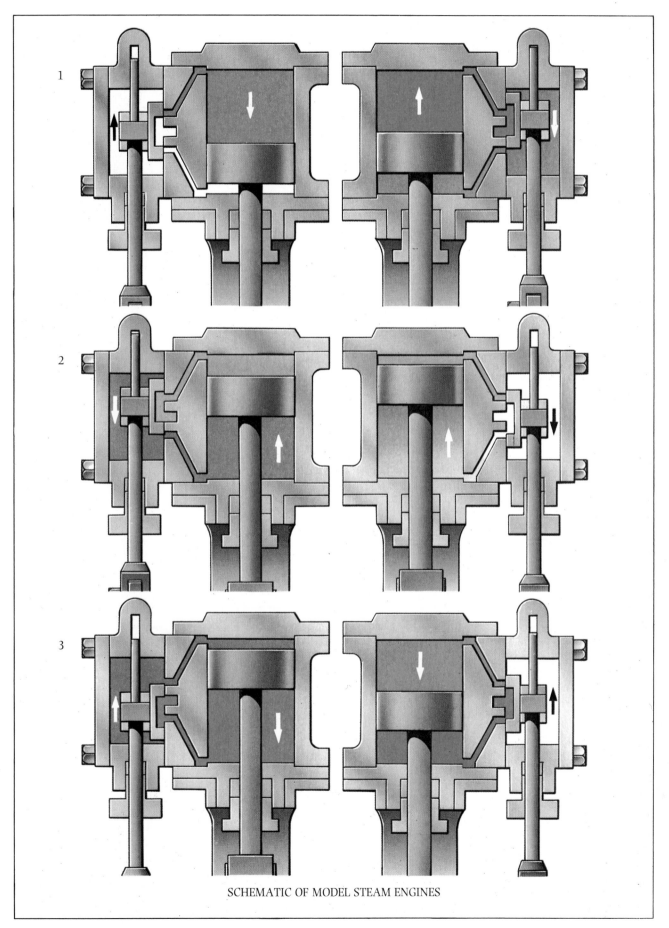

SCHEMATIC OF MODEL STEAM ENGINES

On the model, the effect was made by resorting to a technique which I learned in guitar making. A quarter inch stringer, in ramin hardwood, was sawn at $\frac{1}{4}$in intervals in an engineer's vice to a depth which stops just short of the cut through point. I used a fine tooth metal hacksaw, owing to the brittle grain of ramin. Thus treated the timber has great flexibility and reduces the stringer to an almost floppy state which will follow almost any contour presented. The "build-out" to the contour of the shoulder was achieved by an increasing sharpness of bend emulating the incredible shape of the original. Once the many little saw-cuts are filled with glue, the stringer becomes rigid and strong in a most satisfactory way

The outcome of all this means that the hull, for the very first time, looks right. The sheerstrake has always played a critical role in every ship's construction, but nowhere more so than in the S.S.G.B. When she was in the Falklands, the Islanders used the hulk as a wool-store for many years. During that time in Port Stanley, someone who appreciated the great strength still left in the iron hull, even in its advanced old age, ordered the sheerstrake to be cut right through, creating a more convenient entry for loading and unloading the bales of wool, in confidence that the ship was strong enough to hold together while afloat in the harbour, which she did for the next 50 years.

Fig 42 (Right) Trimming the brass track with a sandpaper wheel in the power drill press. Fig 43. (Below) Checking for the correct position of the bilge keels against plans and photographic references before fixing. Fig 44. (Opposite) The full size bilge keels on the S.S.G.B. at Bristol.

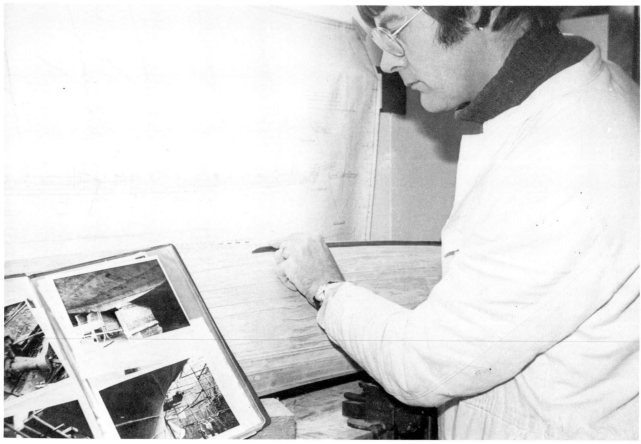

This is the doorway by which the public at present leave the ship.

One might imagine that scuttling a ship by poking holes in the bottom of the hull is a destructive enough thing to do, but it is nowhere near as serious as cutting through the sheerstrake. Yet the appearance of the creeping gap, which at the time of the rescue in 1970 had reached an alarming 13 inches, only started after she had been beached in Sparrow Cove, some few miles out of Port Stanley. Scouring by the tides had removed the support under the stern, leading to this potentially irrevocable damage.

By the time the courageous rescue team arrived, the crack did extend practically from sheer to keel, but on one side of the ship only. It is said that one more bad storm, of which there are plenty on that coastline, would have made a final end of her and that the rescue was literally in the nick of time. Just as an addendum, it is interesting to note that it was not the rivets which gave way, but the plates which split under the strain, proving that the double riveting on this ship was of the very highest order of workmanship.

The Bilge Keels

In the early 1840's, it was still very uncommon for a ship to have bilge keels fitted and it is almost certain that they were not fitted to counteract the rolling characteristic of a large ship's hull. William Froude's experimental work on this subject didn't take place until 1872. Those which are fitted to the S.S.G.B. can more accurately be described as docking keels, and as such have played an important part in the ship's life. When they are first seen, they appear

flimsy and inadequate for the task in hand. They are in fact only $1\frac{3}{4}$in thick and 5in deep on the prototype and therefore present a problem for the modeller.

I was about to represent them in ramin hardwood, sawn into a "T" shape, when I hit on the idea of using some old brass curtain track with the top edge cut off. The original keels were 110ft in length which at 1:48 scale comes down to $27\frac{1}{2}$in. I thought I would probably have to saw down the whole length of 55in, but it turned out that my tinsnips were man enough for the job. The brass track was then trimmed with a sandpaper wheel in the vertical driller and finally filed flat between the two vices, supported underneath by the firm edge of a 3ft wooden ruler. With the top edge removed, the track becomes quite amenable to the idea of following the twist of the hull side and looks very authentic.

The original was riveted to the hull, level with the centreline flush keel, 9ft at either side. Not being over anxious to start putting pins through the hull at this stage, I resorted to our old friend, Araldite epoxy resin, the slow curing one which is still, I believe, the strongest of them all. I do not anticipate losing either of them.

I said that they played an important part in the ship's history, in that the ship has always been steadied by them, giving an already large flat base area an extra "chocking effect" which must have kept her upright through all the lonely years that she was a hulk, and latterly a wreck. Captain Hosken, the first Captain of the S.S.G.B., scraped one of the bilge keels on a reef when he ran into fog off the Newfoundland Bank near Cape Broil on her fourth double crossing in July of 1846, but the fact that the prototype shows no signs of injury is explained by the present bilge keels not being the original ones.

HEAT & WEIGHT

Teamwork

Cross fertilization may sound like something out of a gardening book, but when one is talking about ideas concerned with difficult problems, there is nothing like the opportunity to put your head together with someone else who knows in practice, how large the headache is going to be.

In an almost classic case of meeting just the right man at just the right moment, Geoff Sheppard, a son of the City of Bristol and boiler maker extraordinary, introduced himself to me at The National Model Makers' Festival 1978. Geoff is a loco man at heart and just as Brunel leant heavily upon such men as Daniel Gooch and Thomas Guppy, who from their teens had had experience of mechanical engineering, so am I proud to do the same.

Great ventures are seldom the work of one person, and it is one of the greatest delights to me that in the comparatively small world of model engineering, there is an old fashioned enthusiasm amongst the participants which has to be experienced to be believed.

The Steam Plant

The "Ubiquitous" Stuart Double 10 is now available from Stuart Turner's as a fully machined unit ready for assembly. It is the obvious choice for the S.S.G.B., being powerful, compact and very well engineered. The unit has two cranks at right angles, which means that it will always start without having to be 'turned over'. This is an important feature when it comes to radio control, though this engine was designed long before the arrival of such electronic tricks. The problem at the time of writing this is that the Stuart Double 10 has no boiler in the marine form (that is to say a flue boiler, with a low centre of gravity), to match it.

There is no doubt that 'gas firing' steam units are the answer to the flame or heat problems previously causing irritations to the would-be operator of live steamers. And this is where Geoff Sheppard and his boiler units come into their own. Some original and experimental work has been carried out using different nozzle and canister combinations, to obtain the most efficient flame patterns for different sizes of boiler. I suspect that by the time this is published, his units will be readily available on the open market, but as I write, the drawings for a magnificent 5in × 9in return flue copper boiler are on the board. It is well known that the Stuart Double 10 is greedy on steam, rather than pressure, and therefore an efficient and large boiler is absolutely necessary.

At the outset of this model, I had wrongly supposed that it would be possible to use the Stuart boiler with the external fire tubes (504). This unit is really a 'pot boiler', and as such needs its standard height for air intake and flame, which would bring it just above the deck level. It also puts the weight rather high, but that is not so important as keeping the heat off the underside of the deck. Remember, if you will, the experience which Brunel had with his first ship, *The Great Western* when the boilers had set light to the deck, and Brunel had narrowly escaped with his life, saved by his old friend, Captain Claxton.

In the S.S.G.B., there is a water jacket around the funnel casing, not only as a pre-heat, but to stop any recurrence of his previous experiences. A good clearance is therefore to be recommended on the best authority.

Gas Canisters

The study of the behaviour of gas canisters is also part of the research which has taken place over the last year. It seems that the surface area of the canister is important as far as pressure is concerned, and that a gentle warmth is necessary to keep them from icing up. In the enclosed area of a ship's hull, this is not too much of a problem, but with a constant fierce heat requirement, it may be as well to have a circle of tubing containing preheated water from the boiler to ensure a consistent delivery.

Other Safety Features in Design Stage

Treated purified water, rather than the 'briny' intake of sea-water is obviously necessary for miniature machinery of this kind. Coal was originally stored at either side of the boilers in the centre bulwarks of the S.S.G.B., and this is the sensible place to site the water tanks. In modelling terms there is an immense amount of room for such items, but it is nice to think that the tanks play a dual role in protecting the sides of the hull from excessive heat, as well as providing a constant water supply for the boiler. The delivery of this water into the boiler is by the old fashioned method of a water pump working off the front end of the crankshaft through a regulator. There is also fitted a hand pump for filling the boiler to working level in the first instance.

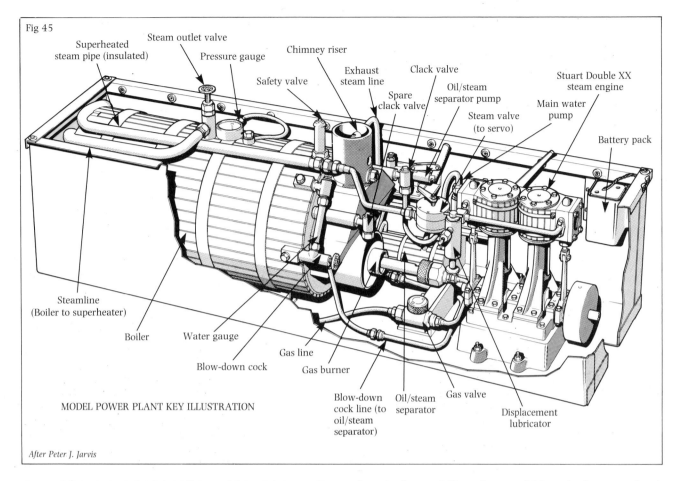

Fig 45

Superheated steam pipe (insulated)
Steam outlet valve
Pressure gauge
Safety valve
Chimney riser
Exhaust steam line
Spare clack valve
Clack valve
Oil/steam separator pump
Steam valve (to servo)
Stuart Double XX steam engine
Main water pump
Battery pack

Steamline (Boiler to superheater)
Boiler
Water gauge
Blow-down cock
Gas line
Gas burner
Blow-down cock line (to oil/steam separator)
Oil/steam separator
Gas valve
Displacement lubricator

MODEL POWER PLANT KEY ILLUSTRATION

After Peter J. Jarvis

Fig 46. Engine against bulkhead.

The Sound of Sawing

The installation of all this machinery means that some of the centre bulkheads need cutting away. This is also the right moment to seal the interior of the hull with a lay-up of glass-fibre strand, which is no job for cowards. I have already been rude about glass-fibre resin paste, but chopped strand is the most hateful of them all. Increasingly I find myself in the haunts of ships' chandlery rather than at the modelling shop, and I bought from our local one, some very wild, hairy looking stuff for the job. Handle it with gloves and caution. The warnings about what organic peroxide can do for you and your living tissue are very explicit and the open air is likely to be your best friend on these deadly occasions.

To lay against all this doom talk, some kind word as far as g.r.p. is concerned, let me say, or rather report something which I heard said by one of this country's leading model ship draughtsmen, that resin is the single most important development in model ship-building that we have seen. I think he is right.

Bowels, Bulwarks and Ballast

From the very outset, the hull of the S.S.G.B. rolled in a pronounced fashion, but true to Brunel's prediction, it hardly pitched at all even in the roughest conditions. Thomas Guppy admitted the word, 'considerable' rolling, but blamed it onto 40 tons of chain on the deck, and high stowed coal at her sides. Corlett points to the truth, that her midship section shape, with its slack bilges and wide water plane was conducive to rolling and her metacentric height or stability was excessive.

Such reports set the modeller thinking when faced with the question of ballast. At an estimated guess, the weight of the completed model without extra ballast will be about 40lb, which although relatively heavy for a model, is light compared with the fully displaced model of, let us say 85lb. So one is faced with a dilemma, a very heavy model,

which is not only difficult to work on, but also back-breaking to launch and recover from the water. Added to this must be the question of strain when the model is out of the water – and that is most of the time. No, when a model is of these proportions, I believe that the weight has to be in one of two forms, either ballast tanks which can be flooded and pumped out, or full sized chain, which can be lowered into the hold(s) as required and withdrawn at the end of the day's run. Chain has the obvious advantage over loose ballast, that it can be easily withdrawn and carried separately from the model.

To this end, much hacking at the bulkheads has had to take place at either side of the engine compartment. It is essential to get the base level down as far as one dare, without weakening the structure of the hull, and here, a sacrifice has had to take place, namely the box girder construction. Although it still exists in the engine housing, its total longitudinal strength is no longer possible as it was originally envisaged. There are however, compensations and I believe, no cause for concern. The hull is extremely strong – fibreglassed on the inside, clinkered in 3 ply birch, and glued with resin glues, to say nothing of the exterior finish in fibreglass paste and several coats of paint. This adds up to a formidable armour which I am satisfied will perform well, particularly when the decking is completed.

The advantage of all this sawing out is a greatly increased accessibility, particularly in the engine room. Of all motive machinery, a steam plant with its 'antimacassar' appeal, needs room both to view and to operate. In passing, I have often paused to wonder why steam engines have such a universal appeal. Electric motors are much more efficient and easy to control. My ship could easily run on compressed air in a splendid hissing silence. One of the new inboard petrol engines would

also be suitable and yet I feel compelled to use steam with all its attendant problems of installation. I have come to the conclusion that the widespread love of steam boils down (sorry) to the human factor. We are attracted by what we know and understand. Steam engines are very like people, much more like people than robots. They hiss and grunt and spit as they grind into action, but with fire in their belly, they are capable of extraordinary output of energy over long periods of time, and none of this magic is lost in miniaturisation.

Heat and Ventilation

Before getting completely carried away in steam clouds of romanticism, an earthly word or two about operational safety. Much has been written and emphasized about boiler safety which it is not my intention to embroider here. Less has been written about the equally important issue of ventilation and heat dispersal.

Basically, the proposition is to put a lighted blow-lamp, with its valve wide open, into the midst of some highly inflammable wood and paint, with a low flash point. If one is not simply building the proverbial 'floating firework' for a one way maiden voyage, then a study of heat shielding and ventilation is an absolute must.

The design of the S.S.G.B. is particularly helpful in this respect and one of the rewards of building a live steamer, is that the ventilators and the like can be put to their proper and original functions.

My inclination is to have a very big safety margin on the heat factor. To this end, I constructed the floor base of the very best quality of mahogany five ply. Next to this, and in the middle of the sandwich, goes $\frac{1}{4}$in Asbestolux sheet, also all the way round the engine compartment. This is followed by a skin of aluminium sheet which keeps

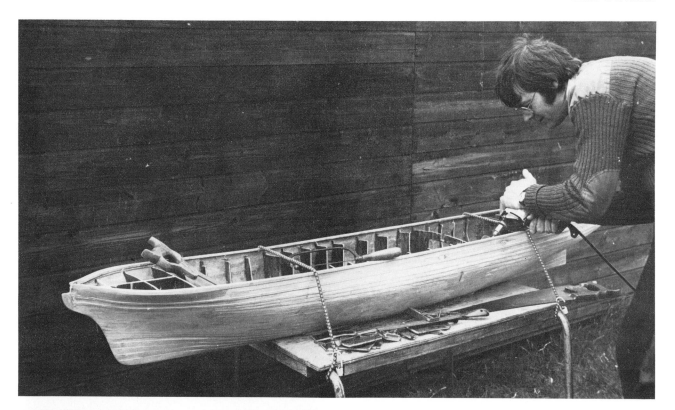

Fig 47. (Opposite) The author's wife and son admiring the egg-box framing before it was sawn out. Fig 48. (Above) Removing the box-girder construction to allow space for installation of the internals. Fig 49. (Left) The large spaces fore and aft of the engine room are the chain lockers, each to hold around 20lb of chain.

grills, at either end of the box, and eventually through the unglazed window lights of the driving wheel housing. Between the decking and the Asbestolux and the aluminium, there is an air gap of about ⅜in, supported by deck beams, which will also give a measure of insulated coolness. The rest, I hope, will return up the flue.

Chain Lockers

At either side of the engine room, the huge chain lockers taking the estimated 20lb of chain each are also lined with aluminium. Besides helping the chain to lie correctly and not to catch or jam on exposed bulkheads, there is a further reason for this lining. This has to do with a possible gas leak, or flame failure. Because butane gas is heavier than air, it lies around in the bottom of boats and is yet another possible cause of explosion. A lined ship however is easier to deal with than one which is full of nooks and crannies.

The Strapping

As it is my intent that the frustrations as well as the joys of building this model should be fully communicated, let me interject that after eight months I am still working on the finish of the hull clinkers. Having corrected the 'shoulder' on the prow into its fully contoured shape, I discover that it subtly alters the angle at which the banded

the Asbestolux in place and further reflects the heat. The sandwich of the three materials is screwed together, so that there is no inflammable glue or vaporisation within what is virtually a chimney amidships. Because this chimney sheath rests on the remains of the bulkheads, it is virtually independent of the hull sides and the bottom.

Ventilation comes through the expanded aluminium

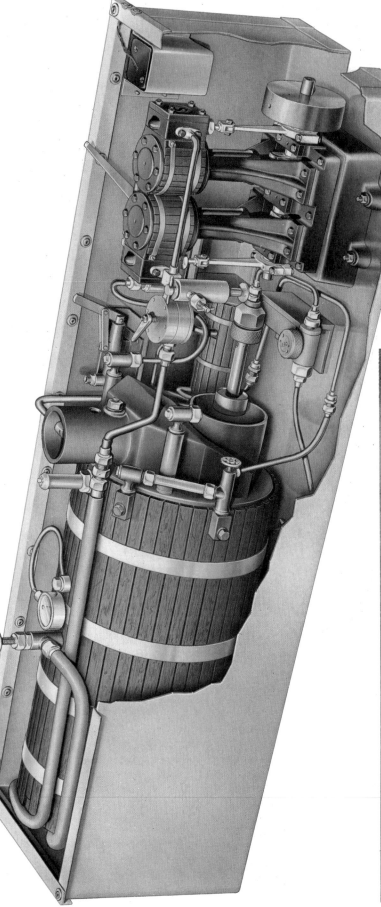

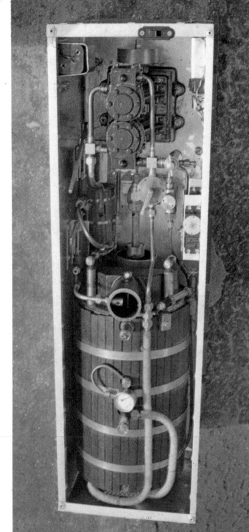

MODEL POWER PLANT SCHEMATIC

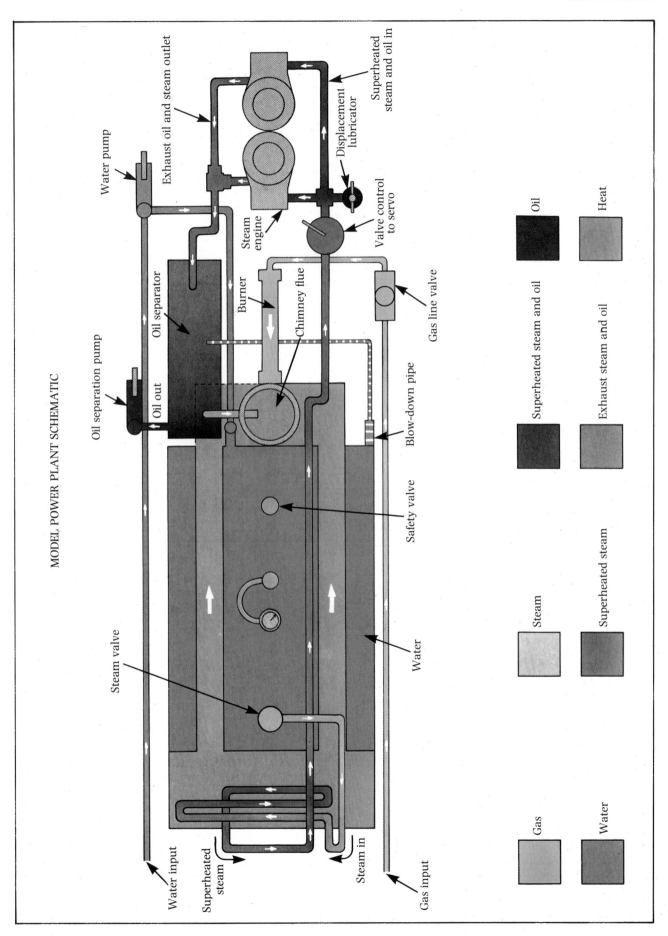

Water pump

Exhaust oil and steam outlet

Superheated steam and oil in

Displacement lubricator

Steam engine

Valve control to servo

Oil separation pump

Oil separator

Burner

Chimney flue

Gas line valve

Oil out

Blow-down pipe

Steam valve

Safety valve

Water

Water input

Superheated steam

Steam in

Gas input

Oil

Heat

Superheated steam and oil

Exhaust steam and oil

Steam

Superheated steam

Gas

Water

Fig 50. (Above) The tubular rivets to hold the strapping in place can just be seen in the photograph. Fig 51. (Right) The raw material for the portholes was a box of spent cartridge cases modified as described in the text. Fig 52. (Opposite) A view of the portholes and strapping of the prototype under restoration at Bristol.

strapping is attached. It is not applied in a symmetrical fashion, but in a way which, viewed from the broadside, appears to be in a straight line. Because of the overhanging bow, however, metaphorically speaking it has to raise an eyebrow in order to give the appearance of straightness. So off it has all had to come and be re-set, but using this time some strips of brass banding which were kindly donated by a local model loco engineer. These are, in fact, marginally undersized in width but absolutely correct in thickness. The fact that they are brass will, I hope, alleviate the sad business of not being able to paint in those mock gun ports that are so much a part of the instant recognition of this ship throughout its history. Unfortunately, after the re-fit in 1846, she was painted black all over with only the gilded adornments picked out in relief. I suspect that the strappings were also painted black, but I intend leaving them 'gilded', not being able to resist the vanity of showing the contours of this hull, over which the strapping passes.

For a quite obscure reason, I found the fixing of this banding to be a laborious job, in that it rejected the usual range of adhesives – Araldite included. In retrospect, it may be that the pencil markings introduced a residue of graphite into the action, although both surfaces were well roughened. Thwarted by three unsatisfactory attempts, I resolved to drill through the brass and rivet it (what else on a ship like this!) with $\frac{1}{16}$in brass tubing; this took nearly two hundred handmade fixings, but does result in the satisfaction of knowing that the banding will not spring off at the first impact blow. Could it also be that subconscious-

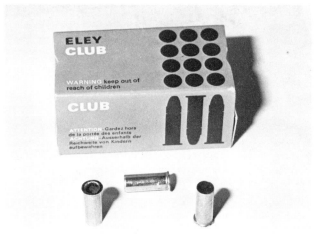

ly, after looking at all that riveting on the prototype, it was necessary to have some proper representation of this method of mechanical fixing somewhere on the miniature?

After seeing the raw hull for almost a year, it is naturally tempting to reach for the nearest pot of undercoat and rid oneself of its 'exhumed' look. In its present state, it looks somewhat like the ship prior to the rescue from Sparrow Cove in 1970 – a ghostly appearance in different shades of grey paste filler with the odd appearance of the levelled timber underneath – a decidedly sickly sight, but full of promise for the future.

Portholes

Shunning the paint brush, certain drillings have to take place in the first instance – the portholes. These are made from spent .22 brass bullet casings, which happen to be exactly the right diameter. The technique for their production is easy enough and involves only the use of a file. The

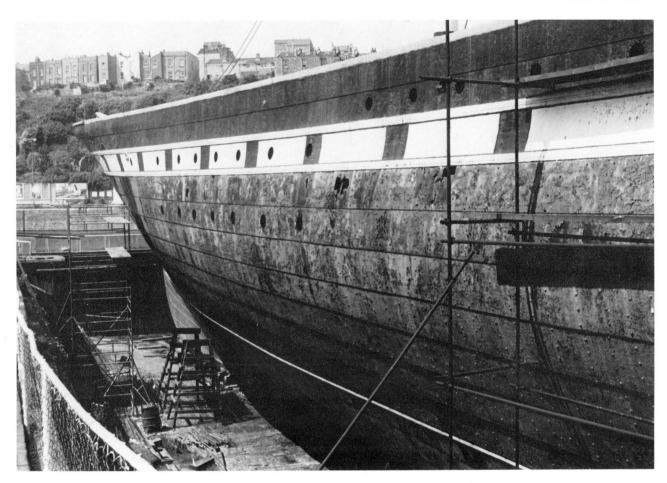

casing is filed down to the breakthrough point on the rim, it is then tapped down from the top (surprisingly) whereupon three more strokes of the file allow the centre to drop away, leaving a thin, but neat circle of brass around the cartridge case. As most proprietory portholes are produced in a rather oversized thickness, these are refreshingly slim, yet appearing to have good depth in that the viewer can see down the cartridge casing, giving the illusion of depth into the hull.

The Bifurcated Hawse Hole

Apart from the portholes, the hawse-pipes outlet must be drilled out. Although the S.S.G.B. now shows both outlets, upper and lower, the original ship sported only the lower exits at the 22ft level. This was an audacious piece of design, cheeking traditional shipbuilders with adventurous daring in the new material. This low lying hawse must have given some trouble, (it would have been difficult to bung in the traditional way) and it was blanked off in the 1857 version of the ship on the Australian Run. Thus warned, mine is drilled through as was the original, but will be blanked off on the interior so as to be watertight. I assume that Brunel was responsible for the 'inhaling nostril' appearance, and as well as having great artistic appeal, the bifurcated hawse was also a piece of practical engineering. The best place for an anchor cable is on the water line. The stem bar must be continuous and it would be impossible to get them close together higher up; set low down, it gave the cables a good lead up the hawses.

The idea that Brunel's ships could be likened to sea monsters which snorted their way across the Atlantic, was quickly seized upon by contemporary journalists. The very name of "The Mammoth" conjured up in their minds the spuming leviathan of the deep, and they were more than happy to trade on rumours of creatures who attacked ships from unfathomable depths, consuming both the vessel and the crew which manned her, leaving nothing but rumour and wreckage. To prove that journalists were thinking like this, consider a report of the departure of Brunel's first ship, The Great Western, at the beginning of the first Atlantic steam race with The Sirius ...

"The Great Western is roused at length. One may see her excited, almost like a living thing. She heaves her huge, whale-like sides, with impatience. Her paddles instinctively dash into the water, as a war horse, when he hears a trumpet, paws the ground, and see, how the fierce breath of a giant defiance pours out of her eager nostrils!" (London Gazette, April 4th, 1838, from "Sway of the Grand Saloon")

At almost the same time as that report was written, the concept of the Mammoth was being dreamed by Brunel. He can hardly have failed to be influenced by the idea of sea monsters, nostrils, hot breath and all. When almost a year ago, I inserted that large piece of stout brass, acting as the stem-post, I was aware that without a metal insert, this part of the model would not have been strong enough to take any impact without injury.

INTERLUDE

Off the Plateau (and on with the Paint)

And so at last, after fifteen months of hull construction and finishing, the first coat of matt black paint has been applied as a primer. Strictly speaking, the painting could have waited until the engineering had been done, but frankly, after six weeks of doing nothing to the model, I badly needed some visible and mental reassurance that I was progressing at all. In the midst of the worst winter we have had for 16 years, I had virtually lost all momentum for the project and had, in any case, to give way to some pressing domestic demands to redecorate the front hall and the loo, on pains of not being allowed to bring my work into the kitchen unless this demand was met!

Matt-Black is Beautiful

I have to admit that matt black is the most interesting paint. It has an ability to introduce instant realism and density, and were it not for the fact that it absorbs oil and dirt marks so easily, I would leave it as a final coat wherever ordinary black was required. Later on of course, it will be sealed with several coats of matt shine. The change

Fig 53. (Opposite) B&P photo of bifurcated hawse. Fig 54. (Below) The hawse hole is clearly seen in this shot of the model as are the remarkable lines.

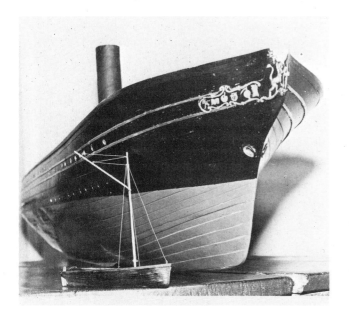

in the look of the painted hull is quite outstanding and the brass banding with the matching portholes, (which are pushed out for the painting process), stand out in a quite resplendent way against the murky matt blackness. Cautionary note here . . . it looks too smart, and something will have to be done about this, in the name of realism.

I am greatly cheered by the result. Certain anxieties have not materialised. I was a little concerned that when the hull was painted, the bulkheads might show slight protrusion; it is in fact not possible to guarantee that this won't happen over long lengths of strip timber, but it hasn't happened in this case. The other matter which concerned me was how the clinkers would actually look when painted. I obviously wanted them to show, and I wanted it to be registered that the ones at the bottom of the hull are thicker than those which clad the sides, but at the same time, not to appear out of scale or over pronounced. I am relieved to say that they conform to this, although I will have to be careful not to overdo the red lead paint when that is applied.

Just a word about application. I use a rough 1½in brush for the ship hull, It was sold to me by our local garage for 'gunking' down the car engine, and where the normal brush would have three hairs, this one only has one. The effect is to leave brush marks. What, I hear from the pressure-can purists, not even an air-brush? the answer is a firm 'no'. Leave the brush marks in even though they are out of scale, they are part of what the eye accepts as natural on a model hull of this size. I want the finished model to have the dignity of looking like a ship, warts and all.

From the Sublime to the Ridiculous – the Lifeboats

The S.S. *Great Britain* carried six lifeboats of some 30ft in length designed to take 80 people each. They were clinker built of iron and had buoyancy tanks sealed into the keels and were the advanced innovations of Thomas Guppy. The fact that the lifeboats were constructed of iron seems particularly impudent when one remembers what people were saying and thinking about iron in the early 1840's – namely that it didn't float and was therefore, by its very nature, most unsuitable. That the Great Western Steam Ship Co. should expect its passengers to trust their lives in an emergency to an iron boat seemed to be laughing fortune in the face . . . a fairly common character trait of its chief designer!

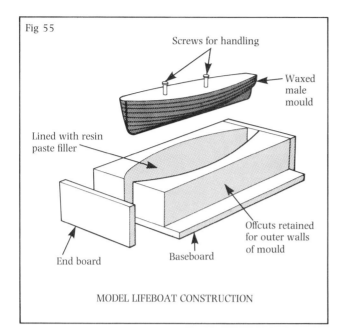

Fig 55

Screws for handling

Waxed male mould

Lined with resin paste filler

Offcuts retained for outer walls of mould

End board

Baseboard

MODEL LIFEBOAT CONSTRUCTION

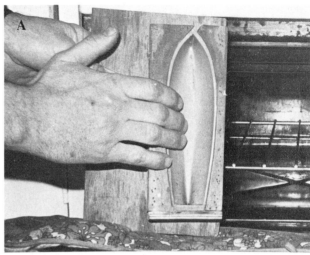

A

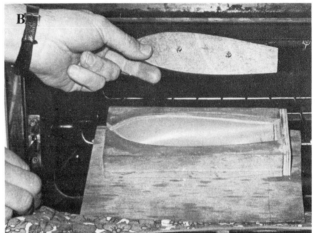

B

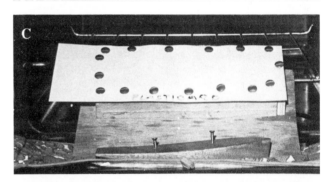

C

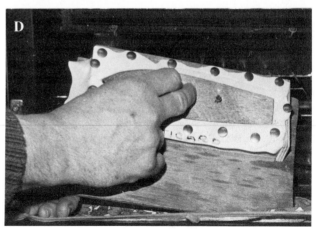

D

Fig 56. Legend for plastic moulding of lifeboats. a) Waxing the female mould with molten wax from the tobacco tin (grill set at 180°C, or number 8, hot). b) Warming the male mould prior to waxing. c) Plasticard (.010) with drawing pins encircling the mould. This prevents Plasticard distorting. d) Male mould pressed well home. e) The result. f) Trimming round the top edge whilst Plasticard is still warm. g) Removing the flash. h) Lots for everyone! i) Fixing the thwarts. Note the black plastic insulation tape with which the hull is clinkered. j) Fixing the thwart battens.

The reproduction of these six auxiliary boats meant for me something untried. I had read articles on plastic moulding and certain aspects of this process were very appealing to me. It is theoretically quick and simple and the product is like the often cursed plastic cup, identical to the one that went before.

Plastic Moulding Process

I decided to go only half way with this process, not to attempt to include the clinker lines, but simply to produce the shape. I bought several thicknesses of Plasticard with which to experiment, and set about carving the shape out of a piece of obechi. This was bandsawn out of a rectangular piece of some $9 \times 5 \times 2$in, and the offcuts were retained for use later. The solid male block was then carved and shaped to the hull lines of the plan and coated with wax; it is also a good idea to put two screws into the top of the male mould so that extraction from the mould is made easier. Next the female mould has to be made. Here the offcuts from the original rectangle were placed together on a base board to form the hollow of the female mould but spaced $\frac{1}{4}$in apart, so as to allow the resin paste filler to key well into the interior walls of the mould. Using the old offcuts saves a good deal of resin paste and makes a useful cradle for subsequent work on the boat.

Having caked the inside of the mould with filler paste, the male mould is pressed into the female until the paste oozes out and up (sounds disgusting!). The male should be

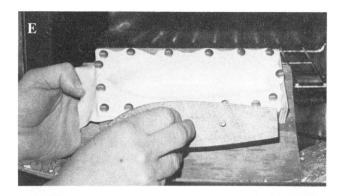

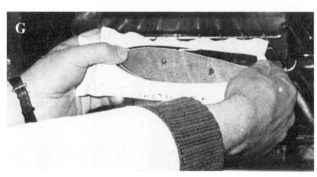

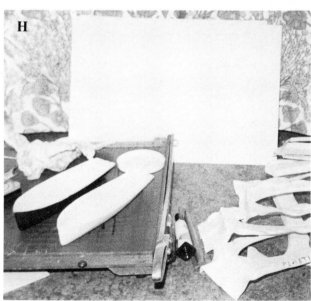

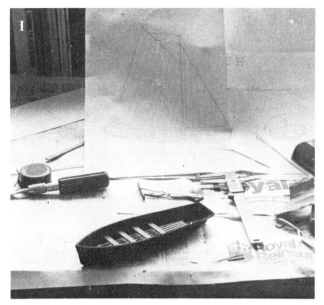

pressed about $\frac{1}{8}$in deeper into the female to allow for trimming off later.

The heat generated by the curing agent of the filler paste melts the wax on the male mould and as soon as the resin has hardened, the male can be withdrawn, leaving a nice smooth finish.

Now comes the only really difficult part of the operation – that is reducing, by the thickness of the Plasticard, the total shape of the male hull. There are fancy methods of doing this, but I will admit that all I did was to score round the outer edges and with a little bit of planing and sanding back, removed the necessary difference of thickness.

Welsh Rarebit en Plastique

All set for the grill then with well waxed male and female moulds at the ready – for all the world it looks as though you are about to enjoy obechi soufflé done to a light turn. Before cooking, (I used a No.8 setting) the Plasticard needs to be pinned all the way round. About 20 seconds under

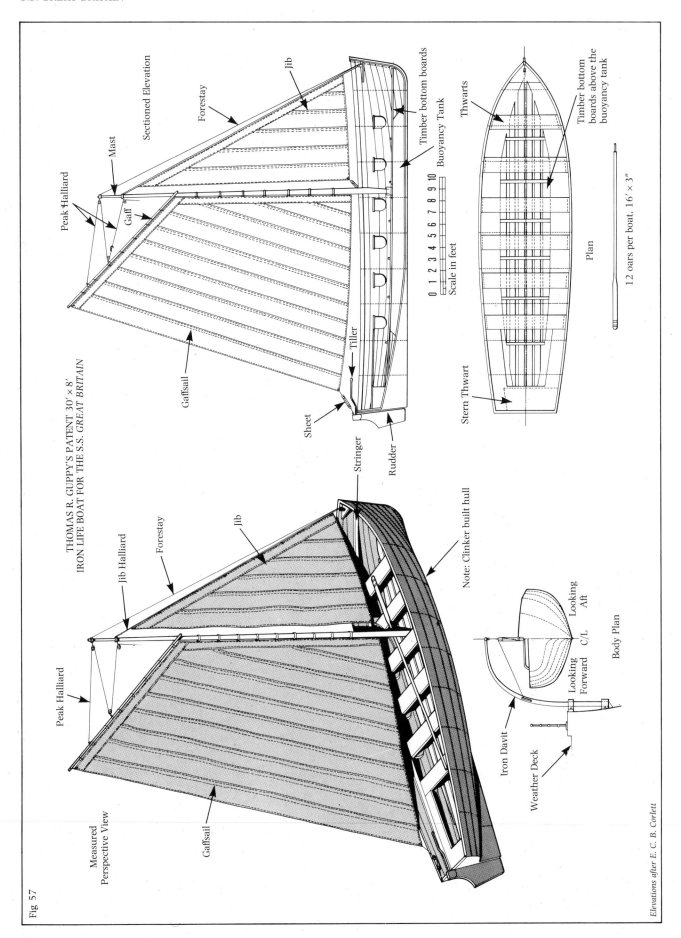

THOMAS R. GUPPY'S PATENT 30' × 8'
IRON LIFE BOAT FOR THE S.S. *GREAT BRITAIN*

Sectioned Elevation

Jib

Forestay

Mast

Peak Halliard

Gaff

Gaffsail

Tiller

Sheet

Stringer

Rudder

Timber bottom boards

Buoyancy Tank

Scale in feet
0 1 2 3 4 5 6 7 8 9 10

Thwarts

Timber bottom boards above the buoyancy tank

Plan

Stern Thwart

12 oars per boat, 16' × 3"

Measured Perspective View

Peak Halliard

Jib Halliard

Forestay

Jib

Gaffsail

Note: Clinker built hull

Looking Aft

Body Plan

C/L

Looking Forward

Iron Davit

Weather Deck

Elevations after E. C. B. Corlett

Fig 57

64

the grill reduces the Plasticard to a consistency of wet chamois leather cloth and you can actually see the plastic start to sink into the mould. Now is the moment to withdraw the female and press home the well waxed male. Ten seconds or so later you can trim round the top edge using a sharp knife, with the male mould still in place. This effectively gives you a ready finished product and I experienced no difficulty in removing the plastic boat from the female mould. Although the thicker plastic gave a very robust result, the very thinnest I had gave the sharpest image, which I preferred. I was anxious not to have it looking like plastic.

In the initial state straight from the mould, it is very flimsy and needs reinforcing. I made the gunwales, inner and outer, from strips of Plasticard and fixed the base,

representing the buoyancy tanks with yet more Plasticard. The clinker lines were then cut from a piece of plastic insulation tape into thin strips and laid, starting from the keel. This process, incidentally, must be done, as always, with planking alternately, for even plastic insulation tape will distort the lines and hog the vessel if you try to do it in any other fashion.

The clinkering strengthens the shell considerably, and a coat of matt-black produces the effect of which I spoke earlier. The wooden interior was then built up in a traditional way using veneer strips, (the duckboards are made of horse-chestnut and flamed maple) with some mahogany for the seats and sail locker. The rudder has the usual fixings, brass capped at the top, and the simple mast and boom are likewise furnished. Each boat will have twelve ramin oars. These loose-footed, gaff-rigged cutters have a charm all their own, and although fairly large for lifeboats, show the immense size of the mothership by comparison.

There was one more general purpose boat, stowed forward of the main mast on what I can only describe as a bedstead, for the practical reason of keeping the boat off the anchor cables which ran beneath it. It was the same size as the other lifeboats, but built of wood for lightness of handling and painted white.

An interesting question for me is whether or not the buoyancy tanks were kept with fresh water in the boats; if so, a very clever and original safety feature was accommodated for the most practical of reasons. Almost certainly rainwater could have been collected and stored like this, and for all the criticisms of iron vessels, this was a feature no wooden vessel had.

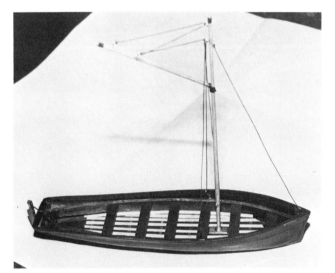

Fig 58. (Left) The model lifeboat. Fig 59. (Below) Finished lifeboat suspended from davits.

WORKING PARTS

Fashioning the Propeller

Ever since the original Mr Archimedes jumped out of his Grecian wash tub in 250 BC (or thereabouts), and shouted "Eureka", loosely translated as "I have found it" (had he lost the soap?), the bath has been a famous place in which to conjure up ideas and hypotheses. This was obvious some six months ago when I realized that the ideal basis on which to build the weird four-bladed propeller was staring me in the face, or in the toe if you prefer. As a piece of hardware for the foundation of the propeller, the bath tap has everything going for it, having not only a centre boss with four arms in a single casting, but being made of brass it possesses all the virtues of easy soldering and a detachable shank.

For a long while I said nothing but eyed it as a spider does a fly when the web is well spun. The one on the wash-basin was even better, but being a coward at heart and knowing where my best interests lie, I had a word with a friendly plumber who produced the following day a somewhat ancient but very solid chromed brass tap, which would amply allow the full bodied twist of the prototype casting.

The original was an interesting piece of work. It was perhaps the most significant change made in the 1846 refit programme. Fashioned in Bristol, it was 15ft 6in in diameter, weighing 7 tons, with a pitch of 25ft. It had a semi-round back, with a flat driving face. I do not know exactly when and where it was made, but the formal report made to the directors of the GWSSCO on 17 Dec.

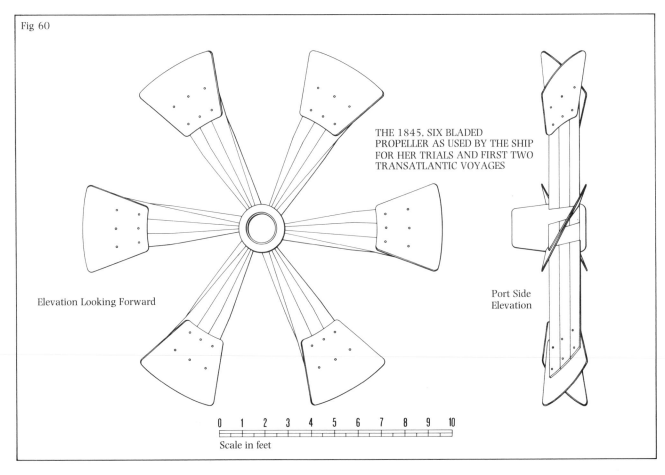

Fig 60

THE 1845, SIX BLADED PROPELLER AS USED BY THE SHIP FOR HER TRIALS AND FIRST TWO TRANSATLANTIC VOYAGES

Elevation Looking Forward

Port Side Elevation

0 1 2 3 4 5 6 7 8 9 10
Scale in feet

1844 following the preliminary sea trials, records Thomas Guppy as saying: "The present (six-bladed) screw has rather surpassed my expectations, but as you have voted that another shall be made and its progress has only been delayed until we can make some observations with regard to this one; I have already consulted Mr Brunel on the subject; it will not be desirable to proceed far with it until we have had the benefit of a few more trial trips . . .

This four bladed propeller was undoubtedly the one intended for the ship on a permanent basis. It was certainly more robust than the six bladed fan, and in section falls between the modern four bladed prop and the experimental one which any visitor to the restored ship in Bristol may view. They are both beautiful objects in their own right, quite apart from their efficient power absorption and their important place in the history of ship propulsion. When I handle this four bladed propeller, I am reminded of a Maltese cross in a three dimensional form and there

Fig 61

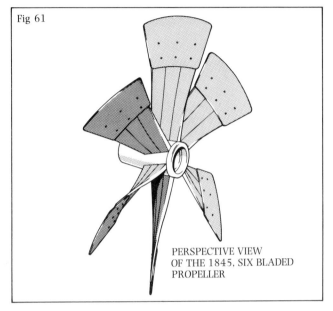

PERSPECTIVE VIEW OF THE 1845, SIX BLADED PROPELLER

Fig 62

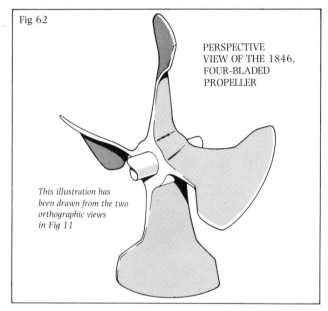

PERSPECTIVE VIEW OF THE 1846, FOUR-BLADED PROPELLER

This illustration has been drawn from the two orthographic views in Fig 11

Fig 63

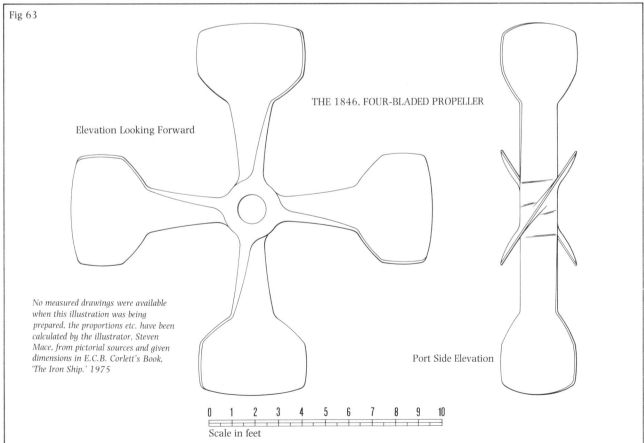

Elevation Looking Forward

THE 1846, FOUR-BLADED PROPELLER

Port Side Elevation

No measured drawings were available when this illustration was being prepared, the proportions etc. have been calculated by the illustrator, Steven Mace, from pictorial sources and given dimensions in E.C.B. Corlett's Book, 'The Iron Ship.' 1975

0 1 2 3 4 5 6 7 8 9 10
Scale in feet

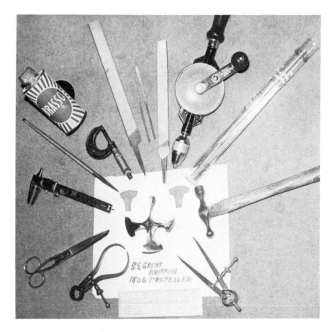

Fig 64. (Left) Tools used for the hand-fashioned propeller of the 1846 refit. Fig 65. Legend for fashioning the propeller. a) Cutting the slot into the tap wing. b) Checking the slot with the piece of brass insert. c) Cutting the palm ends of the prop with the bandsaw. d) Measuring the inserted palm end. e) Pinning the brass through. f) Using the shaper file. g) Applying the heat. Garage proprietor Chris Richards wields the heat gun. h) 'Truing it up' on the lathe. i) The persuader! – or sledgehammer to crack a nut – leading and trailing edges adjustment. Note the flat back of the blade section. It will be very interesting to see how efficiently this performs.

is a certain deliciousness in the feel of the contoured brass, and a certain relief that it was not as difficult to make as I had feared it might be.

Over a long period I studied the ink sketch in Dr Corlett's book. Propellers are very difficult to draw and are one of the classic cases of optical illusion. My other reference was the photograph of the 1:12 scale model of the original machinery which sports a larger replica of the 4-bladed propeller. This is not to be confused with the one fitted to the Thomas Guppy model, which is, sadly, inaccurate, although it does not stop me from being fascinated as to the reason why this model has a four bladed propeller but the original rig? Was the model built before the six bladed propeller, or a very long time afterwards, when the details of the four different propellers had become confused or obscured?

I made the original incisions into the tap-top wings and widened them by the use of all-purpose metal blades. this was still not wide enough to accept 12 gauge brass and so a needle file had to be employed to make the marriage a happy one. The four fins were then cut out of the brass

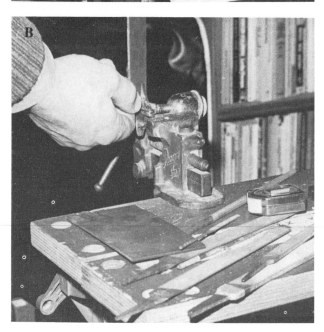

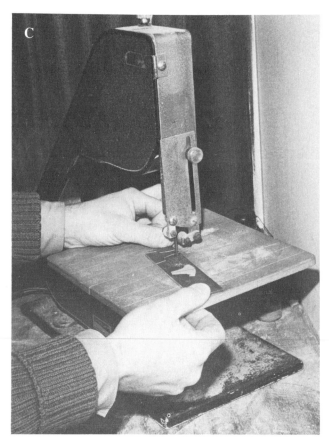

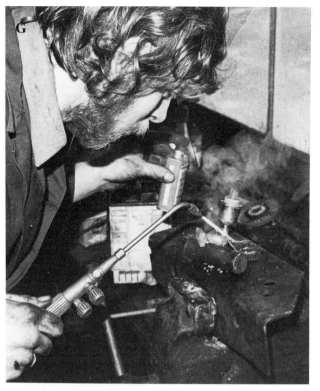

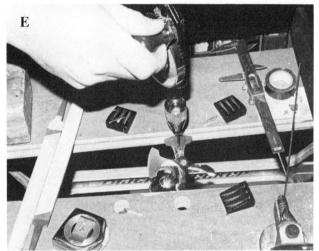

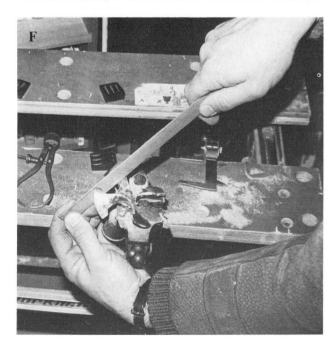

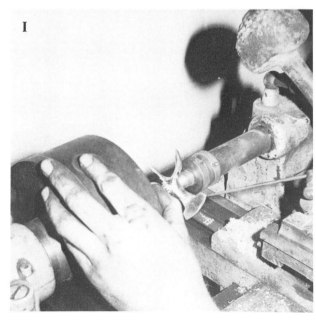

with the aid of the bandsaw, having been previously matched by the use of graph paper glued onto the surface of the brass. They were then clamped and filed as one in order to ensure their regularity. The coarse pitch of the propeller was then applied in three movements starting with the outer part of the fin, and working inwards towards the boss. Plumber's grips and a small engineer's vice were substantial enough to see this job through, although 12 gauge brass is fairly resistant.

Much filing followed this, until the top of the tap began its metamorphosis from bath tap to ship's propeller. The final job of the evening was to pin it through with brass rod, in order to secure it firmly in the soldering process to follow.

Meanwhile . . . down at the garage . . .

Garages, by tradition almost, have a bad press in the eyes of the public at large, but it has been my experience that this is largely brought about by the frustrations of bad components and other people's engineering, to say nothing of clients who want today's repairs done yesterday and preferably at yesterday's prices. That, as they say, is another story. When confronted with a piece of glinting, solid brass, albeit still in the rough, a sparkle comes into the mechanic's eye which is almost as bright as the oxyacetylene torch itself.

In the picture, you will see the propeller awash with 'Baker's Fluid' and aglow with unashamed heat. Here the solder stick is lovingly applied and there is an attention to detail that no exhaust pipe ever experienced. Totally unsolicited by me, the offer then came to 'true it up' on the lathe, and test the leading and trailing edges of the fins. With the exception of one blade (why is there always one?), the propeller ran truly and evenly; a slight tweak with the plumber's grips and a light tap with the mallet on the offending fin, and I departed with a refusal to accept money and a request for the launching date, which I was unable to give.

Plastic Surgery – Restyling the Stern Frame

The price of not carrying out sufficient preliminary research can be a high one to pay. When I originally built the hull, I omitted to appreciate the difference between an iron ship's stern frame and a wooden one. Thus the stern was finished with clinkers flush to it – leaving an inexact profile. Reference to the prototype reveals that, as in all other ways, this hull was innovatory in its unmistakably sleek and streamlined stern frame. This characteristic was hydrodynamically very important in its action on the propeller and rudder. (In passing, I reject totally the notion that the hull design team did not understand the science of hydrodynamics, in terms of speed and efficiency, although I accept that it is anachronistic to label it by the modern name.)

Correcting this grave fault in the model refers me back to one of my opening statements that this undertaking

Fig 66. (Opposite) The full size replica six-bladed propeller being fitted to the restored S.S. Great Britain *under renovation at Bristol Docks. Compare size of propeller with observers below (Photo. David Cundell). Fig 67. (Above Left) Prototype stern frame. Fig 68. (Left) Model hull shown inverted at some stage of development as prototype. Fig 69. (Above) B&P photo. Down among the deep floors and crutches of prototype.*

would require a degree or two of courage. After 18 months work on a hull, the thought of assaulting it with a tenon saw was sufficiently terrifying to put it out of my mind as something which it was too late to rectify; I acquitted myself with such mental excuses as, "It will never show anyway, when the rudder and propeller are in place". Yet it began to annoy me in a festering kind of way. It was wrong. I knew it to be wrong and I couldn't look at the stern without feeling acutely disappointed. Every time I looked at it, I could hear Brunel whispering, as he had done to Captain Claxton at Dundrum Bay, "You have failed, I think . . . from that which causes nine tenths of all failures in this world, from not doing quite enough".

I lost a night's sleep, weighing up the likely outcome of this piece of major surgery. This put me in a sufficiently aggressive mood to make the amputation. Sawing away the clinker strakes soon revealed the stern post and, for all the world, I felt like the orthopaedic surgeon trying to rectify an inborn deformity. In this medical frame of mind, I wished to work as quickly as possible, so that I could put the patient to bed without the open wound showing for too long.

Whilst down there amongst "the deep floors and crutches", I took the opportunity to strengthen this whole area with long wedges of pine wood, firmly resined, giving greater rigidity to the whole area around the stern tube. The wedges were shaped to profile and overlaid with expanded aluminium mesh and filled with resin paste. False continuation of the iron strakes was imitated by a double layer of masking tape being laid along the hull and paste built up to the edge of the tape. The removal of the tape, after the pasting, leaves an edge which satisfactorily copies the original. It is worth saying now, that if I had discovered this method before, I would have carvel built the hull and overlaid it in this fashion, saving what I guess would be about a year's work. That is the price of experience.

At the end of this 10 hour operation, I was able to leave the patient with the major part of the 'plastic surgery' completed. It was a job that I suppose I need not have tackled but I cannot say how glad I am to have it behind me rather than before me. I have heard patients in hospital express the same sentiment.

The Solepiece

The solepiece, that is to say, the bottom horizontal member of the stern frame, is made from a strip of 12 gauge brass, somewhat oversized in scale, for the practical reason of strength and the honest admission that I was unable to obtain any other thickness in strip. I soft soldered to this the strengthening brass wings and triangular support at the base of the propeller frame where it meets the keel of the ship.

Because the ship was originally designed for paddle

Fig 70. (Top right) Final shaping of the solepiece following the major surgery described in the text. Fig 71. (Right) Fitting the solepiece. Fig 72. (Below) The futuristic shape of the lines is well displayed by this inverted pose of the hull prior to fitting the solepiece.

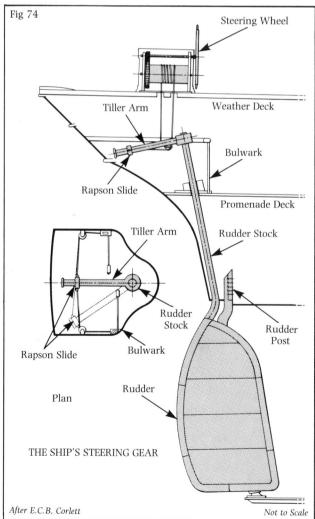

Fig 73. The balanced rudder and propeller round off the attractive hind quarters of the S.S.G.B.

Fig 74

Steering Wheel

Tiller Arm

Weather Deck

Rapson Slide

Bulwark

Promenade Deck

Rudder Stock

Tiller Arm

Rudder Stock

Rudder Post

Rapson Slide

Bulwark

Plan

Rudder

THE SHIP'S STEERING GEAR

After E.C.B. Corlett

Not to Scale

wheels and had "a clean run" astern to the rudder, when the plans were altered, it became necessary to drop the solepiece to accommodate the propeller palms. In comparison with all the other difficulties faced by the midstream rethink of conversion to screw propulsion, Brunel dismissed this small problem as "something which could easily be done, without any expense". By trimming the ship differently, he claimed that it would make no difference to the draught either.

If one looks at the painting by Joseph Walter of the ship being warped out of the Avon dock on 24 January 1845, one can clearly see the propeller blades popping out of the water. Before any accusations can be levelled at Brunel for having miscalculated the draft or not keeping his word to the Directors of the GWSSCO, it has to be appreciated that the final trimming of the ship depended upon deep ballast tanks which had the effect of actually improving the resistance. The picture is correct and yet misleading if one is ignorant of the fact that the ship had to be "dead light" – that is to say no stores, no water and so forth aboard, in order to slip through the lock, something to which I will refer later.

What a splendid turbulence it must have created when the engine was engaged! Is one perhaps allowed the secret thought that Brunel knew full well what that gushing fountain of foam would do in terms of visual effect for all those who came to see this "wonder of the world", particularly Royalty, statesmen, shareholders and rivals? I guess we could soon discredit this ignoble conjecture, for Brunel was engineer first and showman second, even if tempted to extremes of flamboyancy; then, as now, it was speed which counted and not 'pretty sights'.

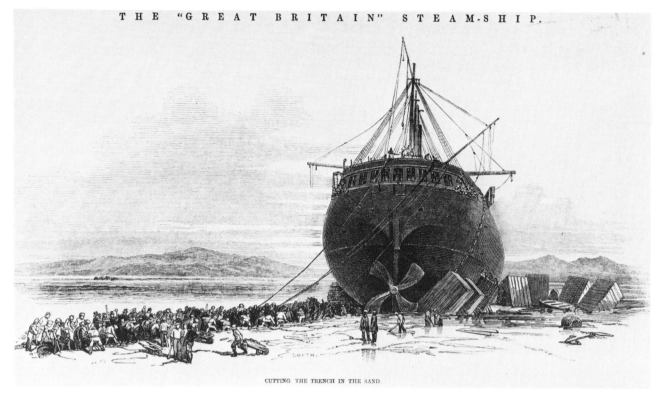

THE "GREAT BRITAIN" STEAM-SHIP.

CUTTING THE TRENCH IN THE SAND.

Fig 75. (Above) S.S.G.B. aground in Dundrum Bay 1846 (copyright BBC Hulton Picture Library). Fig 76. (Right) Despite a very large model, engine room is still at a premium. Fig 77. (Far right) The deck beams and tieplates, showing the curvature of the cambered deck and the restoration of longitudinal strength.

The Balanced Rudder

On paper, this double-cranked rudder, designed by Brunel, looks both innocent and attractive – like a well-sucked lollipop.

Its apparent innocence soon ends when it is discovered how critical its installation has to be for it to function correctly. The underlying and key factor is the angle of the rudder post shaft through the ship's stern member, which you may remember was sawn out before the two spine pieces were joined (see "Hull Strength"). Sad to say, this piece of forethought proved to be out of true by about 3 degrees, which in turn displaced the axis of the bottom pintle. The rudder functioned perfectly well but could not be anchored to the base of the stern frame in its correct position. I fondly imagined that a three degree error would be easy to overcome, and goodness knows how long I fiddled about with it, but angles and axes of moving parts will not function in any other way than that laid down by the original drawings.

I include a sketch of how the original rudder worked using what is called a "Rapson slide", which had been invented in 1839, and is basically simple and very economical on space. The diagram is founded upon a scale drawing in Dr Corlett's book (p.65). The plans show the rudder stock or shaft was fitted immediately behind the rudder post. The angle of the rudder post (80 degrees) continues the line of the shaft by means of this cranked

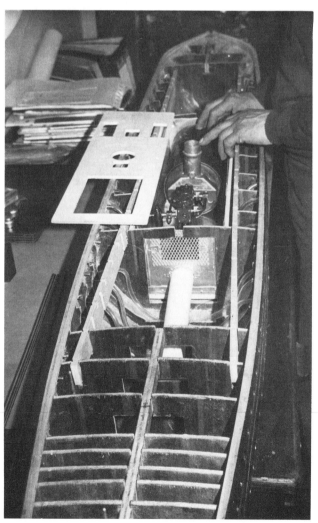

and removable rudder post, which in turn, fits into the pintle at the point determined by the angle of the rudder shaft. It seems almost as hard to explain on paper as it is to fit into the model. It would be rather a tasty feature to have the model work by means of the Rapson slide, but in practical terms I am considering a rather more conventional system for the time being at least.

The balanced rudder, with no central stable position, was a very advanced piece of thinking and application for this early Victorian period. It admirably suited its purpose when under power, but as with all similarly designed rudders, its tendency to 'flop over' when under sail must have required both skill and sheer concentration on the part of the helmsman to avoid. Sadly, the balanced rudder was supplanted in the 1852 refit, following the disastrous episode of stranding on Dundrum Bay, and I would guess from one or two of the contemporary sketches, that it was badly damaged during the time that the ship was "lying like a useless saucepan kicking about on the most exposed shore you can imagine". In fact this same report of Brunel's does go on to mention "some slight damage to the stern ... " Despite the fact that it was replaced, it did form the basis of what is now accepted practice in modern ship-building, and is yet another demonstration of the imaginative foresight of our "man with the top hat".

The Main Weather Deck

The weather deck, unlike the fo'c's'le deck, has a degree of camber on it for the obvious reasons of strength and drainage. Its curvature is gentle but unmistakable. Profile sections through the ship show this camber as being quite appreciable at the forward end, whilst the midship section displays the considerable down-turn as it approaches the "waterway" (deck gutter sluice). Viewed from above, however, this is somewhat obscured by the inclusion of a heavy baltic-pine stringer, which structurally speaking, on the prototype tied all the side frames together.

Producing this deck camber is a bit of a chore in that it involves a great deal of kerfing, but this is 'band saw country', and with a small jig, much of the tedium is removed. The inclusion of two longitudinal tieplates, set between the frames of the model, restores the original box structure and provides a level basis on which to set the deck beams.

Way back, when the bulkhead frames were originally sawn out, I deliberately cut well below the deckline, in order that the deck beams could be built up to the correct level at this later stage. Former experience has taught me that it is much easier to build up the level than to reduce it down. The longitudinal tieplates act as a good means of determining a straight run and both deck beams and tieplates are made from that brittle but strong hardwood, ramin.

Before any gluing can take place, the main engineering works have to be installed, and proper preparation for this includes tidying up the aluminium casing for both the chain lockers and the engine room. Now that the tie-plates are in position, the sheathing aluminium is secured on the inside of the tie-plates using the bulkhead frames on which to rest.

The aluminium engine room protective shield has been made into a waterproof casing, with ventilation through the expanded aluminium mesh at either end of the oblong box. Then there is an oblong aluminium casing protection, necessary to keep the heavy ballasting chain from interfering with the intermediate shaft running inside it.

Interestingly enough, the original intermediate shaft was much as we would view a cast iron drain-pipe today; hollow in section, 61ft 8in in length, but made with wrought iron half-round plates, riveted together (see picture of the mainyard for a similarity of construction). Although this must have given cause for concern, in that it was a long distance for such an unsupported shaft to travel, there is no record of it presenting any problems. The "Solid or Hollow" argument was to go on for many years, particularly with regard to crankshafts, and there was much waxing of eloquent words in the Mechanical Engineering Journals of the day. Yet here was Brunel with yet another 'first' for this ship, an experimental feature which is not perhaps so often underlined as the more dramatic aspects of the S.S.G.B.

And So to Bristol

Apart from the obvious feelings and associations about the boiler being made in the self-same city as the prototype, and the consequent legitimacy of the model to

Fig 78. (Above) The stainless steel tail-shaft being machined through the three-jaw chuck and with subsequent use of the die mounted on the tail-stock. Fig 79. (Right) Tightening up the universal coupling on the tail-shaft.

bear the coat of arms of its birthplace on the transom, it is heartening to know that the residual skills which produced the original are still present today, albeit the men work on aircraft rather than ships.

I have already mentioned Geoff Sheppard, and it is he who is at the central focus of the boiler making process, during which I simply acted as photographic observer. As I use a very simple and rather ancient Kodak 'Retinette' camera, it is to Geoff's credit that he never once objected to the 42in measuring rod for the focal length, which kept appearing under his nose as he went through all the different processes of manufacture.

A lengthy pondering of the layout produced several constructive thoughts, particularly about siting and accessibility. The asbestolux cut-out shows, there are certain immovables, such as the funnel exit and the original driving wheel housing. The major problem lay, however, in where we might site the all important steam take-off. With such a large size of boiler, the headroom is tight. Here we were saved somewhat by the design of the original, which has a hatched grating sited between the two forward companionways, which could be readily used for the purpose. The safety valve presents the same kind of question, and is sited near the chimney riser, so that both may exhaust up the funnel. The diameter of the funnel is

Fig 80

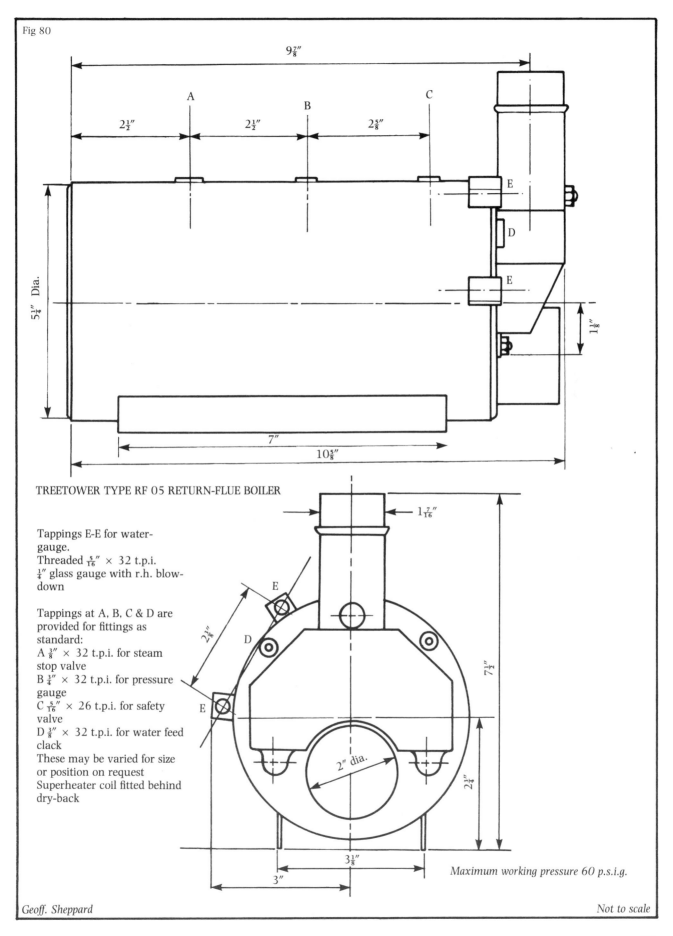

TREETOWER TYPE RF 05 RETURN-FLUE BOILER

Tappings E-E for water-
gauge.
Threaded $\frac{5}{16}''$ × 32 t.p.i.
$\frac{1}{4}''$ glass gauge with r.h. blow-
down

Tappings at A, B, C & D are
provided for fittings as
standard:
A $\frac{3}{8}''$ × 32 t.p.i. for steam
stop valve
B $\frac{3}{4}''$ × 32 t.p.i. for pressure
gauge
C $\frac{5}{16}''$ × 26 t.p.i. for safety
valve
D $\frac{3}{8}''$ × 32 t.p.i. for water feed
clack
These may be varied for size
or position on request
Superheater coil fitted behind
dry-back

Maximum working pressure 60 p.s.i.g.

Geoff. Sheppard

Not to scale

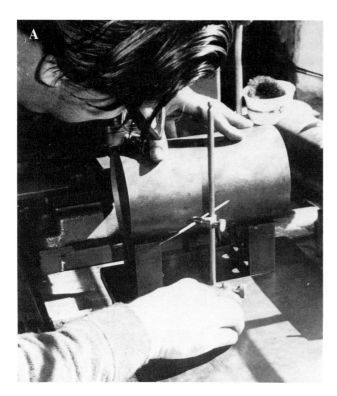

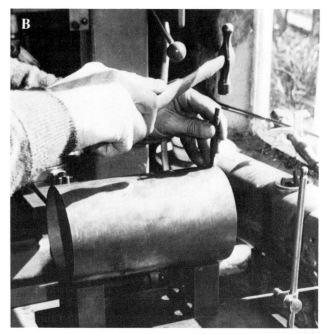

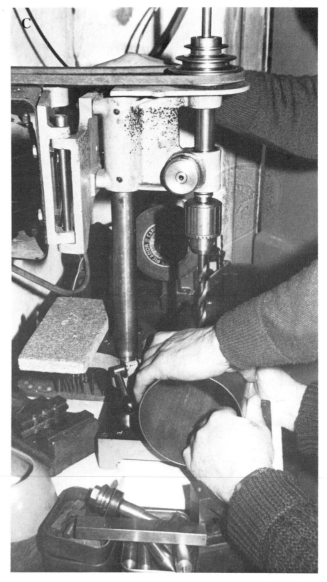

Fig 81. a) Scribing out the boiler shell. Note the flat machine faced table and the supporting "V" blocks which allow for a very accurate marking line. b) "Who pinched my centre punch!" Geoff Sheppard punching the holes for the safety valve and steam take-off outlets. c) Using the pillar drill and an extra pair of hands to drill the steam take-off outlet. d) Gently tapping on the end plates. Note the copper rod boiler stays and the spiral cross-flow tubes of the main flue. e) Marrying it all together. f) Testing the fit of the chimney with the return flues and boiler stays.

large enough to incorporate both safety valve and exhaust gases.

It also became very clear that despite a very large model, engine room space is still at a premium. The yoked gas bottles would have to be moved to the space originally meant for the forward ballasting chain and plumbed in from there. The engine could then be moved under the original driving wheel housing, and there would be room to operate the burner and hand pump much more easily.

One more major issue remained before any work could start, and that was the question of the prop shaft and engine mounting. I had already aligned two $\frac{1}{4}$in inside diameter brass tubes, appropriately angled to allow sufficient height for the engine mounting inside the aluminium casing. Into these tubes is to be inserted stainless steel rod. For the purposes of cosmetic good looks, the stuffing gland on the original is to be replaced by the internal insertion of an 'O' ring at the top end of the final drive shaft. In passing, you may have noticed that all the bilges have been piped to the portholes, so that any water which does get in, can be sucked out by using a conventional syringe. I hope of course, that this will not be necessary, but practical experience shows boating to be a watery business.

Geoff's machine shop has all the air of a 'Holy of Holies', particularly to someone who is used only to the com-

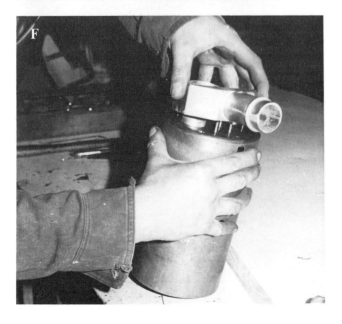

parative crudities of woodworking machinery. For those of you, like me, who heave heavy sighs of envy when they see the glinting precision of an ML Super 7 (Myford Lathe), let me just mention that Geoff won his in a club raffle – fortuitous, to say the least.

The two pictures show the stainless steel rod coming through the three jaw chuck, and subsequently having had the thread put on by use of a die mounted in the tailstock; the Huco universal coupling is tightened on with a spanner. Sort of sickeningly easy somehow, but then that is the way professionals always make it look.

The Boiler

The major task has now to be tackled. Before I arrived on the scene for the day's boiler-making, all the component parts had been loosely assembled. The huge 9in × 5$\frac{1}{4}$in copper tube for the boiler's outer skin, plus the main flue and the two return flues, were all in readiness. This included the spiral cross tubes which are an integral part of the main flue and allow the flame of the jet burner to play directly onto the cross flow of the water inside the boiler at this critical low point. These cross flow tubes have to be soldered with the high temperature silver solder so that they hold steady when the considerable heat is applied to the end plates. Being a smaller tube, of course, it is marginally easier to do this, but nonetheless it has all the hallmarks of requiring both skill and experience to execute with success.

Geoff drilled out the appropriately marked holes for the steam take-off and pressure gauge before departing for the garage, wherein lie all kinds of interesting objects. The extra pair of hands in the picture are not mine, but those of Slim Lacey who was responsible for the delightful piece of aluminium casting which forms the chimney on the end of the return flues.

Holes for the copper boiler stays were also drilled out. I have to admit that I didn't realize such things existed, but for the ignorant like me, they simply stop the end plates from expanding too much when the boiler is under pressure.

Cleanliness being next to Godliness, as the old saying goes, the next proceeding was more like a pre-operative scrubbing up by a consultant surgeon than a man about to solder up a piece of hardware. The table was scrubbed with a scouring powder whilst the boiler was 'dunked' in the acid pickle and subsequently rinsed and cleaned with emery cloth on all the areas to be soldered.

Other preparations included loading up the silver solder rod holders and laying others in readiness for the awkward moment of having to replenish these, when the boiler skin is red hot. Propane gas is the stable companion of the silver solder craftsman. Coupled with this great burst of heat from an industrial size nozzle, is the portable forge surrounded by fire bricks, which retain the heat necessary for the job.

Black and white photographs do no justice at all to the dramatic effect of the intense blue flame on glowing red hot copper, but this was one situation where I thought that I had better keep my 3$\frac{1}{2}$ft distance without waving the photographic measuring rod in front of what was happening.

Fig 82. a) Loading the silver solder sticks. b) Handling the boiler after it has been dunked in the acid pickle, prior to fluxing. c) Fluxing up. d) The first application of silver solder. Note the large size of torch necessary to raise the boiler to red hot. e) Cooling down. f) Pickling and rinsing in containers shown. g) Checking the cavity which will form the super-heated area. h) A rare sight of the guts of a Scotch boiler.

None of the process was easy. Physically speaking, it is very hot work and the jet nozzle has to be kept in exactly the right place for the heat to have sufficient intensity. Just to show how critical the heat factor is, I had to close the door of the garage halfway through the operation because a slight draught was cooling the total surface of the boiler. When I had done this, the glow on the boiler immediately changed and improved the flow of the solder, enabling that part of the job to be finished. The ceremonial dunking back into the acid pickle is preceded by a cooling off period.

The pickle reveals the odd 'worm' (unmelted solder stick), but generally speaking, this critical part of the manufacture is pronounced to have gone well, and a check with the engineer's rule, in the section of the boiler which will act as the super heater, reveals that we are well on the way to producing this most vital part of the power unit.

What of the prototype, and as a secondary question, why shouldn't the internal workings be representative of the original? I admit it would be nice. There is, however, the issue of low/high pressure to be considered. The prototype boiler was of such construction that it required to withstand no more than 5lb working pressure, and was gravity fed, whereas the model version must produce

nearly twelve times that output for normal running.

The following information was kindly given by Commander James Richard, who is in charge of the S.S. *Great Britain* 'Replica' Engine Committee:-

"Twelve furnaces and flues were all divided from each other by water passages, and only came together at the top, immediately under the funnel. There were three steam take-offs and a cylindrical preheating water jacket, surrounding the uptake below the weather deck level. It was not the oval funnel base casing above the deck, restored as rectangular , as is popularly thought.

The S.S.G.B. was fitted for the continuous brining of boilers, that is to say, water was continuously removed from the boilers, in volume about one third of the feed. (N.B. "feed" means the water supply to the boilers, not the steam supply to the engine). As a result, the salt con-

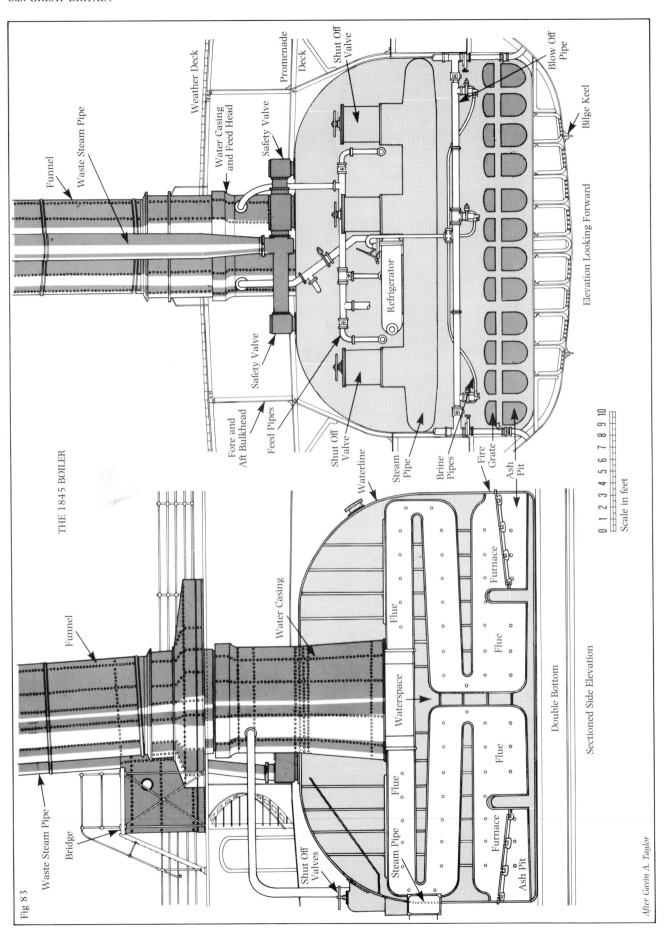

Fig 83   THE 1845 BOILER

Elevation Looking Forward

Funnel

Waste Steam Pipe

Weather Deck

Promenade Deck

Water Casing and Feed Head

Safety Valve

Shut Off Valve

Blow Off Pipe

Bilge Keel

Refrigerator

Safety Valve

Fore and Aft Bulkhead

Feed Pipes

Shut Off Valve

Waterline

Steam Pipe

Brine Pipes

Fire Grate

Ash Pit

Funnel

Waste Steam Pipe

Bridge

Shut Off Valves

Water Casing

Flue

Waterspace

Flue

Furnace

Flue

Flue

Furnace

Steam Pipe

Flue

Furnace

Ash Pit

Double Bottom

Sectioned Side Elevation

0 1 2 3 4 5 6 7 8 9 10
Scale in feet

After Gavin A. Taylor

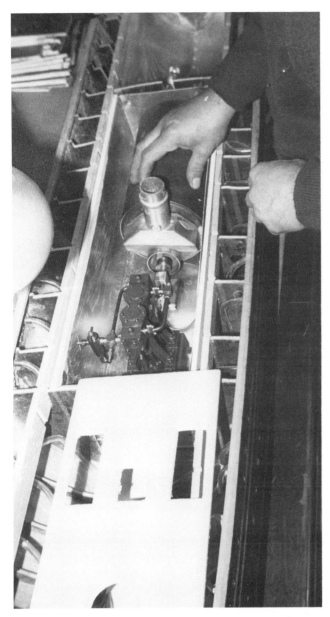

Fig 84. (Above Left) Trying the boiler in the engine room prior to final installation. Fig 85. (Above right) Note the flexible plastic tubing connected to the portholes, providing a ready means of draining bilge water using a syringe.

centration in the boilers would not rise above three times that of sea water, and this kept the rate of scale deposition acceptably low. The alternative process, (available in all ships including the S.S.G.B., whether fitted for continuous brining or not,) was to blow an appropriate quantity of water out of the boilers at intervals, about once a watch, and the overall result was the same. Descaling would be carried out at intervals of weeks or possibly months. The three sections would have been descaled in rotation, but it would never have been planned to descale one section while steaming another except under emergency conditions after a defect or crass maloperation."

With the enlargement of the airpumps and fire flues, the 1846 refit gave a solid 11.8 knots at an i.h.p. of 1,600 at 16.75rpm. At that time, this represented a good

average speed for the Atlantic run, the magical 10 knots having all the appeal then that Mach 2 has for the Atlantic passenger today. The service speed had been comfortably surpassed and both Brunel and Guppy could be justly proud of the ship's performance.

Skylight "One Large Light over the Engine Room"

This is the description given to the main driving wheel housing, which is really nothing more than a glorified hatch, but because of its position on the sparse deck of the S.S.G.B., is undoubtedly a focal point of interest. Dr Corlett, in his profile plan of the ship indicates 12 skylights set within six main frames at either side of the structure. This is affirmed by the Joseph Walter painting, "The Great Britain in a gale of headwind in 1846" (City of Liverpool Museum), but contradicted by the much more famous 23 January 1845 picture by the same artist. Both paintings, however, show that the glazing on the first three skylights has been either removed altogether or opened after the

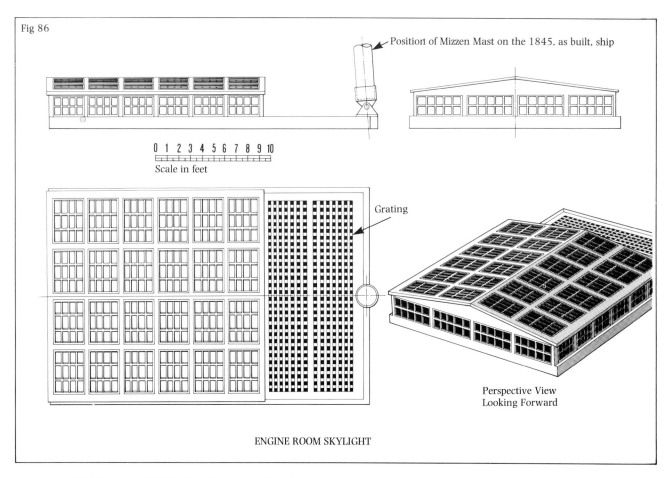

Fig 86

Position of Mizzen Mast on the 1845, as built, ship

0 1 2 3 4 5 6 7 8 9 10
Scale in feet

Grating

Perspective View
Looking Forward

ENGINE ROOM SKYLIGHT

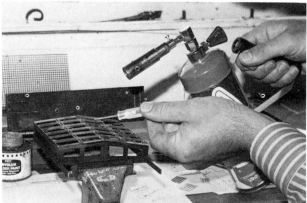

Fig 87. (Left) Soldering the brass frames. The grating is by Aeronaut. Fig 88. (Below left) The Skylight. Fig 89. (Opposite top) Basic frame of skylight laid over drawing; other references to hand. Fig 90. (Right) Funnel. B&P photo.

fashion of a sash window. It does therefore occur to me at least, to think that these skylights were removable to allow maximum ventilation to the hot spot of the engine room below. One is also able to consider that the massive driving wheel would have the effect of drawing down some air from this open hatch. Duplicating the prototype, this hatch has to act as the main source of ventilation and quick access to the engine, which is sited immediately below. It needs to be strongly built so that it does not suffer from frequent removal. I decided therefore to construct it in a composite fashion, with the sides and ends of ply, and the roof of soldered brass angle. This was expensive in terms of time and money but the effect given has a pay-off in the squareness of the framing which speaks of realism. The heat factor here would preclude the use of plastic strutting, and timber would likewise suffer from constant temperature change.

"A Certain Naughtiness"

The passengers, as can be seen in the several paintings of the ship obviously enjoyed a 'sight of the works' through the skylight. What they would have seen was the 18ft primary driving wheel, with its four sets of driving chains

DETAILS OF DECK FITTINGS
OF S.S. GREAT BRITAIN 1843

whirring furiously round, propelled by the muscle of the four great cylinders from deep in the bowels of the ship. The 17ft long water-cooled crankshaft came to within 3ft of the underside of the weather deck and was plainly visible for the promenading Victorian ladies who would never, under normal circumstances, have been exposed to the indelicacies of such a monstrous sight. The panting beast must therefore have been all the more fascinating, having not only Samson-like strength, but also the air of something which "Mama would rather we didn't see".

Queen Victoria, when she inspected the ship on 23 April 1845, was shown a model of how the engine worked, (possibly the one now in the Science Museum, acquired in 1862 from Gibbs, Bright & Co., the owners of the ship; its history before that is obscure), the organisers of the inspection thinking that a "sight of the real thing" would be far too vulgar for the young Queen's eyes. As things turned out, however, they were wrong and following an extensive tour of the ship the Queen surprised them all by asking to inspect the engine room, which thing Thomas Guppy was delighted to do, and must have remained one of the highlights of his life.

The Funnel

Richard Goold-Adams, the Chairman of the S.S. *Great Britain* Project Committee, reports in his book, "The Return of The *Great Britain*", that as early as 1971, the restoration committee had received a generous offer from F.E. Beaumont Ltd., of Gravesend in Kent, to both make and present a replica funnel for the S.S.G.B. free of charge. Goold-Adams underlines not only the gratitude of the committee but also their anxiety to see the funnel erected as "being the most significant piece of symbolism for the early steamship". It served also as a testimonial that work was actually proceeding with the repair and restoration of the ship.

The psychology of funnels could be discussed at great length. What is certain is that from the time of Brunel onwards, the ship's funnel played an increasingly important part in the general appearance of transatlantic travel in the new breed of greyhounds. When one compares the 25ft girth of this 38ft funnel with the 'drain-pipes' of auxiliary craft built only a few years before, the new confidence in steam becomes apparent. Brunel presented his ship with pride in marine steam rather than with an apology for the fact that the motive power was heat rather than wind. (The Admiralty, which specialised in the other sort of wind, would take twenty years to accept the point, but in the commercial world, as sailpower diminished, funnels became bigger and more numerous until we reach a point where a fourth funnel would be fitted, just to balance up the look of a ship.) I have referred previously to the oval base of the chimney, which is simply an air space between funnel and deck.

Before launching into the construction of this item, a word of explanation as to why the restored funnel base is the wrong shape. Instead of an oval form, as is documented for the ship, the restoration base is rectangular with rounded corners. For an obscure reason, so is the The Science Museum model, proving if nothing else, that this ship is full of traps for the unwary. On the prototype, the explanation for the reconstructed rectangular shape is one of speed and cost. On the return from the Falkland Islands, The S.S.G.B. had three large hatches resulting from her final operational days as a three masted sailing ship. In order to save work and money, Corlett suggested the adoption of the sailing ship hatch coaming as the base of the funnel support. Charles Hill and Sons Ltd. were therefore able to proceed with the work without the

Fig 91. (Right) Oval funnel base of Model Fig 92. (Below) The restored funnel and base on S.S. Great Britain at Bristol. Note remarks in text re base shape.

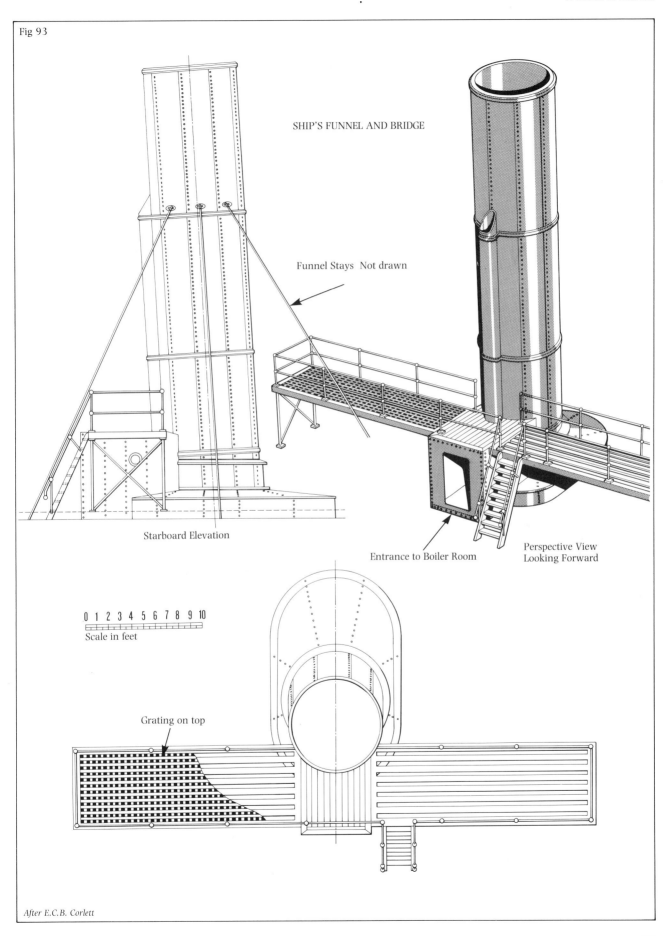

Fig 93

SHIP'S FUNNEL AND BRIDGE

Funnel Stays Not drawn

Starboard Elevation

Entrance to Boiler Room

Perspective View
Looking Forward

0 1 2 3 4 5 6 7 8 9 10
Scale in feet

Grating on top

After E.C.B. Corlett

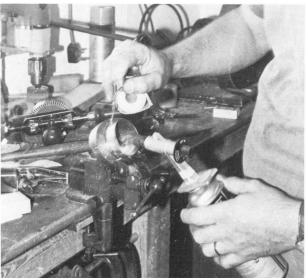

Fig 94. (Above) The author rolled the brass funnel round the tube former mounted in the vice, and joined the seam with a T-section strip. Fig 95. (Left) Soldering the base structure using resin cored solder and a butane torch. Fig 96. (Bottom left) Base and funnel assembled and awaiting final finishing. Fig 97. (Right) 'Elegance and ease'.

necessity of building and underpinning an entirely new support. It is not really a matter of great importance or significance but does demonstrate the sort of practical difficulty in restoring a ship of this kind on a limited budget.

Not having to face such decisions, my casing is oval in shape although the penalty for copying the original, rather than the restoration will be forever having to explain the reason why.

Marking out the rivets, prior to the manufacture of the funnel caused me to reflect on the generosity of Beaumont's Ltd., and indeed all the other firms who have so enthusiastically involved themselves with the many and varied aspects of the restoration. The funnel has been reconstructed in octant section and the heads of the bolts or rivets are very prominent, not having acquired a natural degree of rust in the performance of their duties. The imitation rivets of my funnel were made by the time-honoured method of punching from the reverse side before assembly, the treatment having the effect, of course, of making the brass shim curl in a quite helpful way. Although it needed to be rolled over a metal tube to ensure an even curvature it could not be tackled by hammering, as this would obviously make the rivets disappear as quickly as they had arrived. I found that the best way was to use a $1\frac{1}{2}$in tube ($\frac{1}{2}$in narrower than the ultimate exterior diameter of the chimney) and roll the brass firmly in on itself, much as you would a newspaper. When it was unfurled, it presented itself well for soldering down the seam, with the addition of an inserted "T" section which supports the sturdy elliptical steam-pipe closely attached to the aft side of the funnel.

STEPPING STONE BOOKS

#1 from start to finish!

Co

Sh   s of the
hu   only in
tra   incor-
po

ac   , cabin
pa   of the
                      eration

so that passengers may move with elegance and ease. It is hard for us today to realise just how much a Victorian lady minded an uninvited glimpse of her ankle by a crew member as she stepped onto the weather deck – or at least, she was supposed to mind!

The Victorian ship in many ways reflected the classical four storied Victorian house with its "upstairs and downstairs" layout. The saloon and promenade decks, which included in our ship the innovation of 'boudoirs' in the wings of the latter, were strictly the province of the 1st and 2nd class passengers. These voyagers would have expected the same distinctions of social class on the high seas as they would have done in Eaton Square or Hyde Park.

Terms like "promenade deck" and "saloon deck" denote precisely the fashionable expectancy of the age to wine and dine and stroll at a leisurely pace. All of these things were done at an 'appropriate' time and would have been easily recognisable as the same cultural pattern of London's fashionable society. The stroll on the promenade deck had its exact counterpart in the daily fashion parades in London's parks and doubtless provided *the* topic of conversation when the ladies left the men for their boudoirs and the men were left alone for a glass of port and a smoke.

The 'attics' and 'cellars' of the ship – that is to say the galleys and the fo'c's'le and the cargo decks housed the workforce; this meant the crew, up in the eyes of the ship the engineers, firemen, stokers, galley staff and stewards lived like rats in holes and hammocks in the noisiest and most uncomfortable quarters of the ship.

It would be anachronistic to blame the crinoline skirt for the handsome four foot width of the standard companionway on the ship; it did show great foresight, however, on the part of the design team and meant that later fashion could be flourished aboard without alteration to the upperworks or embarrassment to the wearer who might not have considered some of the restriction of 'life aboard'. Visitors to the restored ship at Bristol can feel the spaciousness of the stairwell and fully appreciate the forward thinking of the original planning.

The design of double doors, which opened on whichever was the favourable lee side of the ship was also a consideration not hitherto shown to passengers, and would, no doubt, have saved many a bonnet and top-hat from certain death by drowning in a head-wind.

Reminiscent of the carriagework of the age, the 'tambour' effect of the fall away from the hatch roofs in semicircular section acts as a streamlining effect externally, whilst allowing internal headroom to the emerging or descending passenger.

There were also header tanks sited under the 'chaise longue' shape, which housed the domestic water supply, fitted at the highest level for maximum gravitational pressure.

The restoration companionways have been handsomely rebuilt and positioned, allowing today's visitors to emerge on the weather deck (still as draughty as ever) and sense, by proxy, some of the excitement experienced by the early Victorian travellers. It is now the Brunel ship which one remembers and the rotting wreck which one forgets, whereas in the first ten years of restoration one could not help being aware more of the immense efforts to preserve the shell and structure, to the exclusion of the more visually rewarding deck fittings.

Apart from the fact that I had to rebuild both the fore and aft companionways, which I originally lifted from the Science Museum plans, they did not cause any trouble. All eight doors work, which necessitated producing 32 cranked hinges but as I tried to emphasize in my introduction, it is important that such items work, in order to give an inhabited appearance, which all full size ships have. It also adds spatial depth and hints at the hidden world below decks.

Here, and perhaps only here, is one allowed to indulge and wallow in high gloss varnish. At the period in which this ship is being modelled, a major refit had just taken place, on a ship which was relatively new anyway, and so one might legitimately expect a spick and span appear-

ance on the upperworks, alas to be destroyed on the prototype by the ignominy of stranding off the coast of Ireland at Dundrum Bay, exposing the new paintwork to the wildest ravages of the sea for a whole year.

Ironically, this stranding, whilst breaking the already strained resources of the GWSSCO, proved finally and conclusively to all doubters the indestructibility of the iron ship, in a way that no other demonstration could have done.

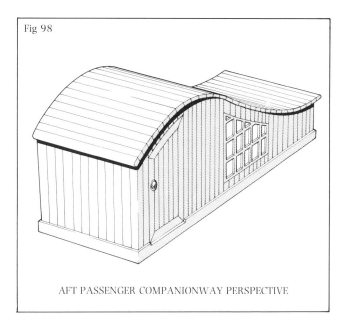

Fig 98

AFT PASSENGER COMPANIONWAY PERSPECTIVE

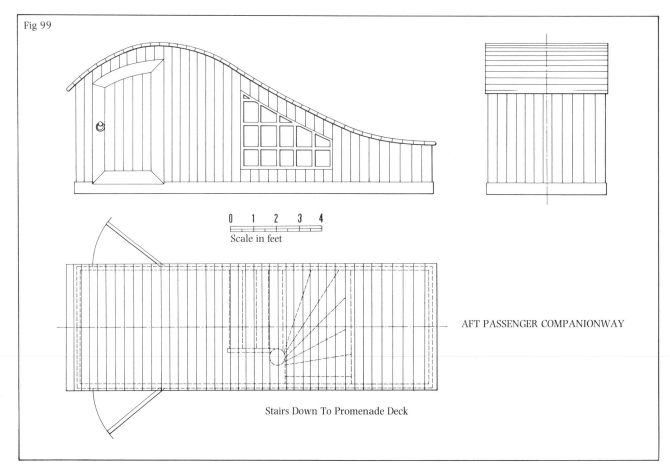

Fig 99

0 1 2 3 4
Scale in feet

AFT PASSENGER COMPANIONWAY

Stairs Down To Promenade Deck

For a whole year, monstrous storms raged at the stranded vessel on this most exposed shore off the coast of Ireland, and it is certain that under similar circumstances, a wooden ship would have gone to pieces in less than a week.

An Age of Light

The Victorian period is spoken of as an age of light, and perhaps the most outstanding witness to this was the building of the Crystal Palace in Hyde Park in 1851. Joseph Paxton, who designed it, drew on experience gained in planning the huge conservatories at Chatsworth House in Derbyshire. The design combined efficiency with elegance, to display manufactured goods from all over the world. With the Victorians' fascination of all things mechanical and novel, the Exhibition of 1851 was enormously successful.

Brunel, at the spearhead of advancing mechanical science, constructed two circular skylights, one on the weather deck and one below in the saloon, with exactly the same thoughts in mind, namely that through these "conservatories" at the stern of the ship, passengers could see all the moving parts of the rudder mechanism as the ship proceeded on the voyage. These little skylights take their place alongside all the memorabilia of the Victorians' obsession with anything and everything involving

Fig 100. (Top left) Aft companionway, restoration. Fig 101. (Left) Forward companionway, restoration.

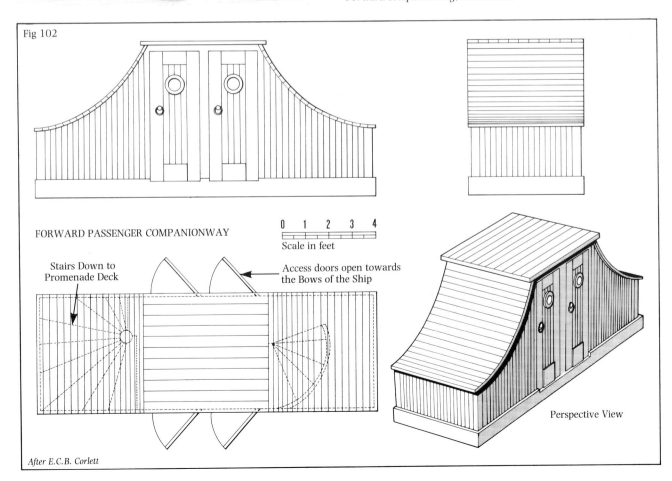

Fig 102

FORWARD PASSENGER COMPANIONWAY

Scale in feet
0 1 2 3 4

Stairs Down to Promenade Deck

Access doors open towards the Bows of the Ship

Perspective View

After E.C.B. Corlett

mechanical motion, from musical boxes to knife polishers.

For the modeller, the little "Summer-house conservatory" presents a challenge. No doubt there are a dozen different ways of setting about a construction like this, but I had hoarded away a Perspex typewriter spool case, which I judged to be about the right size, but had never bothered to measure. It turned out to be too big; in order to reduce the diameter by $\frac{1}{2}$in it was necessary to cut the rim, sawing out the centre before rejoining the circle. This I managed to do, coupling it with a warming session in front of a fan heater. I thought that if it didn't craze, it might well snap, as these spool cases are moulded originally, and therefore none too flexible. As predicted, it did craze slightly, but as it was whitened from the interior in order to emphasise the window framing, one cannot in fact see the slightly shattered effect which appears as no

Fig 105. (Bottom) View of restoration work on the weather deck showing circular skylight. Fig 106. (Opposite top) Model deckhouses.

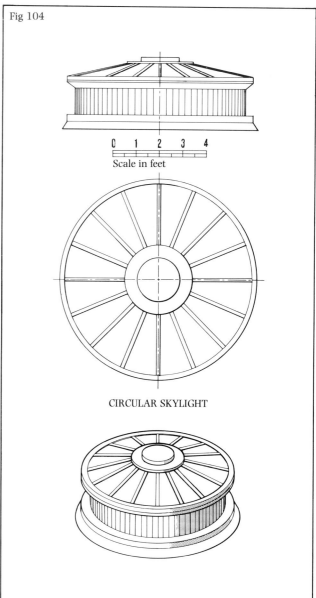

Fig 104

Scale in feet

CIRCULAR SKYLIGHT

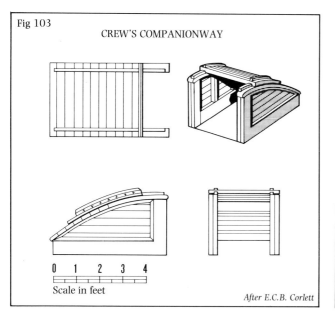

Fig 103

CREW'S COMPANIONWAY

0   1   2   3   4
Scale in feet

After E.C.B. Corlett

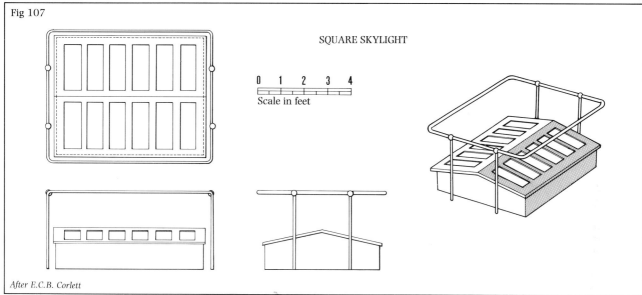

Fig 107

SQUARE SKYLIGHT

0 1 2 3 4
Scale in feet

After E.C.B. Corlett

more than frosting. Good fortune, which often seems to follow the magpie, had provided a little external lip which acted as a support for the roof section and ran parallel with the base.

The roof was none too straightforward either, and I thought of all the modellers who scratch build shire wagons and gypsy caravans; the roof of the conservatory was almost certainly made by someone with experience as a wheelwright, from whence the original must have derived – a sixteen spoked wheel with a 15 degree negative angle on the centre boss, tyred round twice with a veneer strip. I turned the centre boss out of a piece of

precious Spanish mahogany in the chuck of the electric drill. It is perhaps just worth mentioning that with large modern chucks a great deal of turning for models in wood can be done without the use of a lathe proper, and for personal preference, I would back the vertical drill stand as being of greater value than the lathe if a choice has to be made between the two.

It is often impossible to say how long something took to make, and so it may be of some interest to mention that the little summer house took a full twelve hour day to fashion, but left me at the end of a satisfying day with a completed item which I had really enjoyed making.

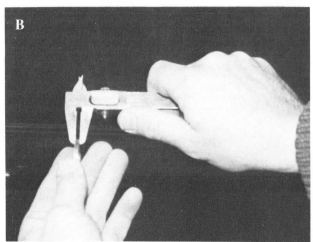

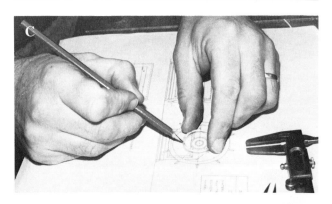

Fig 108. The steering wheel. a) Sawing out the plastic wheel centre. b) Checking the width at the circumference. c) Marking out the 36° angle from the lovely restoration drawings (E.C.B. Corlett). d) Checking the fit of the belaying pin into $\frac{1}{16}$in brass tubing. e) Marking out with the scriber ('lower left six, nurse – drill and fill'.) f) Drilling out for spokes. Note the use of miniature chuck in jaws of electric drill. g) Pinching the centre spoke with sharp nosed pliers. The flat is drilled out to take axle. h) All spokes in. i) Veneering the outer edge. j) Piercing through the veneer for the belaying pins. k) Four in and six to go! l) Just needs the box.

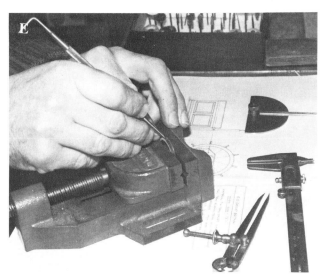

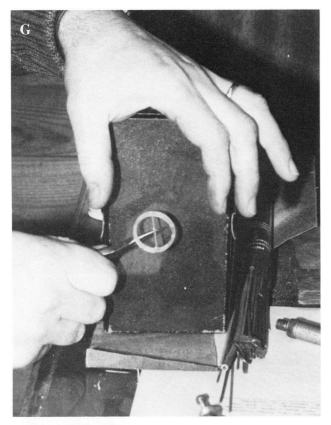

The Ship's Wheel

In every Hollywood movie to do with ships and the swash-buckling days of sail, the hero helmsman is there, standing on the wrong side of the ship's wheel, steering the vessel (backwards?) through the storm with the same ease and nonchalance that a croupier uses to spin the roulette wheel. The real thing was somewhat different.

When I first saw the Thomas Guppy model in the Science Museum, I recall as one of the distinguishing

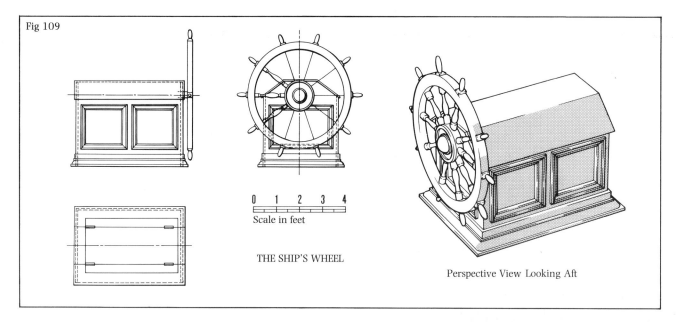

Fig 109

THE SHIP'S WHEEL

0 1 2 3 4
Scale in feet

Perspective View Looking Aft

features, the unusual upward facing steering apparatus, that is to say, the wheel running parallel with the deck, after the fashion of a standard capstan. There is great logic to this, in that as many as ten men could steady the action of the rudder in high seas, which was not uncommon practice before the introduction of steam power-assisted steering. Despite the Guppy model, the case against such an arrangement on this particular ship is pretty strong, the most compelling of the arguments being that there was very little room in the quarter galleries to house the necessary mechanism, and none of the interior sketches detail such a thing. There is no real doubt about the true facts and I was lucky enough to have the restoration drawings from Dr Corlett.

The wheel rim was started with the aid of a perspex ring, of the correct diameter. It was marked off and drilled out to accept ten spokes made of $\frac{1}{16}$in brass tubing, the first of which was inserted across the full diameter of the wheel and pinched in the centre where the axle boss would fit. The remaining eight spokes were fed through the holes in the rim, pinched with sharp nose pliers and centred to the boss.

Now different things amuse different people, but one of the striking features of any properly made ship's wheel, are the different segments of the solid timber from which it has been fashioned, and the way these catch the light as the wheel revolves. In order to reproduce this, I veneered the segments at 36 degrees around the circumference and inserted the brass banding on both the inside and outside diameters. The proceedings were literally rounded off by the insertion of proprietary belaying pins (Graupner), which fit snugly through the wheel rim into the brass tubing, adding realism as well as strength to the whole structure of the wheel.

In that it is not possible to buy a ten spoked wheel as a proprietary item, and certainly not a segmented one, it is quite a challenge to build a convincing free-lance wheel and see just how accurate one can make it. On the principle of building it from the outside in, rather than working from the boss outwards, one can achieve credible results without a great deal of fuss.

Fig 110. (Above) A ship's wheel looking for a ship. Fig 111. (Opposite top). Original Trotman Anchor. Photo B&P. Fig 112. (Right). One of the author's completed model anchors.

The Anchors

King Midas of Phyrgia, besides his well known trick of being able to turn everything he touched into gold, is also credited, in Greek Mythology, with the invention of the anchor. In reality the ancient Greek sailors used baskets of stones until the time when it seems likely that Tuscan seamen established the use of the double hook and stock that we would recognise as the standard Fisherman's anchor.

Those fitted to the S.S.G.B. were an improvement on the common bower anchor in two major respects of practical design. The curved arms of the anchor were hinged at the crown of the shank, allowing the fluke of the anchor

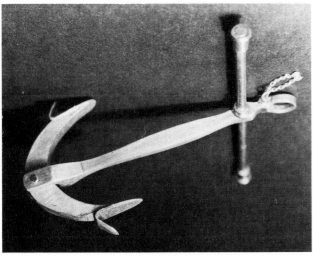

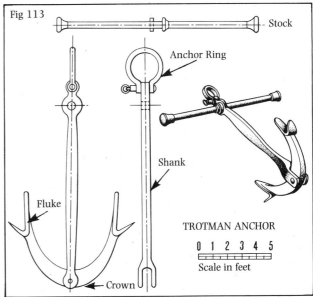

Fig 113

Stock

Anchor Ring

Shank

Fluke

Crown

TROTMAN ANCHOR

0 1 2 3 4 5

Scale in feet

arm to be pulled flush with the shaft. This meant that when the anchor was engaged with the seabed, the cable chain would not foul on the protruding fluke, even though the ship swung round in a full circle.

The other practical improvement in this transitional stage of development was the removable anchor stock. The fixed wooden stock with its banding hoops gives way to the portable anchor stock with its nuts and forelock chain, making stowage easier with fish tackle over the bows. A few years would elapse before the introduction of the stockless bower anchor that must have done away with the whole undignified process of hauling these enormously unwieldy objects off the bottom of the ocean floor.

The patent design employed by the S.S.G.B. was known as a "Trotman Anchor". It is made of iron, and as it survives it therefore presents no problems in terms of research. I had the continuing delight of using the Corlett drawings in their production.

Brass, being the poor man's gold, would not I think have offended old King Midas, and certainly the gold dust of the filings at the end of the day give us a foretaste of the historical fact that our ship was saved in order to service the Australian gold-rush in the 1850's.

The cutting and filing of brass by hand was the only

alternative to casting the pair of them in brass, a method I would have seriously considered, had there been more than two of them to do.

The shape of the shank has a beautiful and slender contour to it which ends in a jaw or yoke which accepts the pivoting arm; it is however, the bird's beak flukes, looking like baby starlings in a nest, which complete the aesthetic appeal for me. Even in a miniature form, it is a remarkable efficient piece of digging equipment, and judging by the bent shank of the prototype, it must have gripped the sea-bed with great tenacity.

The Trotman anchors were suspended from old fashioned catheads, and they weighed nearly four tons apiece.

Fig 114. The Anchor. a) Drilling and pinning the shank. b) Final fixing by silver soldering. c) Filing the spine to shape. d) After shaping. e) A helping hand to remove plate . . . f) . . . filed to shape as the flukes. g) The model anchor photographed above the Corlett drawings of same.

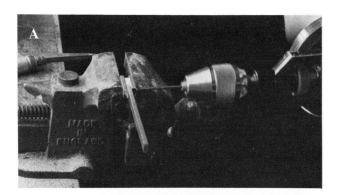

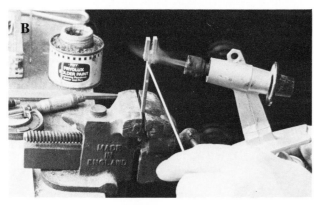

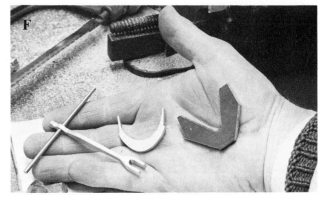

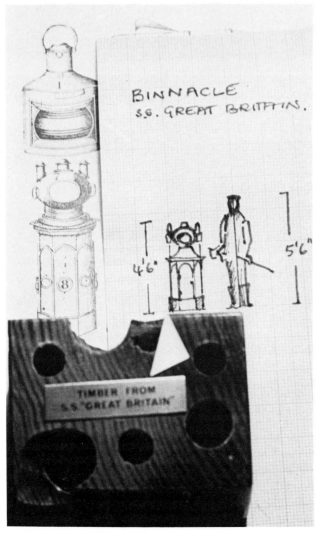

Fig 115. (Above) The author's first binnacle with soft iron spheres for compass corrections. Fig 116. (Left) The binnacle pedestal made from original ship's timber. Note the size of the teredo worm holes in the offcut.

The Binnacle

It has been a long established tradition that the binnacle on a sailing ship should serve a double purpose, primarily as the central piece of navigational equipment which could be seen by day and by night, and secondarily as a small circular cupboard with front opening access, where the current charts could be stowed for constant reference as the voyage proceeded. It was the second factor which set my mind thinking that, with some care and a bit of luck, my binnacle could also play a dual role.

For associative reasons, pieces of original ship's timbers have often been used and incorporated in models by the men who have sought, not only to copy the original, but also to graft into it something of the spirit of the prototype. As a piece of folklore this romanticism seems to be universal, and is as old, by tradition, as ship-modelling itself. The off-cut which I bought in the trading shop set up beside the S.S.G.B., was so riddled with teredo worm holes, that it was selling as a desk-top pencil holder. No wonder the old sailors and harbour-masters feared the attack of ship's weevil so much, when the adult worms have a boring capacity of anything up to half an inch in diameter.

Nevertheless, I determined that somehow this small block could be used even though it had the outward appearance of a piece of gruyere cheese. On turning it over in my fingers as well as my mind, it suddenly dawned on me that, although the wood wasn't up to much, the holes were splendid. What I needed to make this binnacle was a hole with a bit of wood around it. Well it seems churlish to use a drill when a worm has bitten a hole especially for you with its bare 'teeth', and one particular hole was a

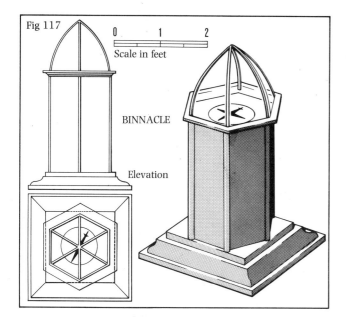

vertically drilled job of exactly $\frac{3}{8}$ in, perfectly suiting my requirement. I cut round the hole and planed it until it looked like a bamboo stick. I needed only $\frac{3}{4}$in in upright length for the binnacle base, and it is of interest that in this length, the worm had deviated only $\frac{1}{32}$nd of an inch off centre.

Planing the pitch pine, which was of course part of the ship's cladding added in 1882 for the purpose of strengthening her – it also helped to preserve the ship – I was surprised by two things, namely: the still resinous nature of the wood, waxy and clogging on the plane blade after 98 years, and the still pungent smell, so reminiscent of the carpenter's shop. The worm hole in this piece of wood will act, not as the receptacle for a scale chart of the Atlantic, but as the secret hiding-place for my maker's message (also an age-old custom), so that the binnacle base will be both a relic and a repository combined – the dual role preserved.

The top half of the binnacle was fashioned from a contemporary design in Captain H. Paasch's Marine Encyclopedia (1890) of which I have a facsimile copy. It is worth mentioning that the brass bowl head, looking for all the world like a diver's helmet, was made from a brass drawer handle retainer, which is ideal for the purpose, as it not only has a tapped base, but also is hollow on the inside face. A whisk of the file makes the sloping face, and with the addition of a glazed and hinged surround, the navigational nerve centre of the ship begins to look as it should. The central compass card is made from a piece of Plasticard, $\frac{1}{8}$in diameter, which was first of all scribed with a metal marker and the radiant lines rubbed in with pencil graphite. This gives a razor sharp line, the only problem being that the scribing process has to be done first onto the Plasticard, which then has to be punched out separately with a specially sharpened section of brass tubing. Centralizing this can be tricky, and I ended up having to make three before I got it right.

Exactly what happened to the prototype binnacle is unknown to me, but my suspicions are that it was taken for inspection following the Dundrum Bay stranding in

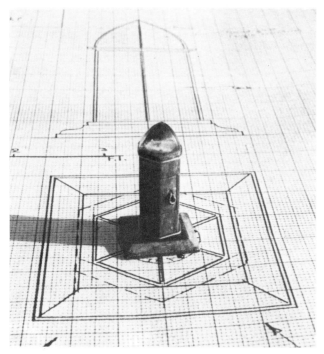

Fig 118. (Left) New binnacle drawing as submitted by Corlett. Fig 119. (Below) S.S.B.G. Aground at Dundrum Bay. Copyright BBC Hulton Picture Library. Fig 121. (Right) The real windlass capstan positioned just abaft the foc'sle, (1882 position).

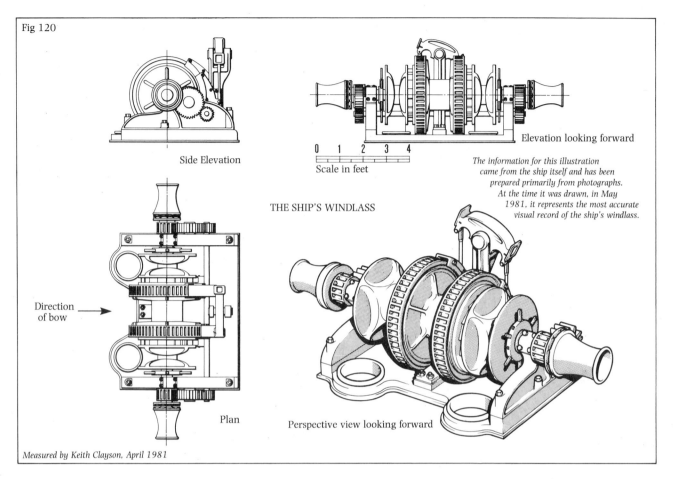

Fig 120

Side Elevation

Elevation looking forward

Scale in feet

The information for this illustration came from the ship itself and has been prepared primarily from photographs. At the time it was drawn, in May 1981, it represents the most accurate visual record of the ship's windlass.

THE SHIP'S WINDLASS

Direction of bow

Plan

Perspective view looking forward

Measured by Keith Clayson, April 1981

late 1846, although there would have been little point in doing this, as its very removal from the large mass of iron now like a stranded whale on the beach, would have upset the delicate compass correction simply by being taken out of the particular magnetic field.

The effect of a large mass of iron on a magnetic compass was one of the points on which cynics and doubters exuded much venomous nonsense. The truth of the matter was that it had been adequately demonstrated by no less a person than Professor Airy, the Astronomer Royal, in 1838, that compass error could be easily compensated for by the use of soft iron bars, appropriately placed. This was actually carried out five years before the launch of the S.S.G.B., on the iron ship, *The Rainbow*. Without any foundation, compass error has been pointed

to as a possible reason for Captain James Hosken's embarrassing and crippling arrival on the Irish beach, but I am fairly certain there was nothing wrong with the mechanism.

Judgement given by Professor Sir George Airy was not always to be trusted. He announced in a pamphlet that the Crystal Palace would certainly blow down; he damned the Atlantic Telegraph Cable Project, saying that it was a mathematical impossibility to submerge a cable at so great a depth, and if it were possible, no signals could be transmitted through so great a length. Perhaps his classic piece of misinformation was to advise Sir Thomas Bouch, chief engineer in charge of the Tay Bridge project (1871), that the greatest wind pressure to which that bridge would be subjected would be 10lb per sq ft. When the Forth Bridge was opened 19 years later, Sir John Fowler, the consultant civil engineer for the Forth Bridge (with Benjamin Baker), remarked dryly, "I do not believe in astronomy being a safe guide for practical engineering."

(New research by Dr Corlett has revealed a 6-sided pedestal with a compass card viewable from either side of the helm. This is the design for the restoration; mine has been altered accordingly.)

The Windlass

The windlass of the S.S.G.B. is a delicious piece of hardware, which I have been, as it were, saving up till the end of the meal.

The prototype, remarkably, survives, and there is

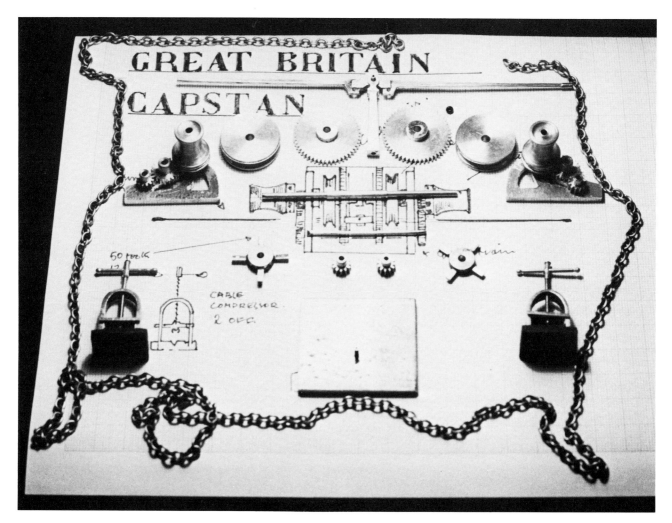

Fig 122. (Above) Windlass parts before assembly, superimposed on working drawing. Fig 123. (Right) The model windlass stands over a photograph of the original, pictured in 1968, during the survey when the ship was still in the Falkland Isles.

sound evidence to indicate that it is the original as fitted at the launch of the ship in 1843. The historical corroboration comes from a description of a piece of agricultural winching equipment, the "Etzler Iron Slave", which ends with the words, "like that fitted to the S.S. *Great Britain*," as a kind of selling point. The description fits well. The mechanism was operated by an up and down pumping action, which activated a ratchet and pall on a cross head, which in turn slowly inched in the studded links of the anchor cable through the hawse, a job which involved up to two dozen men at a time. When hawsers and smaller cables were being hove in, there was a dog clutch mechanism, which enabled the main cable lifters to be disengaged, allowing the lighter work to have a faster ratio of gearing.

Was this windlass another 'first' for Brunel? It seems more likely to me that he spotted an item from the world of farming or forestry which would be directly applicable to the task of hauling, not only the majestic "Trotman" anchors, but also the 40 tons of chain that went with them.

The 50 toothed brass gears which form the basis for the model of the toothed drums are not from the Meccano box, but supplied by a ship modelling company. They look to me as though they are spur gears, and give or take a tooth, are in accurate scale for the task in hand. The cable holders and warping ends were turned on a local lathe, whilst the spoked brakes were fashioned from (0, happy day) brass curtain runners. If it all sounds too easy, let me not forget to mention the trip to the casualty department

of our local hospital, late at night, for a tetanus injection – the result of sticking a needle file through the base of my thumb. The nurse's needle in my leg was a rather kinder experience.

Although fiddling fingers are generally discouraged, I do like items such as a windlass to work. It's strange how one can almost instantly tell the difference between static representation and proper miniaturized working. The eye is a hard task-master to serve.

The pair of "Compressor Stoppers" were designed to choke the cable against the sides of the navel pipes and prevent it running out, and also to stop it altogether until the cable could be bitted and secured. The prototypes look a bit tired and bent, but they are almost certainly original partners of the windlass and survive to tell the tale of a hard working life.

Fig 124. (Above left) Close-ups of the Etzler Iron Slave, still only partly finished. Fig 125 (Left) Finished windlass.

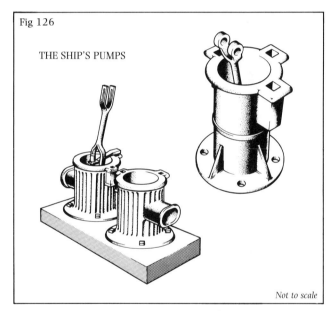

Fig 126

THE SHIP'S PUMPS

Not to scale

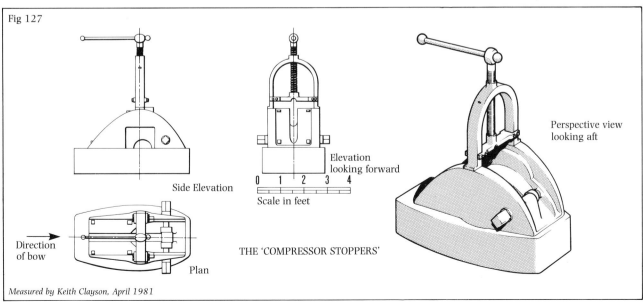

Fig 127

Side Elevation

Elevation looking forward

0 1 2 3 4

Scale in feet

Perspective view looking aft

Direction of bow

Plan

THE 'COMPRESSOR STOPPERS'

Measured by Keith Clayson, April 1981

103

Weather deck

1st class dining saloon

Passengers of the 1840's

Crew brawling

FITTING OUT

Fitting Out

On 19th July 1843, the S.S.G.B. was at last launched, or more accurately, she was undocked and floated out, to the cheering of the citizens of Bristol and the great relief of the GWSSCO. In carnival mood, Brunel arrived on the footplate of a GWR locomotive, driven by his old friend and colleague, Daniel Gooch, drawing the Royal Coach with the Prince Consort aboard.

After a lengthy detour round the Bristol Dock area, His Royal Highness finally named the ship by throwing, with great force, a second bottle of champagne which shattered against the iron plates, showering dockworkers below the dais with splintered glass. The first bottle of champagne should have been released by a lady called Mrs Miles. She was one of the GWSSCO's directors' wives and had launched the Great Western in 1838. Amidst some commun-

ications confusion with the tug "Avon", the ship began to move prematurely, and the intended bottle simply fell into the water. This was a bad omen, coupled with the fact that the ship's name had been altered twice, and gave old sea dogs the opportunity to shake their heads and mutter about iron plates, multi-masting and the wrath of God which is visited upon young men who tamper with tradition.

At the time of the launch, the six-bladed propeller was fitted and so were the six masts, but these only temporarily, as they would have to be removed later in order to reduce the draught and allow free passage through the upper lock ... a very critical operation.

Fig 128. (Below) Lithograph of launch, July 19th 1843. Copyright, National Maritime Museum. Fig 129 (opposite). Site of fitting out.

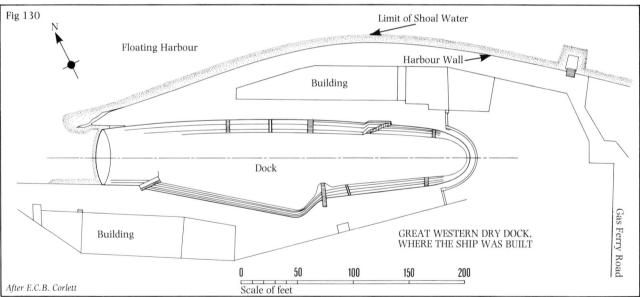

Fig 130

N

Limit of Shoal Water

Floating Harbour

Harbour Wall

Building

Dock

Building

GREAT WESTERN DRY DOCK,
WHERE THE SHIP WAS BUILT

Gas Ferry Road

After E.C.B. Corlett

0   50   100   150   200

Scale of feet

The profile of the upper lock basin dictated to the original hull design team the midship section of the S.S.G.B. As lightly laden as possible, the vessel should have been able to slip through the upper lock with only inches to spare. As we shall learn, the theory did not quite match up to the practice.

The GWSSCO had a choice between fitting the ship out in the Cumberland Basin, which lies between the upper and lower lock gates, leading into the River Avon, or using the floating harbour opposite the GWSSCO graving dock. Fitting out in the Cumberland Basin would mean, as they thought, that the ship could be easily released, but being the narrow neck of the bottle to the Bristol Docks, the presence of the vessel would have greatly inconvenienced other shipping using the extensive dock area. The GWSSCO was already in bad odour with the Bristol Dock Co. and any thoughts of a further loss of revenue and inconvenience were more than the Bristol Dock Co. could

A

B

Fig 131 a & b. (Opposite) Remarkable mirror image comparing the famous 1844 photograph (Copyright National Maritime Museum, Greenwich) of the original vessel by the pioneer photographer Fox-Talbot, with the photograph of the model, both shown at the 'fitting out' stage. Fig 132 (Above) Fitting out. At last it looks as though it might work.

stand. Thus the ship was fitted out on the North side of the floating harbour, opposite the graving dock, just below the gas works. In this position, the famous photograph was taken by the pioneer photographer, Fox-Talbot, thought to be the first photograph ever taken of a ship. It is a most useful source of original information and demonstrates that the technical revolution at this period in history was not simply confined to boats and trains, but had an all embracing nature about it.

For four years the Bristol Dock Co. had had on its Minute Book a resolution that the lock-gates should be widened, not only to release the S.S.G.B., but more importantly from their point of view, to bring extra trade from the new breed of paddle steamers which the old lock-gates could not accommodate. A mixture of inertia and internal conflict had failed to produce any alterations, despite the GWSSCO's willingness to carry out the work. It took all of Brunel's influence and persuasion to get the necessary permission to release the ship, and the final "rape of the lock-gates" on the night of 11th December 1844, was the inevitable conclusion to the besetting sin of the Dock Co. having done nothing to improve the access. Brunel's old friend, Captain Claxton, supervised the final emergence of the ship into the River Avon on the morning of 12th December 1844. That same triumphant morning steam

was raised by chief engineer, H.S. Harman, who initially set the engine revs to 6rpm, giving a speed of 4 knots. Marvellous moment.

The Raising of Steam

There has been an interesting but unintentional parallel between the building of my model and the building of the original ship. It confirms the statement that a fully working model takes one man about the same amount of time to build as it requires for a shipyard workforce to complete the prototype. I originally estimated a meagre two years for this model, but it has become quite plain that it will not be finished in under four years, and that the delays and frustrations endured by the Building Committee of the S.S.G.B. must also be experienced by those who seek to follow in their footsteps, albeit on a smaller scale.

The fitting out of the engines on the S.S.G.B. took five months, and, almost to the day, it has taken me the same amount of time. Naturally our engine-rooms look rather different, despite sharing the same motive powers. There is however an all-pervading atmosphere which the blood-brotherhood of steam engines emits, no matter what the shape or layout of the different units may be.

With a mixture of gas, water, electricity and oil it is very easy to let an engine room assume the look of a snake pit, with each piece coiling itself around the last item fitted. If the engine room is not to look like a plumber's bag, then the layout must be as carefully planned as the rest of the ship. The obvious thing is ease of access for operation and maintenance, but this is sometimes thwarted by the demands of the prototype and calls for a compromise.

Where this does happen, and particularly where it involves safety, items such as shut-off valves should stand in their own right and are part of the difference between a working model, and that pale shadow in a glass case, one simply for display.

Of primary concern in the raising of steam is keeping the vapour hot once it has left the boiler. The good looks which are given to even the plainest boiler by wooden cladding and brass bands are at the beginning of the insulation chain. Thereafter, the superheated steam pipe and the exhaust system are all jacketed in string binding and the cylinder heads encased, adding realism to function.

One of the reasons that the engines on the prototype gave rise to some disappointment was a lack of insulation. Thermodynamics as a science was not wholly understood at the time, and the massive sizes of the cylinder heads necessary for low pressure engines like those used on the S.S.G.B. aggravated the condensation problems no end. When one considers that it would be possible to drive a small family car through the 88″ cylinder bore, we can more readily appreciate the enormous surface area constantly cooling the laboriously produced steam. Other factors also reducing the general running efficiency of early

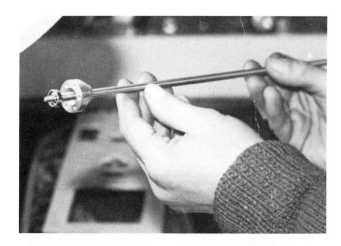

Fig 133. (Top right) Propeller shaft and thrust bearing. Fig 134. (Right) Final drive section of propeller shaft with thrust ball race sealed housing. Fig 135. (Below) Pipe bending around the lagged boiler.

Fig 136. (Above) Engine room temporarily assembled. Note timber cladding around cylinders. Fig 137. (Left) Soldering the water tank.

was, for the first and last time, fresh. This gives me the excuse to mention that I have changed my mind about the positioning of my freshwater tanks. Instead of siting them amidships, abreast of the boiler in the wings of the ship, I have placed a single tank for'ard. The reasons for this are simplicity of operation and keeping the centre of gravity as low as possible. I am no longer concerned about heat transference to the sides of the ship, as I am satisfied that the casing will not allow this to happen. Positioned for' ard, the water supply will help as ballast, and is well out of the way of other items. Jacketed, for the purposes of using previously heated water from a thermos, it will provide residual heat to the offside of the gas canisters, themselves sandwiched between the superheated end of the boiler and this tank of warm water. Even on a cold day, I believe that this will provide a sufficiently warm poultice to keep the gas supply from freezing up without too many complicated pieces of plumbing. The water tank has an overflow system which is piped into one of the portside portholes; all one has to do is to keep pouring the water down the inlet pipe until it starts to come back at you ... somewhat reminiscent of the "Little Boy of Brussels".

Doing my best to avoid obvious vulgarity, the blow-down cock situated immediately beneath the boiler sight glass will also discharge itself in a similar manner, but with a great deal more force, via the oil separator. This fitting ensures a clear and accurate reading of the water level in the boiler, and periodically needs releasing for this purpose.

With the hull inverted, possibly for the last time, one final job remains with the completion of the top member of the stern frame which is made of brass strip set in GRP resin. It houses the all important top pintle through which the rudder stock (brass rod) passes like a hinge pin. As with the prototype, this allows the rudder to be removable, an important consideration in both model and ship. The

steamships really stemmed from the use of salt water in the boilers, encrustations of which insulated the boiler plates from the furnaces. Like badly furred kettles, the boilers stubbornly resisted the exertions of the stokers to maintain the meagre 5lb per sq in pressure, the salt-baked lining acting as insulation in reverse. No wonder then, that on average the S.S.G.B. consumed 60 tons of coal in just 24 hours.

On that special day, the first day's steaming, 12 December 1844, the water in the boilers of the S.S. *Great Britain*

1845 LONGITUDINAL ELEVATION

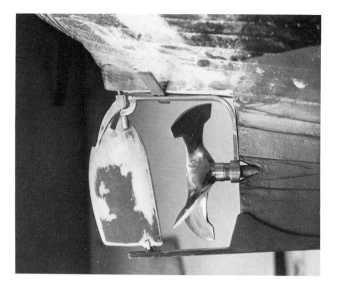

Fig 138. (Above left) Prototype removable rudder. Fig 139. (Above). Annealing the copper coupling. Makeshift fire-brick forge. Fig 140. (Left). First steaming – a very special moment – 7.00pm May 17th 1980.

Magic Moments. 17 May 1980, 7.00pm.

Apart from the launch itself, the first raising of steam gives life to the dry bones of a ship in a way that nothing else can. The birth of any steam model takes place on the first firing up, and is a long awaited and anxious moment. For this special occasion, I was delighted to welcome Geoff Sheppard in the role of chief engineer with his wealth of knowledge and expertise in this field.

Prior to any thoughts of ignition, the copper coupling tubes needed annealing, to give softness and flexibility to make the final assembly an easier process. The copper tubing is heated to a bright orange and then quenched in cold water, reducing the strength of the tubing to the extent that it is easy to bend by hand. Firebricks make this process of annealing very much easier, and a makeshift forge, as seen in the picture, increases the usefulness of even a small butane gas torch by its heat retention.

With all the pipe-work linked, a flame test on the burner gave every indication that we were in business, leaving little else to do other than try it all out under steam power. As the boiler pressure rose to 20psi, spanners were flying around the engine room as in a Grand Prix wheel change adjusting and tightening up nuts, valves and couplings.

As one might have predicted, this was the moment when I ran out of film in the camera, and before I had time to change the roll and return to the scene, the chief engineer had it all pulsating away like an industrial sewing machine on a bonus scheme!

Steam is the strong silent one, with all its thrust delivered with hardly more than a serpent's hiss. Unlike other forms of power unit, it has all its muscle present at low revs from the moment the steam valve is opened. This ability to show its strength at low revs is one of the secrets of just why it is steam models look so effective: be they locomotives, traction engines, or Victorian steamships, they all share in this same magical appeal.

final drive shaft has also to be sealed to the hull with a stern tube fairing leading up to the propeller stuffing gland, (a raced bearing with an 'O' seal). The original was made watertight by a "leather and copper" stuffing gland, but had Brunel had the advantage of silicon rubber, no doubt he would have used it, at least in a working model. The hull is now finally watertight, I hope and trust.

THE UPPER WORKS

Laying the Sub-deck

The inordinate amount of time which it seemed to have taken to get the first piece of sub-deck laid stems from a mixture between caution and fear that some item which I will need to get at in the future will have become totally inaccessible by, as it were, 'nailing down the lid of the coffin too soon.'

Whereas modelling in the long term requires the mind to be adjusted to the concept of nibbling away at tiny objects for months on end, every now and again it is necessary to undertake a major piece of woodwork. I think of decking as being the flesh which covers the bones of a ship, and it is certain that covering the bulkheads dramatically changes the whole feel of the model, giving it a new confidence. It also has the effect of making it appear larger than ever.

The fo'c's'le is the first area to be tackled. Richard Goold-Adams, the chairman of the S.S. *Great Britain* Project, records in his book, "The Return of The Great Britain", that the decking of the fo'c's'le was one of the very first pilot schemes to be tackled in 1973 on the rescued ship. This job needed doing very badly, not only to give the ship a water-tight interior, but also to arrest the corrosion which had been much accelerated by the rain which falls over Bristol, containing an industrial fall-out with elements of sulphuric and hydrochloric acid, not of course present in the Falkland Islands.

As can be seen from the pictures of the model, card templates are back in action once more, following the internal shape of the 'shoulder' in its double twist action towards the prow. To follow this contortive shape, some $\frac{1}{16}''$ birch ply was cut on the short grain of the sheet. This makes it thoroughly amenable and obviates the need for soaking and steaming the strips of wood.

One of the most difficult technical tasks in building model ships is to get the correct deck levels. The S.S.G.B.

Fig 141. (Left) Card templates are back in action. Note the flat fo'c's'le. Fig. 142. (Below) Deck curvature by pre-treating the plywood.

Fig 143. (Above) "Down three steps onto the main deck", the prototype fo'c's'le. Fig 144. (Right). The model subdeck.

is no exception to the rule, but it does have the unusual feature of a flat fo'c's'le. Normally one furrows the eyebrows at the sight of a model with a flat deck of any kind, but in this particular instance, Brunel designed it so, adding to this unique feature diagonal iron strapping and planking for increased strength – another departure from the famous model in the Science Museum which depicts the common practice of planking fore and aft.

Down three steps onto the main deck, a tip worth mentioning which will help to achieve even deck curvature, is that of painting on a light mix of Cascamite resin to the underside of the raw plywood. Allow it to soak for approximately fifteen minutes, and then wipe it off with a damp rag and allow it to dry. As it dries out it will curl very gently, giving the ply a curvature which can still be flattened, but which has an inbuilt camber which is self-assumed. It must be fixed to the deck beams before the untreated topside is overlaid or painted or it will simply flatten out as counter-shrinkage takes place.

The warping of wood on removable deck hatches has often proved a nuisance to model boat builders. There inevitably seems to be one corner which refuses to align with the curvature of the deck, and has either to be screwed or clasped in some way, making emergency removal rather awkward.

The solution to this suggested itself to me in the product of a company who use a backing of aluminium foil to

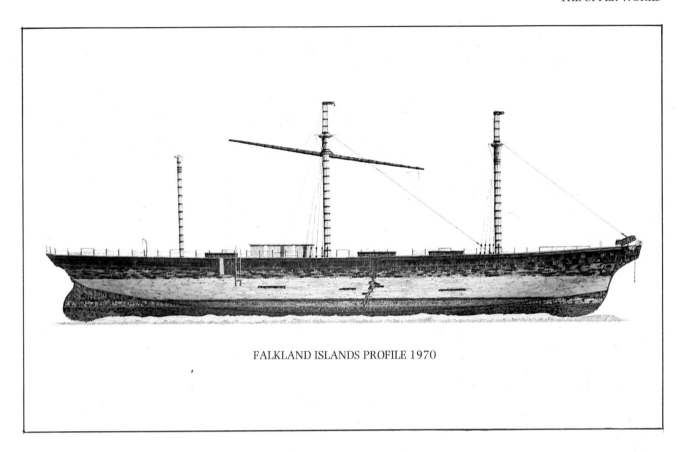

FALKLAND ISLANDS PROFILE 1970

Starboard-broadside of model

Fig 145. (Above) Planking the deck, prototype . . . Fig 146. (Right) . . . and the model.

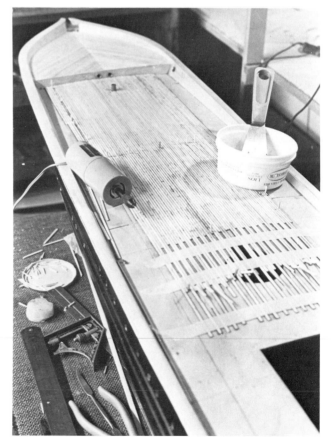

facilitate the use of their veneers, (Rollwood Ltd.) Aluminium, which can be given a slight camber before adhesion to the underside of the deck hatch covers, and can always be adjusted according to the directions in which the wood decides it will move. In old fashioned English, it can be 'bent straight'.

I am anticipating some trouble from the long cover directly over the boiler. The combination of heat and steam are after all, exactly what has been used to make wood bend and twist in boat building for many hundreds of years. You will see therefore, quite extensive use of aluminium sheet, set between the deck beams, not only to reflect the heat, but also to counteract any tendency to 'curl its bottom lip'. It is as well to remember that direct sunlight can play the same trick in reverse, and whereas a hot summer's day may appeal greatly from the operational point of view of model boats, it can spell a deal of trouble with a timber-built ship model. By the same token, finished models should not be placed in rooms where direct sunlight can shine on them, a point to be checked out if you loan a model for exhibition purposes. Speaking as someone who has been nurtured on the construction of musical instruments, I am aghast when I see an un-shaded shop window full of guitars and the like in blazing sunlight. If you step inside the shop, you can hear the contortive agony of wood on the move and smell the destructive effects of the sun's rays on hot varnish and raw

Fig 147. (Above) Diagonal planking on the fo'c's'le. Note use of cocktail sticks as treenails. Fig 148. (Left) "200 lengths of 2mm wide lime strips".

timber. What a contrast to the high set windows of our national museums, where these dangers were well appreciated by our predecessors in their initial designs? The greatest fear in these establishments comes during the winter months, with the dryness of permanent central heating demanded by the public expectancy for comfort. This dryness is slowly destroying exhibits which have survived all the other dangers of history, in some cases for three or four hundred years. Humidifiers do not appear to be able to counteract moisture starved air, and the only real remedy would seem to be to turn off the heating and provide visitors with an extra overcoat and a pair of woolly socks. Maybe the energy crisis will force us back to the use of the old coke stoves which were much more suited to the requirements of heat for human beings and preservation of the exhibits they have come to see.

Planking the Deck

I have hinted previously that one of the fascinations of wood is its chance to play out several roles in the latter felled stage of its life. The planking which is now almost complete on the ship in Bristol is just such a case in point.

In July 1970, Ewan Corlett 'phoned Richard Goold-Adams with the snippet of information that the Royal Navy were pulling down one of their barracks at Portsmouth, and that he believed, if they acted quickly enough,

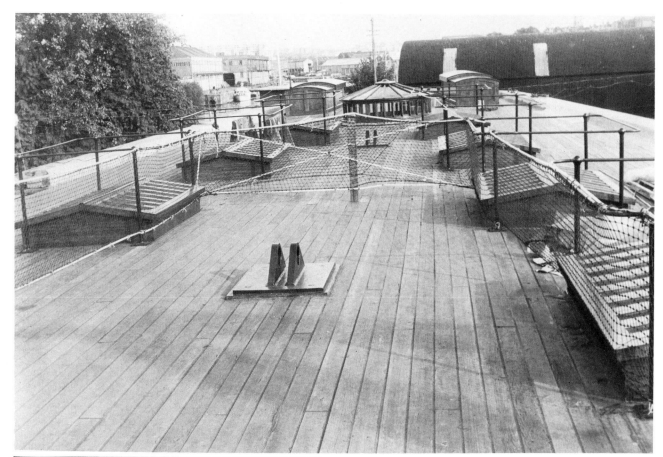

Fig 149. (Above) S.S.G.B. prototype, deck planking, looking aft.
Fig 150. (Left) "The Crack" (Drawing by J.C. Cave, ASAI).

they would secure the flooring very cheaply. Without any cash whatsoever to spare, they got the lot for £4,500, delivered free; a wonderful purchase made possible by the generosity of John Smith M.P., at that time still in the House of Commons as Member for Westminster.

Aboard the prototype at Bristol, there has been criticism that the decking purchased 10 years ago, has only just come to completion, and that this delay has caused unnecessary damage to the interior of the hull. Besides the many considerations of time, skill and money, such judgement should be tempered by a proper understanding of the structural problems caused by "The Crack" and the paramount importance of ensuring that the hull was absolutely stable before any of the upper work could be undertaken. The main deck has taken some $2\frac{1}{2}$ years to complete, the lengthiest and most difficult part being the waterproofing, which has included the laying of a sub-deck, much as in the model. The original red pine planking on the ship was 6″ deep and 5″ wide, with a total of 79 widths amidships. Mine is laid in that most choice of modelling timbers – lime – purchased in a pre-sawn bundle – 200 lengths of 2mm strip, which is almost perfectly to scale. I, too, could have done with a redundant barrack floor!

Caulking

The sub-deck plays an important part on the model, in that it gives a level surface on which to lay the planks, and perhaps even more usefully, it means that the planks only have to be glued on their bottom sides and not along the caulking lines, where glue seepage is difficult to deal with. Herein lies a problem, the question being how one may best get the true effect of caulking? I resist all talk of black glue; I hear tell of those who use negative photographic strip, literally caulked in between the planks, but that, to me, just sounds like a different form of torture. Hopefully, I've come up with some sort of answer which is neither painful nor expensive.

Three-quarter stern view of model

Three-quarter bow view of model

Geoff Sheppard, superintendent, engineer and boiler maker, looking decidedly pleased (Photo by Ben Mowll)

First you must take a trip to your friendly doctor to secure a used hypodermic syringe so that you can inject new life into one of those felt tip marker pens. The little reservoir cup which acts as the friction grip to the main body of the syringe (which you don't need on this occasion, but accept the gift if it is offered,) is sufficient to hold enough ink for about 40ft of planking. The felt tip needs to be well moistened, hence the necessity for the extra injection of ink. I found it easiest to draw the plank over the pen nib rather than the more conventional way of doing things. The result of edging the plank with ink is to give a very realistic thin black line, which just occasionally wavers as when, in full scale, the hot tar on the oakum has been spilt. When the two planks are faced together the result is very striking. Need I say – use an ink which is both waterproof and undisturbed by whatever finish is later applied.

A properly laid deck will always pay visual dividends, and whereas many tricks in model-making can be made to deceive the eye, ships' decks are almost impossible to fake successfully. Even a raw amateur can tell by the different colour and grain of timber, whether or not the modeller has bothered to lay the deck by individual strips, or whether he, or she, has short-circuited the job by some other means.

Fig 151 (Above right) Modified felt tip pen for use as a caulker. Fig 152 (Below) Visual dividends of a planked deck. Fig 153. (Below right) Flying bridge, prototype.

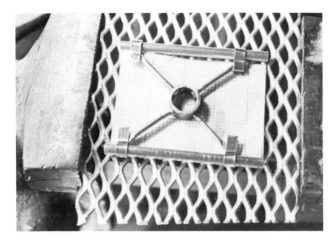

Fig 154. (Above left) Flying bridge support on griddle, ready for soldering. Fig 155. (Above) Flying bridge support, made from brass tube and strip. Fig. 156. (Left) Prototype flying bridge support.

bridge over a stream, the banks of which have been swept away. It did provide an accessible lookout platform and something on which to put navigation lights, but perhaps its most immediate use was to give the captain and officers of the watch a special place of retreat from all those adoring ladies. The steep and narrow gangway aloft would have been a deterrent to even the most intrepid of these, though the real reason for the restrictively steep angle was the tightness of fit between the bottom of the gangway and the engine skylight, out of which rose Wednesday mast on the prototype 1843 ship. This also accounts for the fact that the gangway has to be offset from centre. Taken all in all, it is an untidy piece of design which points to Brunel changing his mind about the propulsion, ridding himself of the paddle steamer but not of all its trappings.

When the ship arrived home from the Falkland Islands in 1970 at Avonmouth, a hurriedly erected platform using scaffolding was mounted before the historic passage up the river Avon was undertaken, the ship moving for the first time in 34 years on her own keel. It would seem, therefore that a rostrum is useful in navigationally tight circumstances, and its retention quite understandable. It must have been a draughty spot in a headwind, and indeed Keith Griffin's modern picture of the ship details some canvas protection fixed to the stanchion rail, which would have given basic protection to the captain's frock coat-tails but not much else. No wonder they all grew beards.

The Flying Bridge

If you are inclined to think that the flying bridge looks somewhat of a spatchcock affair, serving no real purpose, then you would have guessed at half the truth. It seems certain that it was designed to fit between the paddle boxes on the original specification for the ship, before the courageous decision was taken to use screw propulsion instead of the cumbersome paddle. With the paddle boxes removed it would seem that nobody had quite the heart to depart from the practice of steamers at this period and well beyond, to have an elevated platform. So there it remained, looking flimsy and awkward, like a country

Fiddley Grating

To say that the flying bridge is a straightforward case of fiddley grating joined to stanchion rail is to make light of two rather tricky items. Fiddley grating and its production in miniature has been much discussed. It seems everyone has his pet way of going about the task, and the jigs and tools for its production multiply daily. The key factor is to match the width of the timber strip with the width of the sawblade kerf (cut). You really need to know the blade width before anything else can start to happen. With the strip and the kerf in exactly the same width, there must follow absolute uniformity in the spacing. The depth of the

123

cut to just over half the thickness of the strip is not so critical, but the width must be spot on. You are, in practice, locking wooden teeth together, and it can be very unforgiving if the teeth are not evenly spaced.

The radial arm saw is a wonderful way to cheat, and as an aid to making over 700 joints in the bridge alone, this machine tool really comes into its own, but I do hesitate to show a technique which will be available only to a few, when in practice, the effect can be achieved with a tenon saw and mitre block. The finest I have ever seen was made by hand with a hacksaw blade in the scale of $\frac{3}{16}$":1'. It does require hardwood, the closer grained the better. Mine is of walnut, and they are often executed in boxwood or lime, although I found that mahogany shatters, which is hardly surprising with a nine inch circular saw blade and a castellation of $\frac{1}{16}$". Do watch the size of the finished hole. In full scale practice it is less than the width of the timber, which means that for the modeller, the sawcuts must be made as close together as you dare to go, and herein lies the skill, because it is bordering on the impractical to produce them absolutely to scale, but a real challenge to flirt on the fringe of the impossible. In the end it is most satisfying putting the converse grains together and there is no real substitute in the emulation of the original, unless, of course, you join the ranks of the unabashed and buy it ready cut from one of the splendid continental firms.

Fig 157. (Right) Fiddley Grating. Wooden teeth locking together. This grating was found to be too coarse and was not used on the final bridge assembly. Fig 158. (Below) Stanchion rail for bridge using the 'ring eyes'. Blobs were soldered into the top of the $\frac{1}{16}$in diam. brass tube.

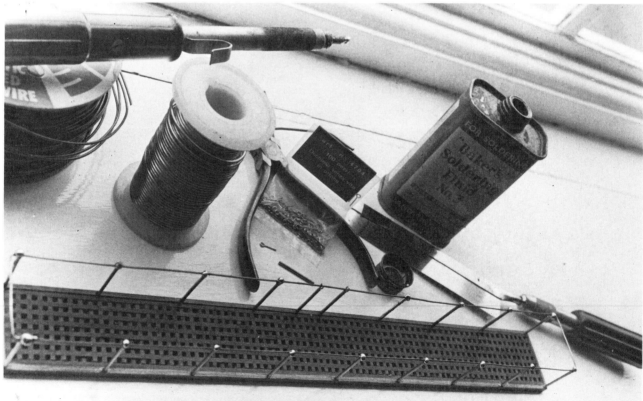

An impressive turn of speed (Photo by Ben Mowll)

Stanchion Post (for Bridge)

Having fiddled with the fiddley – my bridge is actually attempt number three – what about the wretched stanchion posts? Unlike the grating, which if you want to buy it is reasonably priced, stanchion posts, lathe-turned in brass are understandably very expensive, so a suitable method for home production is well worthwhile considering. I have tried lots of different ways, but recommend the following, if only for its simplicity of production and its cheapness. In essence, it is $\frac{1}{16}''$ O/D brass tube for the stanchion post with a brass jackstay soldered to the top of it. (A jackstay is like a "screw eye" without the screw thread. Marketed as "ring eye – plain end", at current prices they are literally two a penny.) The simplicity is enhanced at the time of fitting the wire rail to the post, because the jackstay will assume its own level in the end of the brass tube, even if the tops of the posts are not exactly uniform in height, allowing the rail to determine the straight line. The solder blob is produced by a quick dab with the soldering iron, using an upward movement before the solder starts to run. The colder the brass is, the easier it is to make a nice round blob.

Stanchion Rail

The stanchion rail is nothing fancy – garden PVC tying wire with the sheathing removed. It is a very soft wire which is almost too obedient but stiffens somewhat with solder. Cheap and useful, it will be mentioned again when I reach the subject of rigging.

The rhetorical question is; how do you get it straight when it has been coiled? Easy – but I didn't know until the secret was passed on to me by no less a person than John Cundell.

Roll the wire on a flat, hard surface along its length, with the flatside of a steel rule (or piece of hardwood), backwards and forwards, and out come the humps, kinks and bumps with hardly any resistance. The system works with copper and brass tube as well as fuse wire, and is a tip well worth remembering.

Fig 159. (Right) The final assembly of the model flying bridge, a delicate and awkward construction. Fig 160. (Below) An echo of the prototype.

Fig 161. (Above) The wood-turning lathe . . . £10 the lot! Fig 162. (Left) Turning the capstan. The round nosed gouge.

The Capstan

Given the historical fact that the S.S.G.B. was the first ship to have a piano on board – "needs tuning badly" – the musical centre of this ship remained at the drumhead of the capstan.

"Come all you young fellows who follow the sea,
  To me way, hey, blow the man down,
  Now pray pay attention and listen to me,
  Give me some time to blow the man down."

The fiddler or the ship's piper sat on the drumhead of the capstan barrel whilst for hours the sailors stomped around to the powerful beat of the shanty, their sea boots working in concert with the rhythm of the words.

There was some criticism of the verbal content of the sea shanties by the passengers. Recorded in "The Cabinet" – the news-sheet composed by the passengers on the special trip which carried the Eleven of the All England Cricket Team (December 1861) – is the suggestion that there was an "open field to compose some spirit stirring songs, with dedication to the S.S. *Great Britain*, which would cause the composer's name to be handed down in the records of the ship and his memory cherished with a feeling of respect."

A lingering interest in folksongs of all kinds leads me to believe that an original set of stanzas would often include the composer's name on the last verse. In that most singable outlaw song, "The Ballad of Jesse James", the final verse goes as follows:-

  "This song was made, by Billy Gashade,
    As soon as the news did arrive,
    He said there was no man, with the law in his hand,
    Who could take Jesse James when alive."
  (From a collection by Alan Lomax)

So, by land or by sea, if you wished to be immortalized

"She sits upon the water like a racing gig".

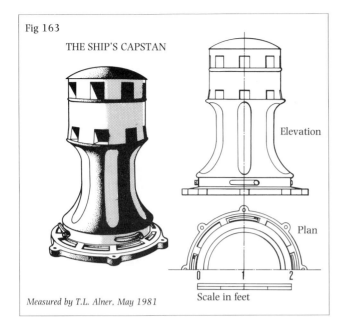

Fig 163

THE SHIP'S CAPSTAN

Elevation

Plan

0   1   2

Scale in feet

Measured by T.L. Alner, May 1981

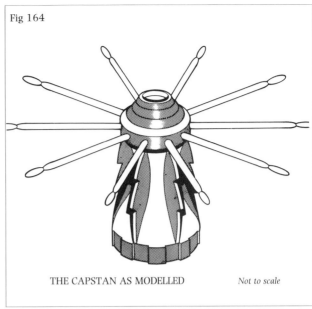

Fig 164

THE CAPSTAN AS MODELLED   *Not to scale*

Fig 165. (Left) The indexing jig. Fig 166. (Below left) The capstan in the jig, being drilled in situ. Fig 167. (Above) Filing groove to accept whelp.

alongside the hero or the event, or in our case the ship on its way to challenge The Australian Cricket Team, then the easiest way to do it was indeed to write yourself into a 'shantey'.

In conclusion, the critic, in his article in "The Cabinet", congratulated the Boatswain and his mates upon the "vigorous manner in which they pipe their ditty upon their whistle." Although there are several poems about the S.S.G.B., I don't know of any that were structured into the 6/8 rhythm of the shanty, although I suppose that the challenge remains open?

The construction of the capstan obviously required lathe-turning, and after several seasons of neglect in the back of the tool cupboard, out came all the bits and pieces which together constitute the wood-turning lathe. A basic outfit this; (what do you expect for £10 the lot at 1963 prices?) with variable speed on the drill it is possible to turn out quite nice work. The capstan barrel, which forms the centre column, is shaped rather like a senior chessman, worked in the main with the round-nose gouge and parting tool. So far so good. Unfortunately the lathe does not

129

run to having an indexing attachment, so how is it possible to mark out accurately the pigeon holes for positioning the ten capstan bars?

The jig is very simple and mighty useful for the accurate marking out of wheel bosses etc. of all sorts and sizes. I hope that the photographs will be self-explanatory, but the principle is as follows. Drill through the centre of the boss, or capstan barrel in this case, so that it is possible to fit the workpiece onto a tight-fitting spindle suspended in a U-shaped channel. On the end of the spindle is mounted a cogwheel (any cogwheel with a suitable number of teeth will do,). This acts as a divider head which can be used to give exact divisions: drill a locating pin-hole through the channel; when this hole is plugged, the locating pin will lock the movement of the spindle in the "V" tooth of the cogwheel. My spindle and cogwheel are from the Fischer-Technic range, and usefully have friction grip, which is easily done up and undone using only fingers. But I underline the fact that any cogwheel and spindle would do.

With the capstan loaded between the channel, the incisions are put in with a fine tooth blade saw, through a previously sawn groove which acts as a guide, rather like a mitre-box. With the workpiece still on the spindle, the jig can be clamped to the drill stand base and drilled 'in situ'. Surprisingly easy and accurate. On a full-sized capstan

whelps are let into the barrel of the capstan in order to give greater grip. On the model also, these are located by the markings of the indexer and grooved out by the use of the 'pillar' needle file.

Cocktail sticks do nicely for the capstan bars, whilst the pawls on the base of the barrel, which stop the capstan running back under heavy load, will be represented by the previously mentioned ring eyes, plain end and slightly bent.

Fig 168. (Right) Dressing back the whelp. Fig 169. (Below) Cocktail sticks for capstan bars.

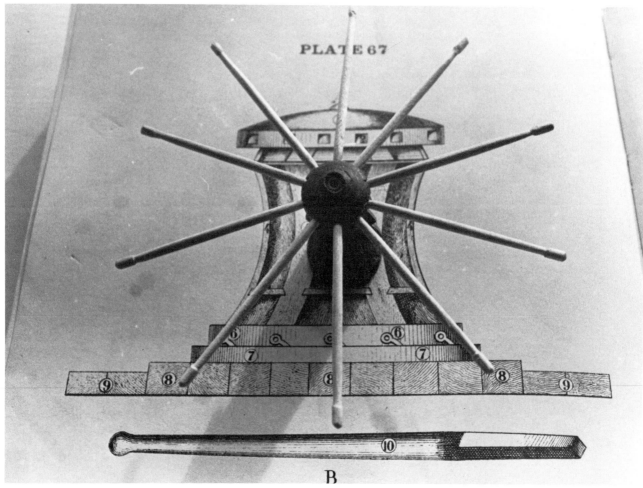

MASTS & RIGGING

Masts

Only number 2 mast of the original 6-masted ship was stepped right through to the keel. This has always been thought of as the Mainmast, but was known by the sailors as "Tuesday" in order to avoid confusion between number four mast and the "foremast". Thus on the original rig, the six masts took their names from the days of the working week, from Monday to Saturday. (This overcame the problem for the sailors alright, but I had the greatest difficulty in pursuading a knowledgeable schoolgirl that the ship had only six masts and not seven, as she was adamant that there was one for every day of the week – ah, well.)

Apart from number 2 mast, all the others were hinged at the base and supported by wire rigging, with the apparent intention that all the sailing gear could be lowered away in its entirety, thus reducing wind resistance, a truly auxiliary concept of sail. One might have imagined that the novelty of these hinged masts allowed the promenade and saloon decks to be free from the interference of masting pillars, giving an air of uncluttered spaciousness to the interior decor. However, there was a row of supports down the middle of each saloon, including almost certainly one under each mast, with the exception of number 3, for which it is proving very hard to find adequate support in the restored ship. Perhaps it never had adequate support, and this had a bearing on its removal in 1846.

The hinged masts and iron wire rigging were an engineer's solution, which did not appeal greatly to

Fig 170. (Left) Masts temporarily positioned. Fig 171. (Below) Section through one of the original masts.

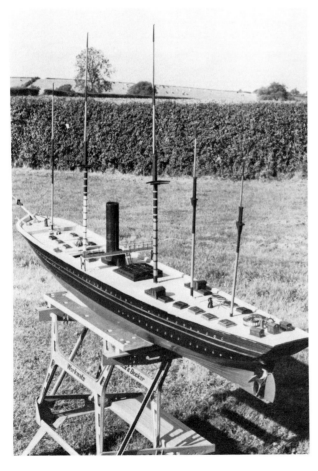

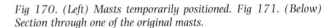

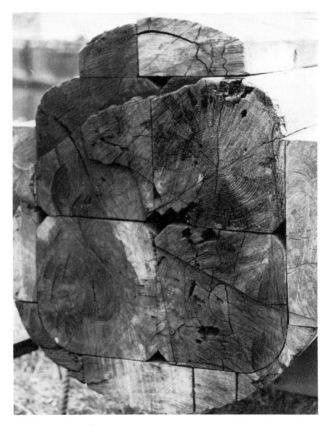

THE "GREAT BRITAIN" STEAM-SHIP, NEWLY RIGGED.

seamen. Captain Hosken obviously resisted these 'improper' deck fittings and at the first opportunity did away with them, replacing Brunel's modern thinking by stepping the refitted masts right through to the keel, and ordering hemp in place of wire for their support.

In order to improve the manoeuvrability of this excessively stable ship, Wednesday mast, situated immediately abaft the funnel, was removed altogether. Thursday was made to the same dimensions as the Main mast, with the addition of secondary masts attached to them, which allowed the goose-neck (jaws of the gaffs,) to run without the interference of the hooped bands of these enormous multiple tree trunks. It is possible that the 'trysail' masts, added to Tuesday and Thursday, were made from the original timber masts made redundant by the requirement of extra length through the decking to the keel. Both Tuesday and Thursday were now square-rigged with the addition of top-gallant masts, and this would have shifted the axis of sail further aft, and improved the handling of the ship when under sail.

The new rig gave the ship a height and majesty which overcame the sneers and snipes that this ship was a dumpy little steam-boat which lacked the elegance of its contemporary (particularly American) counterparts. Not many people would have seen her with this rig, as the stranding episode on Dundrum Bay took place only five months after the ship had assumed its new look. Although the period was very short, the Illustrated London News had one of their artists draw a fine and detailed pen-and-ink broadside view, and Joseph Walter painted at least two oil canvasses of the ship in the new rig, pounding against fierce headwinds, so that the documentation for this all

too brief spell in the ship's life is sound and good.

It came as somewhat of a surprise to me, when I first stumbled into this period of shipping, that masts are not simply round poles. Wherever one mast is fitted to another, or the base of a mast is stepped into a keel, the circular section changes to square in order to prevent the mast twisting on its own axis.

My particular method for the production of masts is to begin with a square section of timber and keep it square as the reduction process is taking place, only rounding it off at the very last moment. This ensures straightness in the taper and helps the difficult business of setting in the cheeks or houndpieces at the base of the lower trestle trees.

A hand-planed mast will preserve something of this original character, particularly if a mature piece of pitch pine with a nice straight grain can be found. In days gone by, the broom handle and the church pew alike were made from this timber, with its properties of strength and flexibility; it didn't even have time to get expensive before it was all used up, and now one is indeed lucky to find a piece, lurking in the back of a garage or attic, posing as a tent pole or a garden hoe. Where I found my piece is a classified secret, but it has been stored for a few years in my special faggot bundle, awaiting the circular saw blade and a new life in a totally changed role.

Hand-planing into the round is a choice job, from which I derive great pleasure, particularly from the scent of the wood. In order to keep a check on the reduction, (and it is very easy to overdo this process, simply because of the enjoyment of the exercise) I use makeshift shooting boards of different thicknesses, so that the plane is prevented from going below a certain depth, even if I should get carried away.

The square footing ends of the upper masts are always preserved, of course, so that they may be 'fidded in' to the cross trees in the correct manner; the hoops on the hounding of the main masts were made with the help of a small tube cutter, (useful tool) slicing up a brass tube like so many cheap wedding rings.

Fig 172. (Opposite) ILN pen-and-ink broadside. Copyright The Illustrated London News, 16 May 1846. Fig 173. (Below) Display of the ship's six yards with all the fittings attached. Fig 174. (Right) Masts and yards before assembly. Fig 175. (Bottom) Yards and spars temporarily positioned.

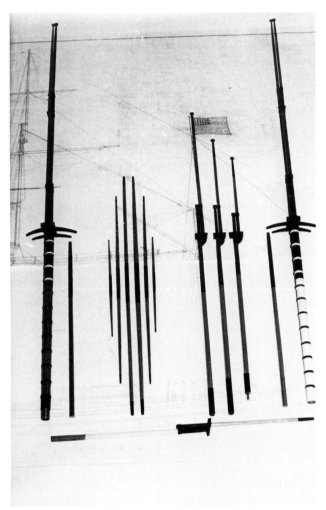

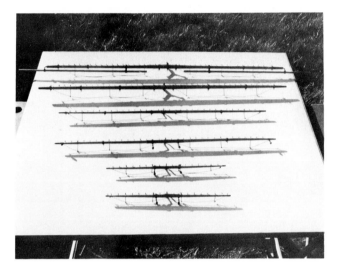

Early in 1971, Henry Elwes made the offer to the S.S.G.B. Project of six masts from the Gloucestershire Forestry Co-operative, of which he was a leading member, five for the masts and one for the bowsprit. This handsome gift of local timber has been seasoning ever since, and to date only the bowsprit is in position, although it cannot be too long now before the familiar and attractively raked masts are firmly seated in the cast-iron caps, attached to the hinging deckplates.

The mainmast, which was originally made of iron, has been restored in tubular steel section, weighing a total of $6\frac{1}{2}$ tons and finally completed in October 1977. In its turn it will be used as a samson post to haul the foremast into position when the time comes. My references show this as an iron mast, painted white with contrasting black hoops, differing from the 1846 Thursday mast, built to the same dimensions, but of timber only, and no doubt influenced by the thinking of Capt. J. Hosken rather than Brunel, in his attempts to rid this ship of its thorough-going modernity.

Yards and Spars

The constant factor with both yards and spars is their undernourished, flyweight appearance The temptation for the modeller is to leave them overweight because it is almost unthinkable to reduce them to such a spindly profile, hardly thicker at the extreme ends than the proverbial matchstick. The question constantly posing itself is, "surely a ship of this size would have required something more robust than these puny-looking little yards to propel it through the ocean?" The answer inevitably is that the feebleness of the timber relied heavily upon the support of the standing and running rigging, and the skill of the master. Such miscalculations as there were, resulted in the loss, not only of the yard, but often the mast

Fig 176. (Below) Four tons of iron spar, the largest ever made. Fig 177. (Bottom) Main yard. Truss bow 1852. Fig 178. (Opposite) Prototype bowsprit. B&P photos.

Fig 179 a & b The ship at the Falkland Islands and being brought home. (Drawings by J.C. Cave ASAI).

as well, causing considerable chaos and danger on the decks below. One of the Joseph Walter paintings depicts a dangling top-gallant yard in gale force winds, hanging like a loose tooth from the topmast as though to prove the point that fierce headwinds often caused structural damage. Needless to say, this was not the painting shown to prospective travellers.

The famous main yard, now displayed beside the ship, is a relic of the 1857 period – four tons of iron spar – the largest example ever made, 105ft long, and a hazardous problem to dismantle before the sea voyage on the pontoon from the Falkland Islands. Strangely, this yard, with its cruciform appearance, added to the 'Golgotha' image of the slowly dying ship in Sparrows Cove, which, prior to the rescue in 1970, was certainly destined to be the final resting place of this stubborn old lady. This mournful

sight, set against the deserted hills around her, might not appear to many people to be the beginning of a great re-kindling of interest, but moved Ewan Corlett to write his famous letter to *The Times* in November 1967, challenging the nation at least to document, photograph and fully record this Crown wreck and, at best, to rescue the ship for Britain.

Sails

There is little doubt in my mind that the so-called "romance of sail and sailing ships" has a strong connection with thinly veiled maidens ashore. The undeniably voluptuous shape which a billowing canvas assumes when filled with a strong sea breeze has finally seduced many a reluctant sailor back to sea, leaving his second love for his first. One might like to consider that the fore-topsail of Nelson's flagship, the *Victory*, shared a remark-ably similar shape to the forefront of Lady Emma Hamil-ton, something which no doubt gave the Admiral great

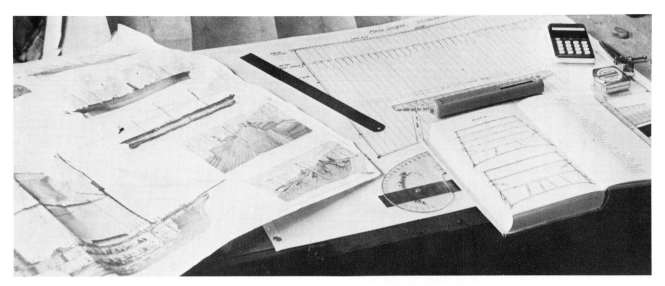

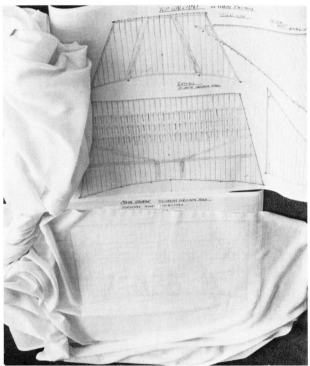

Fig 180. (Above) Scaling up the main course from the drawings produced by the Bournemouth & Poole College of Art, Technical Illustration Dept. These scale drawings are produced as a wall chart. Fig 181. (Right) The use of cotton voile for the sails. Note the realistic folding qualities of this material and its translucence. Fig 182. (Bottom right) Materials. Molnlycke-Spun Syntet No. 9705 for attaching rope to outside, No. 9796 for lines and main machining; marked orange stick; dark macrame waxed linen thread for Bolt rope; fine round-tipped machine needle Singer No. 2045, for fine and synthetic materials; fine string "Zübehor"; Staedtler ultra-fine fibre tip pen No. F/Lumocolor S.313 F, permanent dark brown.

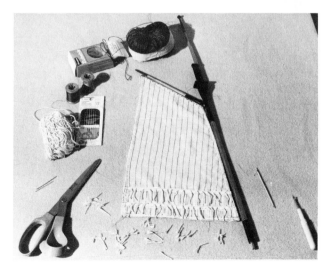

pleasure in his lonelier moments.

The preservation of the chimerical effect of snowy canvas means that a ship modeller must choose a material for a suit of sails which will in no way blot out the form of the ship of the spidery nature of the rigging. Sails on a real ship, when the light is in the right quarter, hide very little of the form, like the scantily dressed dancer whom the ship imitates as she ripples across the ocean. I maintain that sails must appear as cumulus clouds and not as sheets of stiff white cardboard. So many otherwise excellent models are spoilt by carrying overweight linen sails, no matter how lovingly sewn or presented.

In that it is not possible to scale down linen, as one might a mast or a deadeye, it is today possible to use materials which give the effect of lightness and translucence. Those materials employed by the fashion trade which are designed not to obscure feminine charm are particularly suited to miniature sail-making. I chose cotton voile, a man-made mixture of 67% polyester and 33% cotton voile. This material folds realistically, an important point when brailing up sails, is transparent enough to trace from the sail-plan, and is non-shrinking and virtually non absorbent. I would hasten to add that its wind-holding properties are poor, but that is the compromise it is necessary to make for realism.

The making of any suit of sails is a most painstaking business, and accounts for the high regard in which the sailmaker was held aboard ship. It is a tempting option for model shipwrights to leave the yards bare, or do a mock furling job rather than take the plunge with a complete set of canvas.

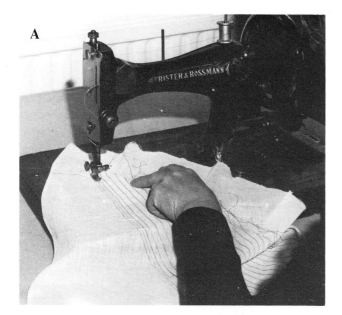

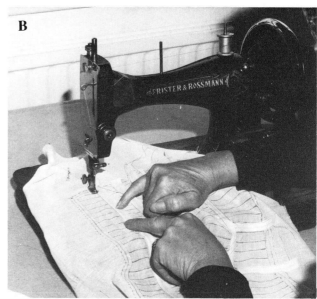

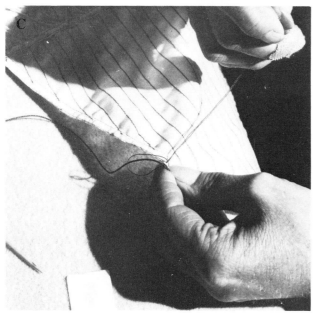

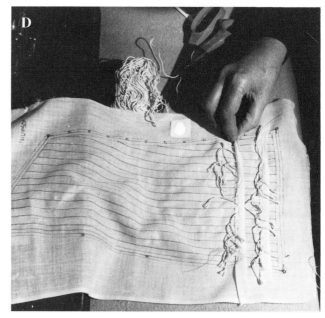

Three things finally decided the prevarication in my mind. The first was a sight of Mike Taylor's S.S.G.B., a picture of which started the magazine series in March 1979 (Model Boats;) the second was an experience of disappointment that when my model of the "P.S. *Sirius*" is under exhibition conditions, without a reflective white background, the rigging lines become almost totally lost; and thirdly, by far the most important consideration, the availability of someone capable of undertaking the work for love, because the work is much too hateful for simple monetary reward. My mother-in-law, was trained as a seamstress by those most exacting of teachers, the nuns, who ensured that not only was patience instilled as a virtue in their girls, but that the work from the convent was of such a standard that it would fetch in the pound notes at the annual summer fete.

Labouring under the misapprehension that there were only three sails to do, she agreed in principle to undertake the job. On receiving my parcel containing the scale draw-ings for thirteen sails, with an option on a further five, there was a certain amount of squeaking down the 'phone. Suffice to say, blood is thicker than water, even sea water, and after she had made a visit to the optician, she forwarded to me within a fortnight, two of the neatest jibsails imaginable.

The legend and the photos show the technique she used, and speak loudly enough for themselves, although where one summons the determination for its execution is quite another matter.

The sails took nearly three months of concentrated 'week-end' work. Surprisingly perhaps, the jibsails, with their sharp angles presented the hardest task in keeping the work neat. Obviously, the whole undertaking required a great deal of dedication and precise machine and hand sewing. Other observations would also include that, despite a fairly loose weave on the cotton voile, when it is all sewn it is so strengthened that I am inclined to revise my opinion as to its wind holding property, which may not be

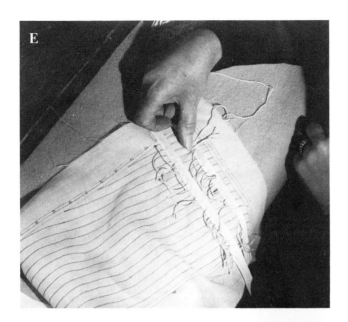

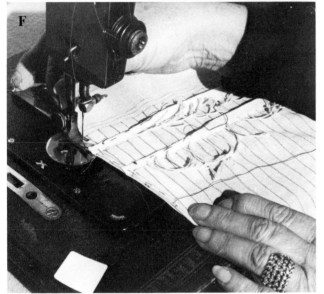

Fig 183. Sailmaking. a) Straight lines to be machine stitched, (approx length of stitch 3mm). b) Machine stitch bias binding (reef band) lines to sail to hold reef points. Top only should be machined to allow access for insertion of reef points. c) Insertion of reef points. Darning needle threaded, should be inserted through the back of sail (leave string attached to main ball of string). Next measure 1½″–2″ in length from cut end of thread and eye of needle, make a knot, ease string through to outside of bias. Now cut string from main ball, allowing 1½″–2″ from back of sail. d) Bias binding now sewn down at bottom, after having inserted reef points. e) Machining down all edges with bias binding: 1 row close to edge, 2nd row approx ¼″ (to hold down turned in edge). f) Attaching rope to edges. Hand stitch the bolt rope with thread No. 9796 (dark) to outside edge of all sides of sail, making loops where required. g) Making loops. For measuring size of loops, use a marked orange stick, pull string to size required and stay stitch securely. h) Finished topsail.

so bad after all. I read with great interest, Mike Taylor's article in July 1980 (Model Boats), in which he states that sails, far from the usual understanding of pushing a ship through the water, actually create a vacuum on the leeward side. Now there's something not even Nelson knew.

The S.S. *Great Britain* was launched as a six masted schooner, carrying 16,000sq ft of sail. As such, Lloyds were faced with registering a ship with a "bit of everything", which means that the vessel makes a classic study of contemporary rigging and sailmaking, as well as a unique example of steam and screw propulsion. By 1846, the sail plan was heightened from the original rig and increased to a possible 'full wardrobe' of 20,000sq ft of canvas, improving the sea-keeping properties and giving the ship a balanced and almost classical appearance, with five masts and twelve sails set. There were possible combinations of a further five sails, including some 'spencers', themselves a modern form of try-sails, introduced generally to take the place of stay-sails between the masts.

It was Brunel's avowed intention that this ship should be handled by a greatly reduced number of crew, thus keeping down the running costs for the GWSSCO. The modern rig reflected the economic stringency, particularly as originally launched, although the return in the 1846 rig to hemp instead of wire rigging must have meant an extra work-load for the crew in terms of adjustment and maintenance.

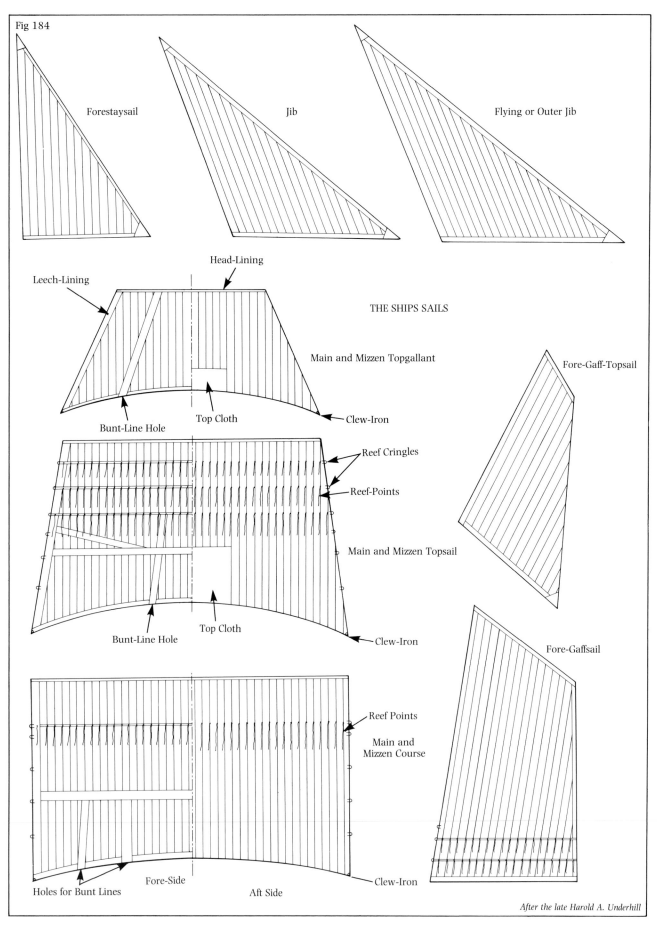

Fig 184

Forestaysail

Jib

Flying or Outer Jib

Head-Lining

Leech-Lining

THE SHIPS SAILS

Main and Mizzen Topgallant

Fore-Gaff-Topsail

Bunt-Line Hole

Top Cloth

Clew-Iron

Reef Cringles

Reef-Points

Main and Mizzen Topsail

Bunt-Line Hole

Top Cloth

Clew-Iron

Fore-Gaffsail

Reef Points

Main and
Mizzen Course

Holes for Bunt Lines

Fore-Side

Aft Side

Clew-Iron

After the late Harold A. Underhill

Ropemaking Materials

Ropemaking is a very ancient art. According to some Egyptian tomb paintings, fishermen on the Nile were making hemp ropes in 2,600 BC, which means that quite apart from the technique involved in its manufacture, they must also have discovered how to grow, crop, soak and rot away the pith of the hemp stalk and beat it until the cortical fibre was separated. From this process, the resultant hemp fibre was ideal for ropemaking and allowed for a good grip on the cordage, as it still does today. Jute is in the same family as hemp, and I do have some carpet jute in my ditty box, for modelling purposes, my personal favourite is waxed linen thread, the sort which upholsterers use, which is usually bought in a hank rather than on a spool. The light gauge Macramé thread is also a winner – there is one that is the colour of creosote, finished with a slight sheen on it. I use this for shroud lines. 'Coates' glacé finished cotton thread is also to be found in my rigging box along with the less satisfactory

cotton crochet threads. All are darkish in colour, going from ashen grey to nut brown, and all the threads are made from natural rather than synthetic fibres. The old enemies, sunlight and temperature variation, cause sagging and stretching in some synthetics which, in extreme circumstances, can cause bitter disappointment. Watch this with some kits, even quite expensive ones, as natural fibres are costly and it is one way in which manufacturers can cut costs, so do check this point at the outset. Coal and oil, from which all the nylons are derived, certainly have a place on board the S.S.G.B. – below decks, rather than above them.

In general terms, the more variety used in gauge and thickness as well as colour, the more realistic the model will appear to be. Keep the colours dark and the gauge light. It also ought to be emphasized that the rigging programme must be planned, so that no running rigging is thicker than standing rigging and nonsenses created whereby, for instance, a fore-preventer stay is outweighed by a shroud-line, or a backstay by a ratline.

The finished result must look like the work of a spider rather than a cobbler, something not made with human hands at all; which is why much of the work incorporates the use of fine nosed pliers and micro-surgery tweezers. Apart from the delusions of grandeur which one can entertain when manipulating the swan neck "number sevens", they have my vote for being one of the nicest instruments of all to handle, extending the use of one's thumb and forefinger into worlds previously unknown.

So much for the introduction; now what about the actual production of miniature rope?

The Ropewalk

With a fanfare of muted trumpets, may I introduce you to the mechanical circus of my ropewalk machine – "The All Electric, AC/DC, Stop, Start and Reversing, Worming, Parcelling and Serving Ropewalk Machine . . . with press button footswitch".

All right, so it looks like a mechanism designed by a committee – the same committee which designed the

Fig 185

19TH CENTURY ROPEMAKING

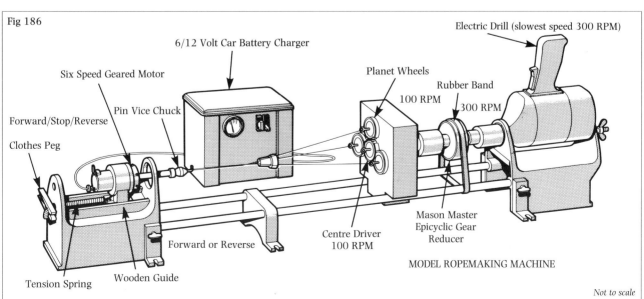

Fig 186

Electric Drill (slowest speed 300 RPM)

6/12 Volt Car Battery Charger

Six Speed Geared Motor

Planet Wheels
100 RPM

Rubber Band

Pin Vice Chuck

300 RPM

Forward/Stop/Reverse

Clothes Peg

Mason Master
Epicyclic Gear
Reducer

Centre Driver
100 RPM

Forward or Reverse

MODEL ROPEMAKING MACHINE

Tension Spring   Wooden Guide

Not to scale

Fig 187. (Above) The all electric AC/DC, worming, parcelling and serving ropewalk machine ... with press button footswitch. Fig 188. How a rope is made. a) Machine threaded up with three strands. b) Controlling the hardness of the top by restraining the movement of the 'top'. c) Sewing up the strands.

camel. The only thing to be said in this machine's favour is that, despite the rubber bands and clothes pegs, it does actually work rather well, though not without a certain amount of operational practice, spinning left or right handed cable rope in combinations of two or three strands according to the required scale thickness. If you ever see left hand laid cable on a model, rest assured it was hand-made and not manufactured.

It warrants a brief description. Any ropewalk will require three main features.

1. The ability to make three hooks revolve slowly at one end.
2. A mechanism to twist the cordage at the other end.
3. The provision of a moving carriage between the centres.

All else, including electric drive, is simply embellishment, and many shipmodellers have made their own hand-cranked versions which I am sure work just as well as mine.

My machine consists of two drill stands joined by some old brass curtain rod, acting as the lathe bed bars but significantly increasing the distance between the centres from the manufacturer's original specification. On the right hand end is clamped an ordinary household electric drill connected to a footswitch. The drill has variable control, set to the lowest speed of 300rpm. The speed is further reduced by an epicyclic, geared chuck down to approximately 100rpm, which is the final speed at which the revolving hooks turn.

The hooks are attached to axles which revolve in the block of wood. The Fischer Technic cogwheels grip the axles and make the hooks turn, clockwise in the case of the

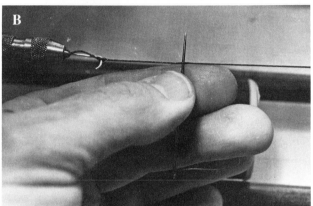

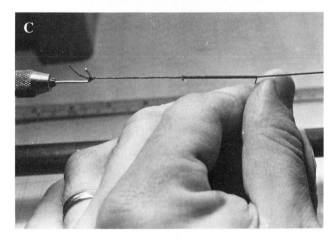

Fig 189. Serving a) Threading up deadeye in preparation for serving. b) Sewing rope at opposite end to the deadeye with serving thread. c) Serving the thread. Note the brass ferrule used for securing the ends. d) Winding off the thread from the bobbin onto the rope.

delicate cordage and means that the work is always under light tension, not only aiding the production of rope, but also assisting the needlework at the start and finish of each length.

How a Rope is Made

Two people wringing out a wet towel will find that the twisting action tightens the fibres of the cloth into a hard core until all the moisture has been squeezed out. The tightness, or technically speaking, the 'hardness' of a rope is made by a similar action, i.e. twisting the fibres in contrary motion from the opposite ends of the cordage. The tighter the twist, the harder the rope becomes as the yarns coil in on themselves.

The action of a ropewalk is both to spin and twist strands at the same time, although it does not in practice have to be done simultaneously. The spinning at the 'cogwheel end' is responsible for the lay of the rope, which can be either left-handed or right-handed, according to the lay of the strands, which must be opposite to the lay of the final rope – thus, left-handed rope must be made with right-handed strands, and vice versa.

This is good news for the modeller, who can normally only get hold of right-handed strands, which are easily converted into left-handed cable, which is exactly what is happening in the photographs. The "top", (a technical term for the conical, grooved stop) controls how tightly the strands are laid together. A 'hard' rope will result from pressing the 'top' against the twist of the rope as it is being made, but the skill is really in getting an even pressure which results in uniform cordage. As the rope is being laid, the distance between the centres of the lathe bed will narrow automatically as the twisting process pulls the moving carriage along the bars.

Don't be either fooled or put off by all these words. Miniature ropemaking is great fun and not at all difficult to do once the machine is set up. I have a strong suspicion that my machine is a bit of a sledgehammer to crack a nut; it certainly incorporates nearly every tool in the cupboard; but at the lowest level it must offer some food for thought

centre cog, and anti-clockwise in the case of the three planet cogs. As we shall see in a minute the three outer cogwheels act as the spinners in the ropemaking process; the centre hook is later used for 'serving' the ropes when they have been laid.

On the left-hand end of the ropewalk, there is a geared D.C. motor powered by a battery charger. In its lowest gear, this motor revolves at 60rpm. It also has the added refinement of forward and reverse and the ability therefore to twist strands into left- or right-hand laid rope. This motor is placed in a wooden channel on top of the original drill stand, with a tension spring fixed to the rear end of the motor mount. This gives fine adjustment to

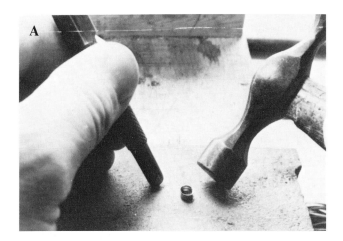

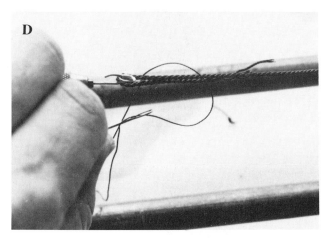

Fig 190. Thimble insertion a) Making the 'thimble' out of brass tube. b) Rope 'seated' in thimble. c) Pinching into oval shape. d) Securing the thimble.

for anyone considering building his own. Ropemaking is also a dying craft which ought to be kept alive now that the old 'line-walks' and rope-houses have largely been demolished.

The exact procedure is to thread up the strands from the three planet wheel hooks to the single driver at the opposite end. A five-second burst on the cogwheel end will spin up the strands in readiness for the twist from the other end. Engage the D.C. driver motor, (I am making a left-hand laid hawser in the picture) having first placed the 'top' between the strands. As the driver motor starts to rotate, the 'top' will immediately start to travel, of its own accord, along the three strands, being squeezed by the action of the rope strands twisting together. The 'top' does not revolve as you might imagine, and finger pressure against it as described earlier will ensure the production of either a hard or, with less pressure, a soft finish to the rope. Approximately every 6″ of rope spun requires a further five-second burst to the cogwheel end, operated in my case by the footswitch, leaving the hands free to deal with the work.

The machine has one more good trick to offer – it will also act as a mechanism which can 'serve' ropes – that is to say, you can wrap thread around a rope which has been previously made, or, as I have done with the shrouds and stays, serve thread onto linen strands straight off the reel. The technique is slightly different in that you use only the centre drivers, working in the same direction, feeding the serving thread off the bobbin and allowing it to wrap itself around the central core. It is a neat way of whipping the turn taken around the deadeyes for shroud lines, and as can be seen from the photographs an effective way of doing an otherwise very tedious job.

Once again, from the pictures, you can see that I have finished the hawser by serving it on the ropewalk. It ought really to have been spliced first, I know, but not only do I suffer from endemic idleness, I have never really mastered the art of splicing. Louis McNeice, the Irish poet, has it in a nutshell when he says, "If we could get the hang of it – entirely – it would take too long." He's right! (from the poem, "*Entirely*".)

The final insertion of a 'thimble' into the eye of the hawser rope is quickly and simply made by slicing off ¼″ of brass or copper tubing and using a blunt punch from either side to make a circular rim around which the rope should fit snugly. A gentle squeeze with pliers turns the thimble shape from circular to oval, and for some reason makes it look more authentic.

Rigging

Before a single rope or stay can be set up on the ship, all the items necessary to anchor the standing and running rigging have to be made and positioned.

Starting at the stem, just above the cutwater, the cloven bolt strap for the bobstay and martingale has to be

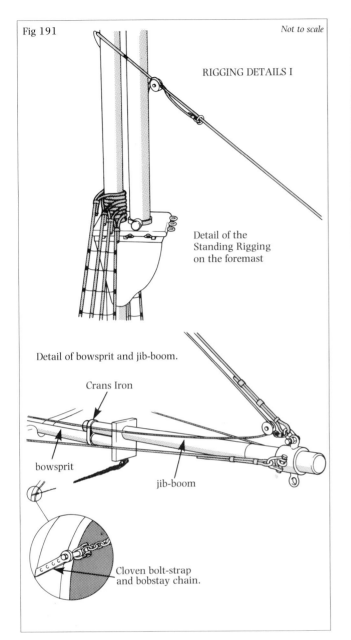

Fig 191   *Not to scale*

RIGGING DETAILS I

Detail of the
Standing Rigging
on the foremast

Detail of bowsprit and jib-boom.

Crans Iron

bowsprit

jib-boom

Cloven bolt-strap
and bobstay chain.

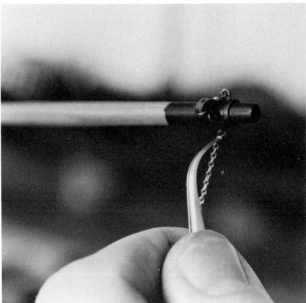

Fig 192. Feeding the martingale (chain) stay through the 'iron' on the tip of the jib-boom, with the 'swan-neck No. 7's'. Fig 193. Bobstay, chain and bolt strap.

fitted just above the bifurcated hawse. The two stays are both made of chain, and provide the total resistance against the back pressure of the foremast shrouds, and act as giant guys against the relentless pull of the shrouds and backstays throughout the whole ship's rigging. So this is where the rigging all begins.

It is perhaps a little surprising that a dolphin striker was not included in the extended rig of the 1846 refit programme, but none of the official sources details one, so that I will have to content myself with its omission.

The pair of knightheads, standing together like guardsmen on parade on the fo'c's'le are not strictly part of the rigging, but they do have the bowsprit slotted into them, and they will eventually have the head-stay downhauls attached to them.

Preparations for setting up the rigging also include the fitting of cleats for the forestays on the masts and bowsprit, siting ringbolts on the deck, the making of ten pin rails containing, in all, 74 belaying pins which will together

secure the falls of the running rigging. The base of each mast has a spider-band and windlass into which some running rigging is secured. 200 jackstays have to be measured and fitted into the yards, along with stirrups, crans irons, quarter iron bands, mast caps, trusses, swivel bolts, yard arm irons and parrels, the last mentioned being the proper name for the iron collars which hold the masts to the yards.

The life-boats and anchors are both suspended over the side of the ship by rigging, in the first instance by davits, and in the second, by catheads. Both these fitments need their own releasing gear which includes cleats, blocks and purchase tackle as well as straps and bolts to attach the non-moving parts firmly to the mothership.

The curved davit arms are perhaps worth a mention in that they are made from guitar strings, (bottom 'E' .042, for the musically or technically minded), swivelling inside brass tubing. The wrapping on the extremity of the string is unwound in order to use the central core of steel as a

145

Fig 194

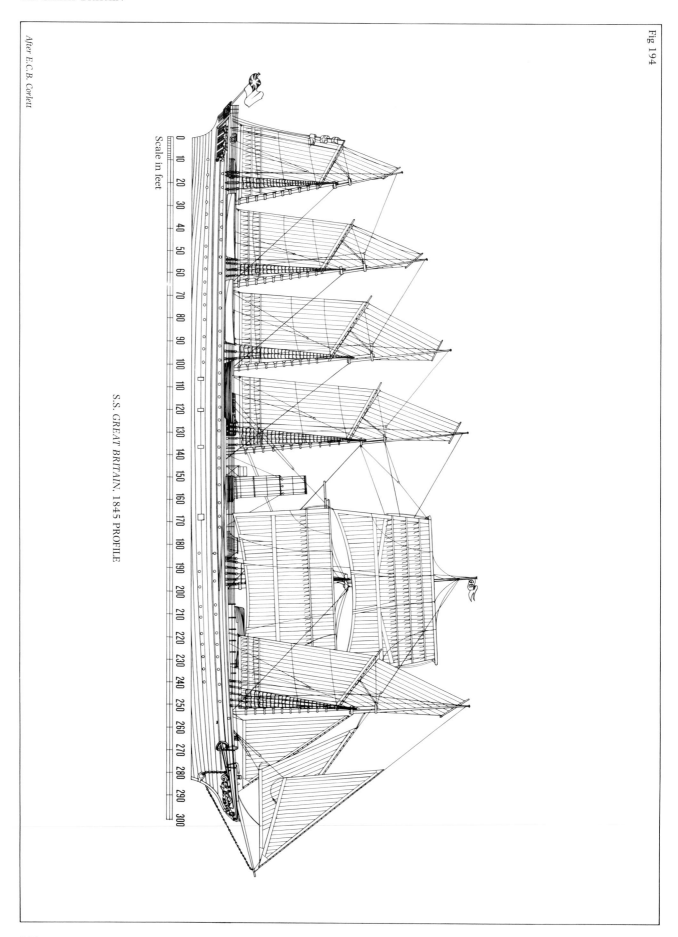

After E.C.B. Corlett

Scale in feet

S.S. GREAT BRITAIN, 1845 PROFILE

0 10 20 30 40 50 60 70 80 90 100 110 120 130 140 150 160 170 180 190 200 210 220 230 240 250 260 270 280 290 300

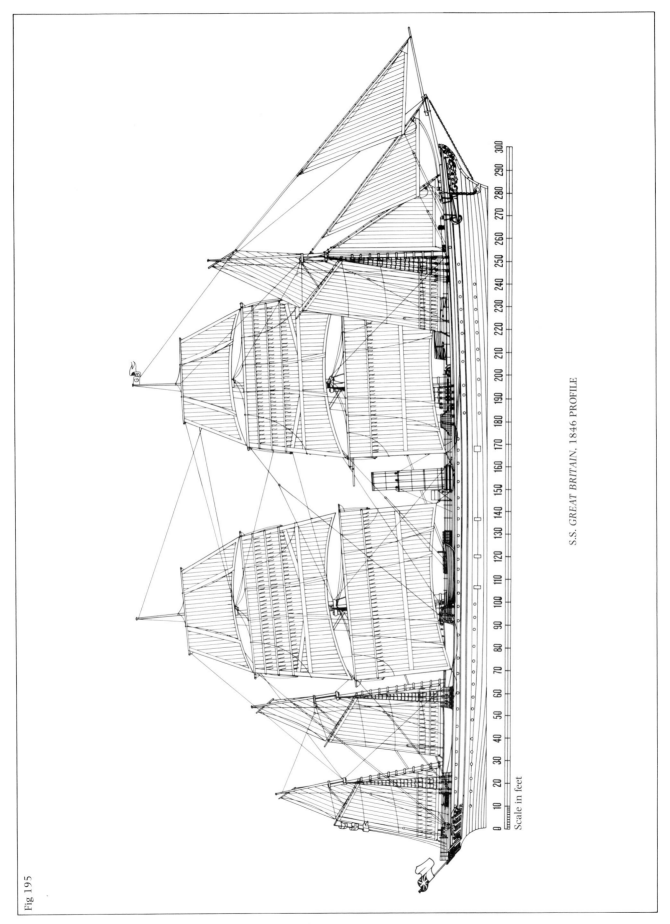

Fig 195

S.S. *GREAT BRITAIN*, 1846 PROFILE

Scale in feet

0 10 20 30 40 50 60 70 80 90 100 110 120 130 140 150 160 170 180 190 200 210 220 230 240 250 260 270 280 290 300

Fig 196. Standing rigging a) Head of Thursday's main mast. b) First glimpse of sail. Flying and outer jib set up. c) Close-up of foremast and outer jibsail.

'chain plate'. These are all drilled and fixed with brass pins through the flange which encircles the vessel.

Standing Rigging

All the lower standing rigging for the ship has been previously measured and served on the ropewalk and is now ready for setting up. I am not over-keen on the eye-splice at the masthead partly out of pure idleness, because it cannot be done on the machine, and partly because it adds to the difficulties of the setting and adjustment of the lines at any later date when this may become necessary. My malpractice is to loop the shroud around the masthead, and with fine copper wire (which disappears into the serving thread), twist and snip the wire, and matt black as though tarred. This means that at any given time I can adjust an individual shroud, without disturbing the others. They are laid up alternately, starting with the foremost, until they look like the children's game of "hand over hand", piled high on top of one another.

The lanyards, which are the lengths of rope used to adjust the deadeyes are set up using spacers, pieces of piano wire bent into a squared 'U' shape, which are inserted into the deadeyes in order to keep them all equidistant from each other. The work at the masthead can proceed with the spacers in situ, the last job being to thread the lanyards through the deadeyes and bring up the tension.

ring-hook to which the blocks can be attached. As these steel strings are naturally springy, accidental knocks leave them unaffected, and even the brass ferrules which anchor these strings to the bridge of the guitar in their bona fide role, can be used for sheaves on the yard arm lifts, so that absolutely nothing is wasted, not even the squeak!

On the model, a total of 58 deadeyes, including those for the backstays, have to be fixed to the gunwale, port and starboard. These anchoring deadeyes have been previously soldered to a small length of brass strip, with a hoop of copper wire which, with a couple of twists and a touch of soft solder, makes the mechanical fixing to the miniature

Fig 197. Ratlines a) "The vexed question of the ratlines"; sewing through 5amp fuse wire. b) Twisting the wire in. c) Foremast completed. Note the wrongly positioned deadeyes with the holes not in mirror image. d) Thursday Mast. Finishing off the lanyards with half hitches.

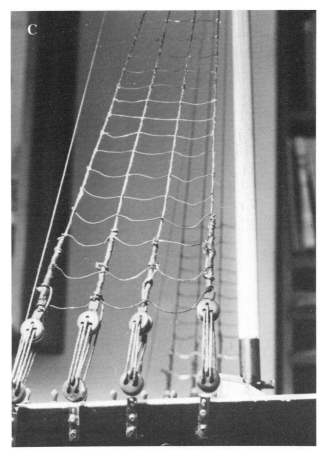

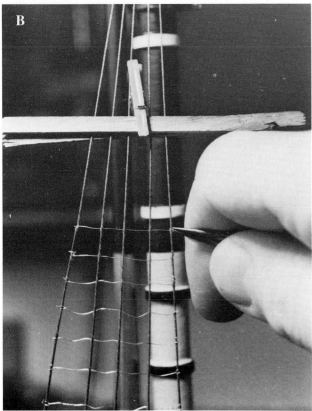

In passing, don't do as I have done, which is to fix the deadeyes with the holes both pointing in the same direction. The triangles of holes ought to be the mirror image of one another, and not as I have done. When I am an old man there is a nice little job waiting to be re-done, and plenty of opportunity to ruminate of the foolishness of elementary mistakes.

Ratlines

Now to the vexed question of the ratlines. To be forthright, you will seldom see miniature ratlines which even remotely resemble their big brothers. The problem is threefold: firstly, the clove-hitch knots are invariably over-

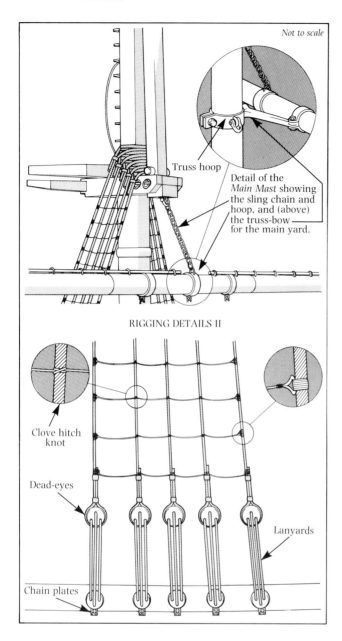

Not to scale

Truss hoop

Detail of the
Main Mast showing
the sling chain and
hoop, and (above)
the truss-bow
for the main yard.

RIGGING DETAILS II

Clove hitch
knot

Dead-eyes

Lanyards

Chain plates

Fig 199. Setting up the standing rigging on the restored ship at Bristol, July 1980.

scale, (how can they be anything else?); secondly, the 'parallels' of the shrouds become distorted with the knots which tend to pull the outer shrouds inwards; finally, and perhaps worst of all, the scallop shape, where the rungs of the ratline should sag downwards with the weight of the rope, actually reverses and pops upwards.

The cure, as with the horses and stirrups on the yards, is to incorporate wire into the rigging; in the first instance I have used brass wire, but for the ratlines, fine soft copper wire is just right. I have spoken previously about the spider's web, here five amp fuse wire will help achieve the delicate weftage required. I thread it through with a needle, using a makeshift cramp, with the help of miniature plastic clothes pegs, which keeps the lines from moving about too much. Once threaded through, snip one end and knot it, and holding the other end, gently make the scallops by pulling the wire down, then secure it at the other end. The scallop shape, whilst looking very effective, also gives you lateral adjustment – in other words, you

can push and pull until the shroud lines are in perfect alignment. A good thick mix of matt-black paint will automatically provide you with the illusion of a knot where the lines join, especially if you leave a hint of the natural colour of the shroud line by only painting across the ratline. The texture of the waxed linen against matt black also adds to the fiction of it all, and is developing in me a very unhealthy interest in how spiders, with 8 legs, a segmented abdomen and four pairs of compound eyes, can actually make a web without a pair of pliers!

The Running Rigging

The cutaway model of the 1845 ship, which was recently commissioned by The National Maritime Museum at Greenwich from Bassett-Lowke, has been rigged according to diagrams drawn up by Michael Leek of the Bournemouth and Poole School of Technical Illustration. In a paper on the subject, published in the Mariner's Mirror,

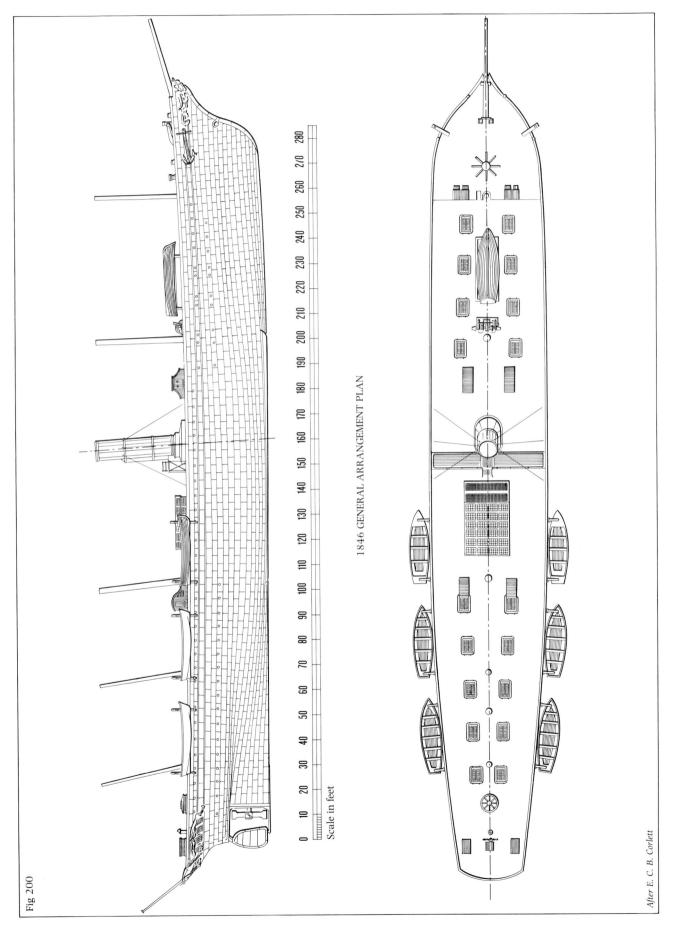

Fig 200

1846 GENERAL ARRANGEMENT PLAN

Scale in feet

0 10 20 30 40 50 60 70 80 90 100 110 120 130 140 150 160 170 180 190 200 210 220 230 240 250 260 270 280

After E. C. B. Corlett

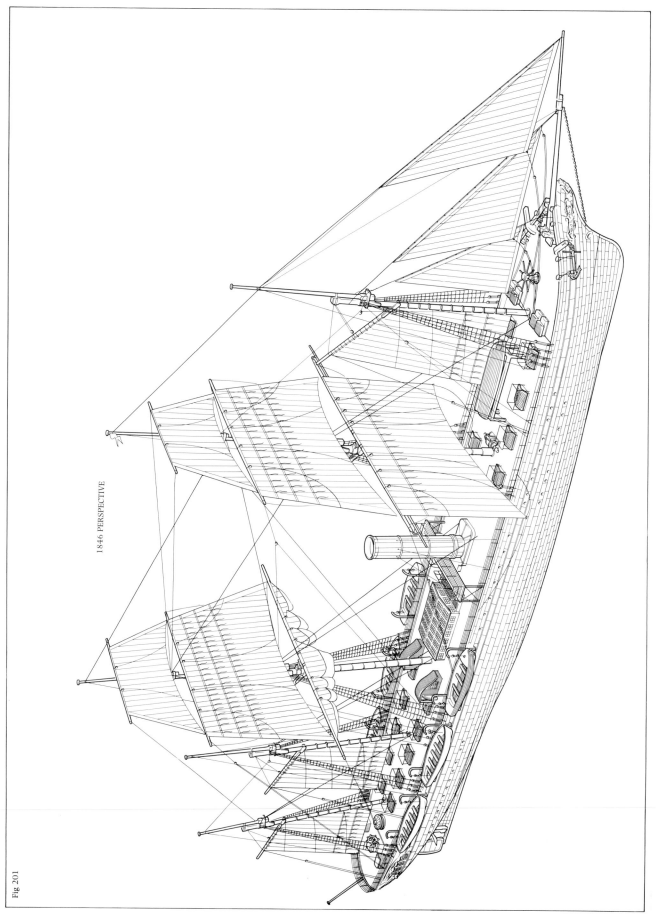

1846 PERSPECTIVE

Fig 201

152

Fig 202

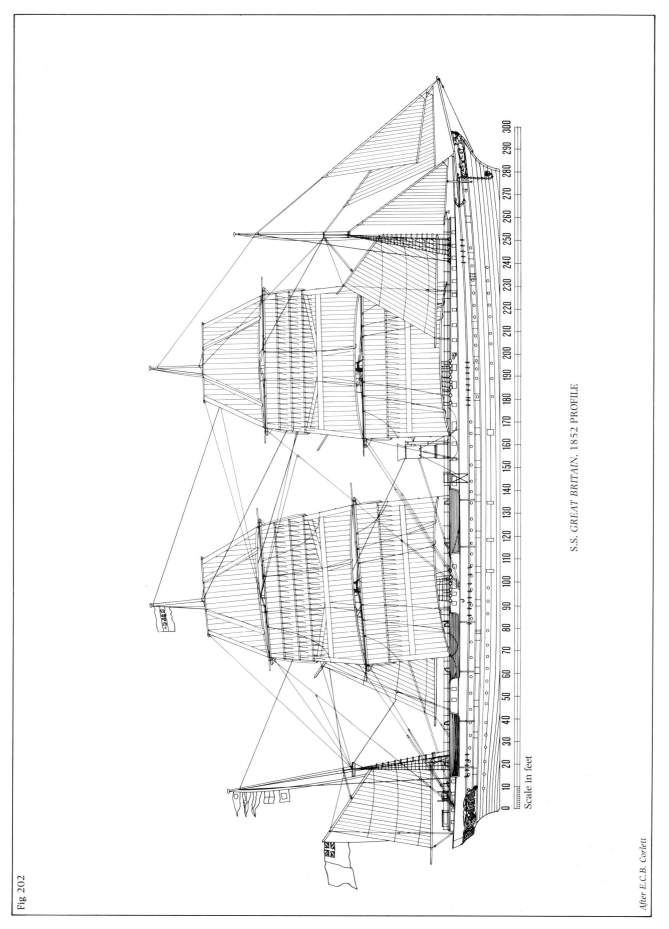

S.S. GREAT BRITAIN, 1852 PROFILE

Scale in feet

0 10 20 30 40 50 60 70 80 90 100 110 120 130 140 150 160 170 180 190 200 210 220 230 240 250 260 270 280 290 300

After E.C.B. Corlett

Fig 203. (Above) Work progressing on setting up the rigging lines.
Fig 204. (Right) Close up of the rigging at the main masthead.

"The Appearance and Lead of the Rig of the S.S. *Great Britain* in 1845", he has gone to considerable lengths of research to establish the workings of the running rigging, which can be used in conjunction with the illustrated drawings. With his permission, I have used this as a basis for a detailed explanation of how the running rigging was set up on the original ship, which may be of more general interest to those looking at the restored ship. The 1846 version is in no way dramatically different apart from the details which I have already mentioned, i.e. the use of hemp rather than wire, the removal of Wednesday mast, and the stepping of the masts through the deck rather than the hinged fittings, as ordered by Brunel.

For purposes of clarity, Michael Leek has used the 19th century terminology for the masts, that is to say, Fore, Main, Mizzen, Jigger, Driver and Spanker, instead of the well established nick-names of the working week which I have used up to the present moment.

"As far as the foremast is concerned, both the jib-stay and topmast-stay are taken out to the bowsprit head where they pass through bulls-eyes which lead the stays aft to be set up with lanyards just below the catheads, on the starboard and port side respectively. As on the Science Museum model, all the lowermast stays consist of single wire, seized in the middle to form an eye which is passed over the lowermast to sit on top of the lower rigging, which in turn sits on the bolsters and trestle trees. The ends of the lowermast stays are taken down and forward to the heel of the lowermast in front, to be set up with

deadeyes and lanyards, either side of the mast, thus in effect making a double but unseized stay. That of the foremast is taken down and set up at a point just forward and on either side of the heel of the bowsprit.

Contemporary lithographs show the ship as being rigged with a total of thirteen sails, viz.; three headsails, the flying-jib or outer-jib, jib and forestaysail; followed by the foremast which set a fore-gaffsail and a fore-gaff-topsail. Next the mainmast which was the only square-rigged mast in the ship. This mast set only a mainsail or maincourse and a main-single-topsail above. The remaining four masts were as for the fore-mast.

Working accurately from the known dimensions of the spars, it has been possible to determine the sizes and areas of the sails. The area as calculated for the illustration on which this description is based totals just under 18,100sq ft. This is in excess of that in the article published in the Mechanics Magazine for September, 1842, which quotes a figure of 1,700sq yd (15,300sq ft.)

The lead of the running rigging on all three headsails and the square sails on the mainmast do not detract from conventional practice and therefore require no further description. Both sails on the mainmast were fitted with reef points, the course with one and topsail with three. Both sails clewed up to the quarters and the yards are shown fitted with a chain sling on the main and a chain tye halliard on the topsail yard, as chain was in fairly common use in rigs from about 1840 onwards.

The Science Museum retains a small poster reprinted

from the original published by The Liverpool Standard, 1 July, 1845, which includes two engravings of the ship at sea under full sail, and these clearly show the three headsails. Furthermore, a beautiful coloured lithograph of the ship is, at the time of writing, on display in the East Wing of the National Maritime Museum, Greenwich, which also shows the three headsails. As both sources are contemporary and as the arrangement of the headstays suggests, I doubt whether these three drawings include much in the way of artistic licence. As a matter of interest, One of the views on the aforementioned poster shows the mainmast fitted with a small topgallant sail, and this must be artistic licence, for the Fox-Talbot photograph of the ship, taken at Bristol soon after the launch, shows no provision for such a sail. Besides, the length of the main-topmast, which is 55ft, is insufficient for a single-topsail and a topgallant sail, even if the latter were to be fitted only as a flying kite for use in light airs.

Studding sail booms and swinging booms were also fitted, both showing clearly in the Fox-Talbot photograph. However, as Dr Corlett says in his book, it is unlikely that these would have been set and evidence has yet to come to light that they were. Therefore the gear necessary for them has been omitted from this description. (The gear for stunsails was never a permanent fixture on any ship and their omission would not therefore detract from the feasibility of this study.)

Mention has been made of belaying pin rails, and before

Fig 205. (Left) Deck fittings and mainmast. Note the stunsail booms, trysail mast and belaying pin rails. Fig 206. (Below) Mizzen course brailed up.

continuing it is as well to draw attention to the peculiarity which exists in all the available material; models, paintings and drawings, contemporary and current. This is the total lack of any pins on which to secure the running rigging. The contemporary model in the Science Museum does show a form of spider-band around each mast, but the number of pins and cleats available would be insufficient for the extra gear which would result from the sails being set. As far as the paintings are concerned, their omission can be understood, to a certain extent, for the originals were drawn to a size which allowed for certain smaller details to be ignored. However, there must be a means of securing the fall part of any rope.

Even for the lead of a fore-and-aft rig like the *Great Britain* which is, by comparison with a full-rigged ship, comparatively simple, provision must be made for the running rigging necessary to handle the sails. This alone has become a definite factor in deciding that belaying pin rails should be included in the illustration. This is in addition to the spider-bands which are fitted to each mast. The belaying pin diagram will be sufficient to show the arrangement and location of the rails and the number of pins to each.

In describing the fore-and-aft rigged sails I will take the jiggermast as being typical. As previously stated there were two sails fitted; a loose footed gaffsail and a gaff-topsail rigged and cut as a lugsail. The gaffsail had three brails per side and two rows of reef points, thus indicating that the gaffs were running and not standing gaffs. As such, both peak and throat halliards would be fitted. On all masts the peak halliards are taken down to a pin on the port side of the spider-band, whilst the throat halliards are belayed to a pin on the starboard pin rail. Each brail goes through a single block seized to the bolt rope at the luff of the gaffsail and down to one of the barrels of what appears to be, on the Science Museum model, a winch which forms the forward part of the spider-band. When working out the lead of the fore-and-aft gear it seemed perfectly natural to take the brails to these winches, so making them brailing winches (this is also in keeping with Brunel's ideas of economy in the rig). Thus to each respective barrel goes the three respective brails for that side of the mast. The final part of the running rigging for the gaffsail is the sheet. The sheet is double, port and starboard, and consists of two double blocks shackled to the clew cringle of the sail. The purchases for these are reeved through the two lower blocks which are secured to ring-bolts in the deck and positioned either side but just forward of the mast behind, in this case the drivermast. The fall of the sheet is taken up from the lower blocks to the first two pins, port and starboard, on the spider-band of the drivermast. The luff of the gaffsail is bent to the lowermast with wooden hoops and the head of the sail to the gaff with earings.

In the case of the foremast the arrangement of the fore-gaffsail sheet would be slightly different due to the fact that the iron frame for the upturned lifeboat is in the way. In order that a point must exist for the fall to be secured my contention is that on the foremast the sheet would be a single only, the fall being taken up from the lower block to a pin on the mainmast spider-band. When going about it would be a simple matter of brailing in the gaffsail, after letting go the lower block from its ring-bolt in the deck,

and then, when the sail is clear of the lifeboat frame, letting it out again on the opposite side; the lower block being re-shackled to a similar ring-bolt opposite the first.

Vangs are also fitted to the gaffs; their set up being as is usually found, and therefore needing no further description.

Above the gaffsail we have the jigger-gaff-topsail. All topsails have been drawn as standing lugs, being set to port. (It could well be that these were set to starboard, if so the procedure for setting up the appropriate rigging as shown on the belaying pin diagram would just be reversed.) This arrangement of a standing lug was arrived at because it was thought that a dipping lug would involve

NUMERICAL INDEX TO THE BELAYING PIN DIAGRAM OF THE S.S. GREAT BRITAIN, AS IN JANUARY 1845.

		Position		
No.	Type	Side	Rail	Gear for which used
A	Knighthead			Downhauls for all headstays
1	Bitts	P. & S.	F-Bulwk.	
2	Bitts	P. & S.	F-Bulwk.	
3	Bitts	P. & S.	F-Bulwk.	Flying-jib-sheets
4	W. Bar.	FM	SB	Fore-gaffsail-brails
5	BP	FM	SB	Flying and fore-jib halliards
6	BP	FM	SB	Fore-staysail-halliards
7	BP	FM	SB	Fore-peak-halliard
8	BP	FM	SB	Fore-topsail-halliard
9	BP	FM	SB	Fore-topsail-sheet
10	BP	FM	SB	Fore-topsail-clewline
11	BP	P. & S.	FR	Jib-sheet
12	BP	P. & S.	FR	Fore-staysail-sheet
13	BP	P.	FR	Fore-topsail-tack
14	BP	S.	FR	Fore-throat-halliard
15	BP	P.	FR	Spare. (Signal halliard)
16	BP	S.	FR	Main-topmast-stay
17	BP	P. & S.	FR	Fore-topmast-lifts
18	BP	P. & S.	FR	Main-tack
19	BP	P. & S.	FR	Main-lazy-tack
20	BP	MM	SB	Fore-gaffsail-sheet
21	BP	MM	SB	Main-topsail-sheets
22	BP	MM	SB	Main-lifts
23	BP	MM	SB	Mizzen-topmast-stay
24	BP	MM	SB	Spare
25	BP	P. & S.	MR	Fore-vangs
26	BP	P. & S.	MR	Mainsail-buntlines and leech-lines
27	BP	P. & S.	MR	Main-clewgarnet and reef-tackle
28	BP	P. & S.	MR	Main-topsail-buntlines and clewlines
29	BP	P. & S.	MR	Main-topsail-reef-tackle
30	BP	S.	MR	Main-topsail-halliard
31	BP	P.	MR	Spare. (Signal halliard)
32	BP	P. & S.	MR	Main-topmast-lift
33	BP	P. & S.	MR	Main-sheet
34	W. Bar.	MZM	SB	Mizzen-gaffsail-brails
35	BP	MZM	SB	Spares
36	BP	MZM	SB	Mizzen-topsail-halliard
37	BP	MZM	SB	Mizzen-peak-halliard
38	BP	MZM	SB	Mizzen-topsail-clewline

Position

No.	Type	Side	Rail	Gear for which used
39	BP	MZM	SB	Mizzen-topsail-sheet
40	BP	P. & S.	MZR	Main-topsail-yard-brace
41	BP	P.	MZR	Mizzen-topsail-tack
42	BP	S.	MZR	Mizzen-throat-halliard
43	BP	P.	MZR	Spare. (Signal halliard)
44	BP	S.	MZR	Jigger-topmast-stay
45	BP	P. & S.	MZR	Mizzen-topmast-lifts
46	BP	P. & S.	MZR	Main-yard-brace
47	W. Bar.	JM	SB	Jigger-gaffsail-brails
48	BP	JM	SB	Mizzen-gaffsail-sheets
49	BP	JM	SB	Jigger-peak-halliard
50	BP	JM	SB	Jigger-topsail-halliard
51	BP	JM	SB	Jigger-topsail-sheet
52	BP	JM	SB	Jigger-topsail-clewline
53	BP	P. & S.	JR	Mizzen-vangs
54	BP	S.	JR	Jigger-throat-halliard
55	BP	P.	JR	Jigger-topsail-tack
56	BP	S.	JR	Driver-topmast-stay
57	BP	P.	JR	Spare. (Signal halliards)
58	BP	P. & S.	JR	Jigger-topmasts-lifts
59	W. Bar.	DM	SB	Driver-gaffsail-brails
60	BP	DM	SB	Jigger-gaffsail-sheets
61	BP	DM	SB	Driver-peak-halliard
62	BP	DM	SB	Driver-topsail-halliard
63	BP	DM	SB	Driver-topsail-sheet
64	BP	DM	SB	Driver-topsail-clewline
65	BP	P. & S.	DR	Jigger-vangs
66	BP	S.	DR	Driver-throat-halliard
67	BP	P.	DR	Driver-topsail-tack
68	BP	S.	DR	Spanker-topmast-stay
69	BP	P.	DR	Spare. (Signal halliards)
70	BP	P. & S.	DR	Driver-topmast-lifts
71	W. Bar.	SM	SB	Spanker-gaffsail-brails
72	BP	SM	SB	Driver-gaffsails-sheets
73	BP	SM	SB	Spanker-peak-halliards
74	BP	SM	SB	Spanker-topsail-halliard
75	BP	SM	SB	Spanker-topsail-sheet
76	BP	SM	SB	Spanker-topsail-clewline
77	BP	P. & S.	SR	Driver-vangs
78	BP	S.	SR	Spanker-throat-halliard
79	BP	P.	SR	Spanker-topsail-tack
80	BP	P. & S.	SR	Spares. (One for signal halliard
81	BP	P. & S.	SR	Spanker-topmast-lifts
82	BP	P. & S.	SR	Spanker-vangs
83	BP	midships, behind wheel-box		Spanker-gaffsail sheet

Key (listed as they occur in the index).

P.	Port.	S.	Starboard.
F-Bulwk.	Foscle Bulwark.	W. Bar.	Winch barrels.
FM	Fore-mast.	SB	Spider-band.
BP	Belaying pin.	FR	Fore-rail.
MM	Main-mast.	MR	Main-rail.
MZM	Mizzen-mast.	MZR	Mizzen-rail.
JM	Jigger-mast.	JR	Jigger-rail.
DM	Driver-mast.	DR	Driver-rail.
SM	Spanker-mast.	SR	Spanker-rail.

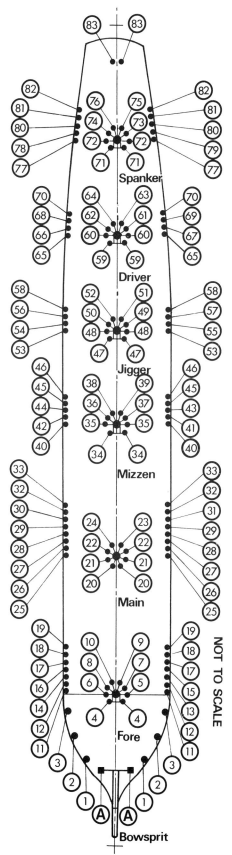

Fig 207. Belaying pin line diagram of running rigging. Copyright 1976, The Society for Nautical Research, and Michael E. Leek. Not to scale. Belaying pins shown inboard of the outline of the ship and pins set inboard of their respective shrouds.

Fig 209

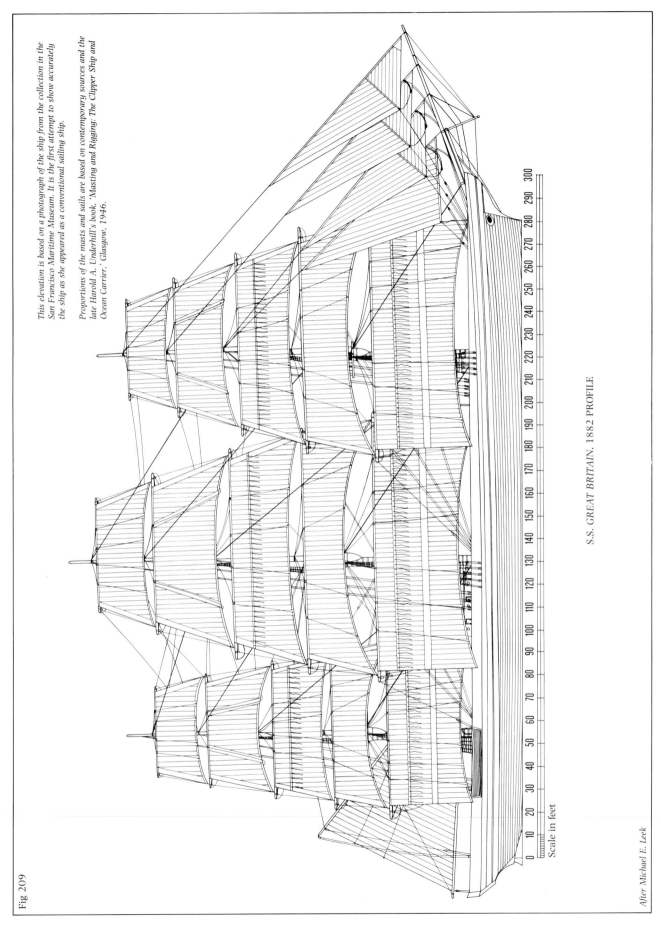

This elevation is based on a photograph of the ship from the collection in the San Francisco Maritime Museum. It is the first attempt to show accurately the ship as she appeared as a conventional sailing ship.

Proportions of the masts and sails are based on contemporary sources and the late Harold A. Underhill's book, 'Masting and Rigging: The Clipper Ship and Ocean Carrier,' Glasgow, 1946.

S.S. *GREAT BRITAIN*, 1882 PROFILE

Scale in feet

0 10 20 30 40 50 60 70 80 90 100 110 120 130 140 150 160 170 180 190 200 210 220 230 240 250 260 270 280 290 300

After Michael E. Leek

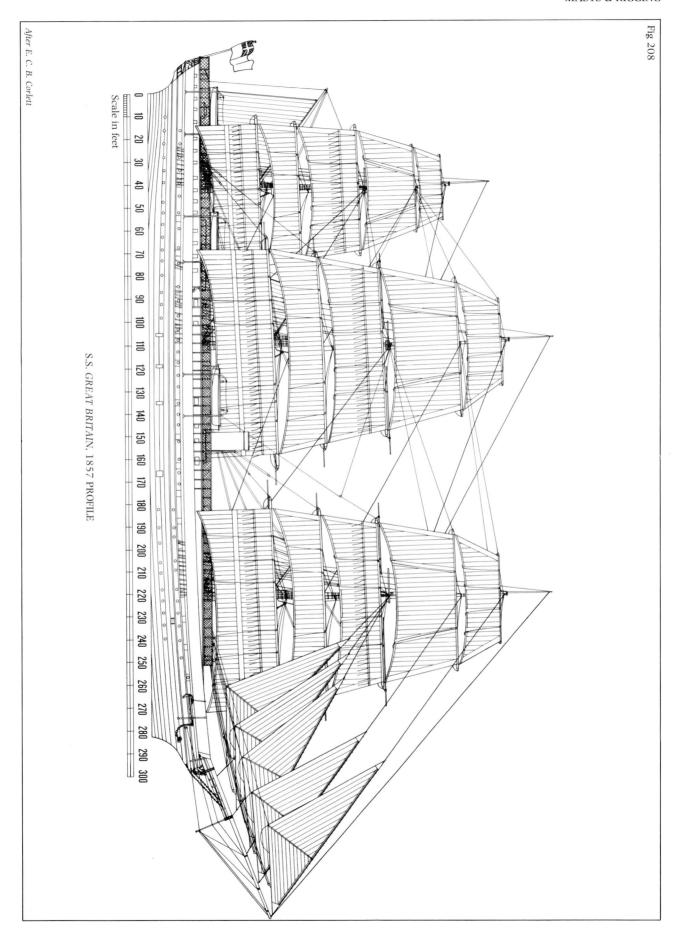

After E. C. B. Corlett

Scale in feet

0 10 20 30 40 50 60 70 80 90 100 110 120 130 140 150 160 170 180 190 200 210 220 230 240 250 260 270 280 290 300

S.S. GREAT BRITAIN. 1857 PROFILE

too much work due to the presence of the gaffsails. A dipping lug would necessitate the tack of the topsail being passed up and over the gaff and so down to the other side every time the vessel went about. This is illogical in terms of time saving.

The running rigging on the jigger-topsail consists of the tack, sheet, clewline and halliard. The first being taken to a pin on the port-jigger pin rail; the others being belayed around the spider-band as indicated in the diagram. The halliard is not directly seized to the yard but to an iron hoop which can freely run up the topmast. An iron hook secures the yard to the hoop, the hook itself being eyespliced to the yard. Earings are used to attach the topsail to the yard. This then completes the description of the rig of the S.S. *Great Britain* as she was when she sailed from Bristol to London in January 1845, prior to her maiden North Atlantic voyage."

(Reprinted by permission of the Editor, Mariner's Mirror, the Quarterly Journal of the Society for Nautical Research, and based upon an article by Michael E. Leek: "The Appearance and Lead of the Rig of the S.S. *Great Britain* in 1845", in the November 1976 issue.)

On the model, my original idea with the rigging lines was to set up only the bare essentials in order to have easy access to the steam plant and its attendant requirements. In practice, it turns out to be almost impossible to leave out any of the lines, as they all play their individual part in the complicated process of making this a truly working model which will sail as well as steam.

In my favour as far as access is concerned, is the size of the model, one might even say the relative spaciousness which the midship section affords. I have been at pains to preserve this by deliberately omitting the lower braces to the main yard, which would be a significant interference across the engine room. Nor can there be a forestay fitted to Thursday mast, or vangs fitted to Thursday and Friday gaff booms as these all pass directly over hatch covers. Otherwise, items are as per the sail plan, with no real restrictions on operation. The braces to the square sails are fitted on a ring system so that the ship can 'go about' without too much fuss. At a later date, I would like to experiment with a servo fixed to the aft capstan which could make this process automatic, but I cannot see that happening just yet even though it is perfectly feasible.

Apart from the mental energy required to rig the ship, the work is pleasant and rewarding. I won't pretend that it doesn't become tedious, but at least it does all show; in fact it is so attracting to the eye, that it rather unfairly grips the attention to the exclusion of everything else.

Finally, in the hints and tips department, I did promise to mention garden PVC tying wire in connection with rigging. For the sliding mast hoops which retain the gaff sails, wrap the PVC wire around a tube, slightly larger than the diameter of the mast, and cut it with a hacksaw along the top edge of the wrapping. Immediately miniature curtain rings will begin to fall – more of the wizardry of M. Taylor, who really ought to write his own book instead of leaving it all to me.

FINISHING TOUCHES

Sandcasting

The idea of sandcasting in a soft metal such as pewter or lead does not readily occur to many people who have not seen it done. In my case, the hesitation stemmed from a basic misunderstanding of what the sand used for casting was like, and exactly how this raw material behaves as a mould making agent. Its use was highly recommended by the already mentioned Mike Taylor, who insisted that as a modelling aid, sandcasting is second to none.

Fig 210. (Opposite) B&P photo. Prototype bollards. Fig 211. (Below) Taking impression from master for the model.

In the consideration of sandcasting, it is necessary to rid yourself of all thoughts of the seaside. Sand used for casting has a consistency and feel which approximate more closely to plasticine than any other material. The sand is as fine as powder and will pick out the smallest detail if handled properly. It compresses so well that it will not fall out of the wooden box frames when they go through the handling processes necessary to reproduce from an original.

Its limitations are only discovered by trial and error. I have to admit that so far I have failed to produce the five bar stanchion rails by this process, but that is not to diminish the many other uses to which it can be put.

For purposes of demonstration, I used the figurine of a woman with a water jar. (The alternative was a fearsome looking plastic soldier firing a pistol: he reproduced in superb detail, but hardly fits into the Victorian scene in the same way as the peasant woman.) She was a tricky subject in that the original was made of clay which could easily have fractured with too much compression. The result was a slight loss of definition, but a quite acceptable degree of detail nonetheless. The bollards which followed, (scale 1:100) were much easier, though not such an appealing subject.

One has to have an original of course, but once a casting has been made, two subjects can be used to produce four and so forth, until your reach the state where you are producing your own private army or navy, as the case may be. My idea is to produce many little castings, particularly of people, which can be used to populate the deck, bringing it all to life. With model ships, I believe that you've either got to have a crowd scene, or leave the whole thing alone and have none.

Lead castings enable a fair amount of arm twisting and torso movement to take place, which makes a difference from the characters all adopting the same pose and looking rather uniform and stiff.

I have used the figurine simply as a demonstration. She is nearer 1:24 than 1:48, but was all I had to lay my hands on when the sun was shining, the lead was boiling and the camera ready to roll.

Casting is enormous fun. You can copy badges, emblems, buttons, drawer handles, jewellery. My younger son even suggested a lead conker, it being the season for such things. Anything which can be left in the solid and which does not, by its shape, choke the flow of molten metal can be easily and accurately reproduced by this ancient process. With more heat and a stouter crucible the sand would accept castings in aluminium and brass, but that's a more expensive story.

Sandcasting

Before you begin, you need the following items:–
1) Pouring frames and locking pins. (thin dowel)
2) Base board. (hardboard)
3) Runner and riser pins. (thin dowel)
4) Metal. (either pewter or lead, pewter is a good deal stronger.)
5) Parting powder. (talc)
6) Casting sand.
7) Ladle.
8) Mallet.
9) Block of wood, to the inner dimensions of the pouring frame.
10) Tray or polythene sheet.
11) Straight edge. (ruler or equivalent)
12) Soft paint brush for dusting the talc.
13) Teaspoon for gouging out the runner hole.
14) Wooden matchstick or toothpick for testing molten temperature.
15) Something heatproof on which to place the hot ladle.
16) Stainless steel knife.

Legend for sandcasting photographs (Fig 212)

1) Emptying the casting sand into the lower pouring frame.
2) Using the mallet and block to compress the sand in the lower frame.
3) Figurine pressed halfway into the flattened face of the lower frame and lightly dusted with talc. Use a soft brush for this. Lightly dust the surface of the sand as well.
4) The upper frame is positioned by two locating pins. Sand is then lightly sprinkled over the top of the figurine, and 'tamped' down by hand.
5) Upper frame almost filled with sand by tamping.
6) Using the block to get extra compression.

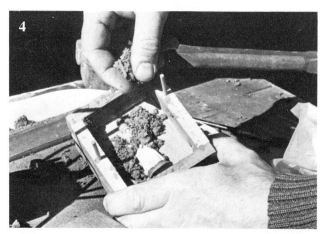

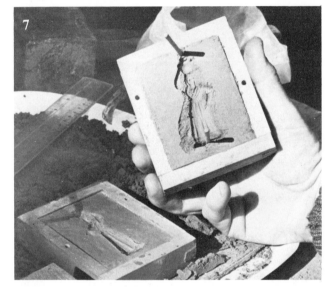

7) Parting the upper frame from the lower one. The original has been removed leaving the cast into which the metal will be poured. Note the runner and riser pins are stuck into the sand at the head and foot of the casting as an 'in & out' for the molten metal.

8) The runner hole is gouged out with the spoon before the wooden runner pin is withdrawn, otherwise grains of sand interfere with the flow of metal, down the runner hole. The whole frame has been tilted to assist the flow of metal. Metal should be heated to approx. 350°C. This temperature can be judged by the charring of the end of the toothpick or matchstick

submerged in the metal for 2–3 seconds. The metal must be hot enough to run freely into the mould, but should not be so hot that a blue/brown film appears on the surface. That indicates overheating and a rough casting may result from it. Skim off any dross floating on the surface of the metal with an old stainless steel table knife.

9) Carefully pour the molten metal down the runner channel of the mould until it appears in the riser channel.

10) Allow two minutes or so for the casting to cool.

11) A bird in the hand . . . ?

Fig 213. *Acid etching a) Initial cleansing of brasswork with iso-propyl alcohol before immersing in the tray. b) Pouring the etching solution into the baking tray. c) The simmering solution of ferric chloride. d) Richard Haines with safety spectacles. Gloves are also a good idea! e) Extracting the first version from the Pyrex heater. f) Checking for the correct temperature of 50°C. g) First version of metal plaque after the etching has taken place but before the letters and screening have been removed and the plaque polished. h) Inspecting the second and final version.*

Acid Etching the Metal Plaque ... Brass Fanfare ...

It is often difficult to determine at what point one has 'arrived' with a model ship, which in a sense, can never be finished. The making of a brass plate must at least indicate a growing confidence that an end is in sight, and that the public will want to know exactly what it is they are looking at and, possibly, have paid to see. Every brass plate is an indication of what you are about to receive; legal advice perhaps, medical help or even a marriage licence. If it gleams with a freshly polished shine, the chances are that the establishment is interested in detail. If the plaque mentions the names of the owners or partners, this silently communicates an air of permanence and solidarity. After 143 years, the S.S.G.B. can claim a standing ovation on both of these counts.

Bas-relief work has been well known to those in the printing trade for a great many years. More recently, with the development of photo-etched electronic circuits, in ever increasing degrees of miniaturisation, this process has also caught the attention of modellers who have to face the demands of great accuracy in the fabrication of small metal parts.

Basically speaking, the process is one of protecting metal from acid attack, by the use of acid-resistant materials. These include specially formulated inks, some paint and varnish, wax and perhaps most usefully, plastic insulation tape. When the metal is immersed in a heat-proof tank or jar, the acid will eat away the unprotected metal parts and bite into any exposed area of metal, with great accuracy.

I had heard some while ago, from two different

modellers, that it was possible to produce bas-relief name-plates by the use of dry letter transfers, which are now readily available in the High Street. Exercising unusual caution, I decided to ring up the research and development departments of two different companies, to try to establish whether or not the rumours were correct. Unbelievably, neither had heard of such a use for their products – both were anxious to know the outcome.

With no more than a rumour and a 'suck it and see' policy, I decided to go ahead and do the artwork on a piece of brass which I cut and hand polished. Then came the problems. The lettering of Letraset, which is perhaps the most well known and easily obtainable dry transfer, is set on stretchy polypropylene sheet. This unfortunately has the effect of allowing the letters to break up when transferred to metal, and their adhesion is thus impaired. 'Pressletta' produce an apparently similar method of lettering, but set on a non-stretch polyester base.

With a gentle heating of the brass plate, directly on the electric cooker ring, these letters detach themselves from the sheet to the metal, using a ballpoint pen to shade them off in the usual manner. 'Preslettas' are set in a waxy substance which enjoys the heat treatment and the fact that the wax melts away with the heat, means that the individual letters part from the base quite easily. It is slow going, because the metal has to keep being reheated, but the result is quite reasonable. The Swarfega comes into the picture as a substance that will remove the unwanted wax which accompanies the letter in a thin film. This must be removed, otherwise it would act as a screen against the acid. This requires great care and results in having to re-do a number of the letters which 'chip'. A few hair-line cracks need to be touched with paint. These cracks appear on the larger rather than the smaller letters. Finally the edge is screened with plastic insulation tape to give a polished edge to the frame.

An approach was made to a local firm, P.T.Coatings Ltd., who are specialist metal finishers. The Managing Director, Mr Richard Haines, experimented with three acidic formulae, the most successful being ferric chloride solution. This acid may be ordered from any chemist shop, and is relatively cheap. Acid etching is accelerated by the application of gentle heat, requiring the use of a pyrex glass jar or heat-proof dish. If you are using a Swiss roll tin, be prepared to chuck it away after the experiment. The solution is not rated as being particularly dangerous, and the process could be done at home, although I say that with some hesitation, more at the level of marital harmony rather than out of considerations of safety.

A one-hour soak in the acid produces an etched depth of approximately 1mm in this solution, (the reaction is enhanced by inverting the plate in the acid). The fact that the acid reaction is not too fierce means that it does not attack paint, or indeed, break down the resin of which these letters are made. The result ... well, see for yourself ...

Cautionary Tales

If you are contemplating a domestic experiment, do have certain things close to hand:
a) water supply and drain
b) washing dish for neutralising the action
c) plenty of rags for wiping spillage
d) pair of long-nose pliers or tongs
e) a controlled heat source, e.g. cooker ring at low setting
f) reasonable ventilation

Heads and Tails

One of the secret personal fears harboured by the gentry who braved the high seas in the pioneering days must have centred on the use of the lavatory. The hideous necessity of the water closet at sea taxed the Victorian reserve about dress and undress to a point verging on hysteria. Only the certain misery of necessity enabled the trapped and captive passenger to use a mechanism which on land would have been rejected on both cultural and practical grounds.

I am uncertain as to whether a Victorian lady was expected to manage such things on her own, or whether a companion was required to assist with the multiplicity of petticoats and so forth. The logistics within a confined space must have been very hampering. (Is it possible that the 'two by two' departure for the cloakroom still practised by today's ladies has its roots in this kind of very necessary mutual assistance?

Fig 214. (Opposite) B&P photo. Two tiny companionways which lead to the heads. Fig 215. (Above) B&P photo. Original all-lead W.C. pan; would have been encased in wood (found on board). Fig 216. (Right) B&P photo. "Hideous necessity", but attractive bowl by A & P Brown, Liverpool.

Not that the English were used to anything very grand in terms of sanitation. The "Window Tax" was not repealed until 1851 which meant that even grand houses which had a room set apart for the purpose, probably forfeited the right to light and air, although the early Victorians recognised the connection between health and ventilation well enough. Lower down the social scale, privies were built apart from the houses and almost inevitably shared with other families in the street.

When the ceramics firm of Doulton & Co. of Lambeth, London, Paisley and Paris introduced their famous "Lambeth Patent Pedestal Combination Closet", it was advertised, (for use on dry land,) as a "water closet, slop sink and urinal, *combined*", and with that word, "combined", I think lay the major problem at sea. On board ship, passengers stuffed any old thing down the traps, using them like dustbins rather than that for which they were designed.

The relationship between sanitation and health was so well appreciated that when a major enquiry into health on the Australian run was conducted in 1854, the members of the enquiring body were told:

"We have generally put four WC's amidships but they have been found to be so great a nuisance that we have proposed to remove all but two – one in the female hospital and one for the single women and to put all the others on deck. They hardly ever get to Australia without being out of order. In the first place, the working of the ship deranges them and then the people who are put aboard are not in the habit of using that kind of convenience and they use it very ill, and throw bones and all kinds of things down it. They are the greatest nuisance that can possibly be aboard ship. It is almost impossible to prevent their leaking. The people do not

understand the plugs and they every now and then set the water going and do not turn it off and then they flood the decks. We have now tried to get them self-acting, but a thing which works very well on shore as self-acting will not act at sea. In fact I confess, we are at our wits' end on the subject of water closets." (Quotation of report, from J.O'Callaghan's "Saga of the S.S.G.B.")

Which lengthy introduction leads me to the construction of the two tiny companionways, immediately abaft the bitts on the fo'c's'le deck. These hatches lead down to the original heads which vented directly downwards from the flare in the ship's bow, a natural escapement. The other place in a ship where the natural shape of the vessel allowed this to happen was in the tuck of the stern, but sea captains disliked the proximity of WC's so close to their quarters, especially when the extra mess resulting from sea-sickness made conditions indescribably squalid. Apart from the 4 WC's in the fo'c's'le, the S.S.G.B. had the initial luxury of 26 WC's amidships, some with exclusive access from the ladies cabins.

A ship, rather like a hospital, is a great leveller. Those who can readily survive the discipline and indignities of a basic change in life-style soon establish themselves as the new elite. A voyage on the high seas creates a new 'pecking order' for the duration of the passage which transcends the social order of things on land. Thus, the natural balladeer, or the good story-teller, or even the clown, becomes, for the time being, an important member of the ship's company. The stuffy, the prudish or the self-styled grandiose person, take on a rather pathetic air when reduced by 'mal de mer', with its gruesome social consequences. It is a remarkable fact that the human body is able to withstand the tremendous gravitational forces exerted upon it in a space launch and flight, and even float about like a wingless insect, but subject it to a gentle rolling with modest pitch and toss, and the human frame is reduced to a state of unmentionable misery.

Contests, Conflicts and Competitions

It would be wrong of me to paint too dreary or sombre a picture of life aboard ship, particularly after the S.S.G.B. entered the Australian service in 1852, now in the hands of her new owners, Gibbs, Bright & Co., of Liverpool. A larger number of passengers (730 max), could now be carried following the refit by the new owners, which had included the addition of a deckhouse running the full length of the ship, and the removal of yet another mast. Various other quite extensive changes in the general arrangements meant a greater suitability for the long passage to Australia, but quite spoilt the lean and hungry look of the Atlantic Greyhound.

There is abundant evidence that enforced captivity aboard ship can produce a youthful spirit in both men and women. It is perhaps an arresting thought that only a ship can throw men and women together for a period of nearly three months with such a prolonged spell of inactivity. For many of the passengers it would be literally a 'once in a lifetime' experience, and they would never again in their lives be so physically close to one another for such a long period of time. It must have elicited both the best and the worst in people. Small wonder then, that there are reports of married women winking at unmarried men and some unsightly bouts of brawling between both sexes; of theft and cheating and carousing after lights out. On the whole, however, The *Great Britain* had a reputation for being a well run ship as compared with some others, borne out of the fact that she was commanded by two very able captains in succession, Bernard Matthews (1852–1854), and John Gray (1854–72). The latter was extremely popular and well respected; all the more devastating therefore was the manner of his death by suicide, or more correctly, his total disappearance on 26th November 1872. The only clue to his demise was the open square transom window of the Captain's quarters. The ship was 30 days out of Melbourne and was commanded on the rest of the homeward voyage by the First Officer.

On the Australian run, passengers danced to the ship's band; they ran contests of all kinds, placing bets on animals and wagers on each other; they dressed up in funny clothes and acted the fool as well as running informal theatrical productions; they slept on the deck when it was too hot to lie in their bunks, then snowballed each other, in the enormous weather variation which the voyage would encounter; they assisted with sailing the ship; they wrote up their diaries and printed their own journal – a news sheet which gave the opportunity to lampoon each other and let off some of the pent-up feelings they had about one another. Some of the articles, although sounding perhaps rather sentimental to us, also express the ambivalence of feeling about leaving their native land for the unknown, showing traces of doubt about the irrevocable step which they had taken.

Whisky drinking had to be periodically controlled by the Master's disciplinary intervention which on occasions would mean clamping the offenders in irons. Whisky was a double edged weapon. (How can something I love so much treat me so badly?) Certainly it helped to pass the hours in the Doldrums and silenced some into a stupefied state, but others were affected in the opposite way, leading to bouts of insults and fighting – yes, ladies included – which would inevitably result in the Captain having to intervene as judge and jury.

The attitude to sickness and death is interesting. We nowadays think of the 'Victorian way of death' as being accompanied by a great show of pomp and ceremony with prolonged mourning and black lace veils. Such contemporary reports as there are indicate that a much more perfunctory attitude was adopted aboard ship. The cadaver was weighted with large lumps of holystone and chucked over the side, not always to the accompaniment of the Book of Common Prayer. One must surmise therefore that during an epidemic of smallpox or yellow fever, one burial service after another would have done little for the morale of the ship and served only to increase the infection. Once an epidemic broke out, it would seep through the ship's company and probably linger until the end of the voyage. Some ships were quarantined and forbidden to land passengers until the disease had abated, which must have been enormously frustrating for all concerned. No wonder captains were forever emphasizing, against very long odds, the desirability of cleanliness and hygiene, which brings me back to where we came in.

Fig 217. B&P photo. Captain's bath. "The desirability of cleanliness". Note interesting position of plug hole!

LAUNCHING & OPERATING

The Launch Coronation Day, 2nd June 1981.

In December, 1844, the headache of getting the completed ship through the Upper Lock to the relative promise of freedom in the River Avon, was a serious matter, depending upon wind and tide as well as "the altering of the masonry of the lock", as Brunel so delicately put it.

The crowds were there, tens of thousands of people, on both sides of the lock, despite a severe frost and a biting east wind. The curiosity as to whether or not "the fattened weasel, grown too big to be released from its hole," would ever emerge unscathed was enough to hold the attention of both the optimistic and the pessimistic alike. The success or failure of human endeavour has always had the element of possible disaster as one of its major attractions for the spectator. The macabre questions silently and secretly pose themselves – will she sink, blow up, keel over, break her back or just plainly refuse to budge?

Brunel wrote a rather nervous letter to Guppy a few days after the undocking ceremony, in which he said, "If all goes well, we shall all gain credit, but 'Quod est scriptum est manet' – if the results disappoint anybody, I shall have to bear the storm and all that spite and revenge can do at The Admiralty."

Fig 218. (Below) The vessel waiting to be launched 2 June 1980. Fig 219. (Right) The author feeding the ballast chain into the aft chain locker.

The night before the launch of the model, pondering on nearly four years' sparetime work spent, and all the publicity which the building programme has received as the ship has grown through the different stages, I felt I shared by proxy some of the weight which Brunel felt on that day. The model was capable of a similar wide range of possible disasters, from the spectacular explosion to downright, abysmal failure, through some small detail missed at an early stage in the building schedule and long since forgotten.

One must, however, plan ahead as though nothing can possibly go wrong, even though the weather report was unfavourable, and gusting winds threatened to spring a mast before the model was even shipped into the transporting van. For this purpose, believing in the old adage

Fig 220. (Above) The moment of launch. Fig 221. (Right) "The fountain of foam in perfect miniature".

that more damage is caused to models in transit than by any operational tricks they may have to perform, I built an 8ft × 2ft launching ramp, with the idea that the model could be handled much more easily like this and even launched on the ramp in a familiar 'pontoon' style. Its width protects the yards and the stunsail booms, and even provides a little 'springiness', so essential to counteract the harsh ride in the back of an average van.

Much photography, even the uncorking and toasting ceremony, preceded the lowering of the vessel into the water. Immediately it was apparent that all the ballasting calculations had been over generous. Six lb in the forward chain locker and twelve in the aft brought her to the correct level, making an all up weight of 62lb. Just like the bride who is waiting at the door of the church, but is prevented from walking up the aisle by the demands of the official photographer, the ship longed to be free at last, but had to be held back – restrained even – whilst shutters clicked at two frames a second.

Her final release brought the original words of the "Liverpool Mail" correspondent to my mind:–

"... the contours presented to the eye are of the most exquisite grace – fine and beautifully rounded in her lines with a gentle sheer, she sits upon the water like a racing gig ..."

(Liverpool Mail, 12th, Dec. 1844)

To be truthful, I had not thought of this model as a sailing vessel which could operate simply and effectively under canvas alone, but as with the full size ship in her day, she does so with ease and charm. Her stunning good looks actually cast a charming spell on the launching party as we all saw for the first time the swan-like grace of her movement through the water.

The mischief of live steam soon changed the whole atmosphere at the waterside with its special brand of humour. From cold, the boiler took about 12 minutes to come to a working pressure; this was already well established; but how, oh how would the propeller perform? Therein lay the all important question. Quite suddenly at the stern there followed the sound of a thousand bubbles, water thrashing, and that fountain of foam so much a part of the original was there in perfect miniature. It was so much more than I could reasonably have hoped for, in total realism, and the turn of speed which was to follow made everyone laugh. She is grossly over-powered,

requiring the gas burner to be turned right down to what can only be described as a very low light in order to muzzle her. This is of course due to the efficiency of the 'Sheppard' return flue boiler and its proven ability to produce a large volume of steam for what is a very greedy but powerful engine. Manoeuvrability, with the addition of a large false rudder bolted over her own, allows an 8ft turning circle – some say it was even less. Given the performance of the prototype, which took half a mile to run a full circle, this modification has to be fitted on the model for use in relatively confined places. It is the only concession and compromise of this replica as against the prototype, and gives the model a lively response on the helm.

Far from being the operational nightmare I had imagined, the model worked like a dream, as though sharing some of the same magic charm as her big sister. She was totally watertight at the end of a four-hour session, with the loss of only one backstay which, I am ashamed to say, simply came undone. She is not, of course, finished, and already there is talk of mechanical feed pumps and reversing gear and stanchion rail and ship's bells – but I'll have none of it – it's three o'clock in the morning, and I'm off to bed.

William Mowll
3/6/81

Fig 222. (Left) Safely under radio control. Fig 223. (Below) The mischief of live steam.

REFLECTIONS

"I get by with a little help from my friends –
I get high with a little help from my friends –
I'm going to try with a little help from my friends."

(Lennon – McCartney)

The hallmark of this whole enterprise has been one of co-operation. I do not believe that any one person could have made this working model on his own, simply because of the variety and breadth of the skills required. I know this would upset some modellers, possibly even prevent them from tackling the task in the first place, particularly those who like to work exclusively on their own and consider it anathema to have anyone else involved. My own point of view is that a shared venture has much more pleasure and fun attached to it, and I also believe that co-operation produces superior results as those involved learn from one another's techniques.

The record of this book, and the illustrative material which it contains, is an attempt to open the workshop door a little wider than usual so that more people may see clearly exactly what it takes to produce a working model, and perhaps even to glimpse what it entails to produce a prototype.

If I need a defence for not having made every item myself, I am in good company. Brunel leant heavily upon the expertise of his friends in a sometimes unmerciful way, their fierce loyalties to him being stretched to breaking point. I would also like to underline the fact that the rescue and restoration programme has been a co-operative venture from its outset, using the skills and expertise of many busy men whose lives were already brimful before the intrusion of the S.S. *Great Britain* and all her heavy demands for attention.

This ship has always been about courage and conviction and not about who was the best engineer or ship designer of the age. The making and completion of the model has likewise been a commitment to prove that it is possible to relive those few brief years in history when sail and steam stood side by side, and to share in the excitement and wonder of the new discoveries of the Victorian Age.

May the experience give you, at least in some measure, the same pleasure it has given me in both the construction of the model ship and, as some will have it, the 'building' of this book.

W.M.

Characters Involved in the S.S. Great Britain Story, 1839–46

Isambard Kingdom Brunel FRS (1806–1859)
Under his father, Sir Marc Brunel, he was appointed Engineer in charge of the Thames Tunnel project (1826) at the age of 20. Chief engineer of the Great Western Railway which included the building of the Royal Albert Bridge at Saltash. Responsible for the design of the Clifton suspension bridge over the Avon Gorge, and the injudicious Atmospheric Railway in South Devon. Chief project engineer for the Great Western Steamship Co. and designer of the three 'Great' ships – the P.S. *Great Western* (1838), the S.S. *Great Britain* (1843), and the P.&S.S. *Great Eastern* (1859).

Sir Marc I. Brunel (1769–1849)
Father of I.K.B. Knighted on completion of the Thames Tunnel, 1841. Patentee of the inverted 'V' engine as used in the 1843 S.S.G.B.

Thomas R. Guppy, Esq.
Bristol merchant. Trained engineer with Maudslay Son & Field; widely travelled; ran Friars Sugar Refinery in Bristol; considerably wealthy; firm friend of Brunel from 1832; staunch supporter and sponsor; Director of the GWR & GWSSCO; Superintendent of the building of the S.S.G.B.

Captain Christopher Claxton, R.N.
Managing Director of the GWSSCO; Quay warden, Bristol Docks; retired naval officer; saved I.K.B.'s life on the *Great Western* in an outbreak of fire in Thames estuary (March 1838); Brunel leant heavily on his practical experience; put in charge of the salvage at Dundrum Bay, 1846.

William Patterson
Ship builder; gave his name to the dock at Wapping, in Bristol Harbour; in charge of building both the *Great Western* and the *Great Britain*, under the supervision of a building committee consisting of Guppy, Claxton and Brunel; Patterson drew up the hull lines for the S.S.G.B.

Sir Daniel Gooch, Bt.
Locomotive designer for the Great Western Railway; broad gauge enthusiast; Chief Locomotive Assistant to I.K.B., 1837; unswerving loyalty to Brunel.

Lt. James Hosken, R.N.
Premier Captain of the GWSSCO; held in high regard by the Company and passengers, but was responsible for stranding the S.S.G.B. in Dundrum Bay, in Co. Down, in circumstances never fully explained; he accepted full responsibility, but the incident spelt disaster for the Company, putting it into financial ruin.

William Froude, Esq., F.R.S. (1810–79)
Engineer, naval architect and mathematician; worked with Brunel on railway engineering projects, but famous for his studies of the behaviour of ship's hulls and hydrodynamics.

Joseph Walter
Contemporary marine artist, responsible for all major paintings of the S.S.G.B.

Francis Humphr(e)ys
Engineer in charge of building the original trunk engines for the first specification that the S.S.G.B. should be a paddle ship. The order to re-design the engines for screw propulsion proved too much for him. (Guppy replaced him.)

James Nasmyth (1808–90). Designed the steam hammer, 1839, which alone managed to forge the paddle shaft designed by Humphrys and marked a great step forward in the whole world of heavy engineering.

Characters Involved in the Rescue and Restoration of the S.S.G.B.

E.C.B. Corlett, MA, PhD, FEng, FRINA.
Ship designer, Burness, Corlett & Partners Ltd.; Home Office Assessor; honorary Naval Architect and technical adviser to the SS *Great Britain* Project in Bristol; author of "The Iron Ship", and, after his survey of the ship in 1968, initiator of the 1970 rescue of the wreck from the Falkland Islands.

Richard Goold-Adams, CBE.
Chairman of the Great Britain Project; author of "The Return of the Great Britain"; financed, with Dr Corlett, the first comprehensive survey of the wrecked ship in Sparrow Cove, near Port Stanley, in 1968.

Commander J.R. Blake, RN.
Project Director of the SS *Great Britain* Project Ltd., Great Western Dock, Bristol.

Commander James D. Richard, MA, CEng, MIMechE, MInstPI.
Mechanical Designer and Technical Historian, in charge of the engine room restoration work.

Charles Hill and Sons Ltd.
Shipbuilders and lessees of the original Great Western Dock at Bristol.

Jack Hayward, OBE.
Prime Benefactor of the Project; his unforgettable phrase, "I'll see the ship home," made possible the initial rescue of the S.S. *Great Britain* from the Falkland Islands at a cost of £150,000.

Ulrich Harms
German Towing Co. based in Hamburg; specialists in pontoon salvage.

Captain Hans Herzog
Skipper of Varius II, the 724 ton tug which towed the pontoon from the Falklands on the 7,400 mile journey home.

Horst Kaulen
Salvage expert, in charge of the operation of the submersible Pontoon.

Lord Euan Strathcona
Project representative who received the formal release of the ship from the Governor of the Falkland Islands, Sir Cosmo Haskard.

Karl Kortum
Director of the San Francisco Maritime Museum; responsible for a series of memorable photographs of the wrecked ship, who with *Bill Swigert*, and American engineer and businessman, unbeknown to the British salvors, were planning their own rescue attempt in the mid 60's; both had a deep interest in the ship over many years.

Eric Gadd
Printer in Bristol; local radio broadcaster with undying loyalty and enthusiasm for the rescue; refused to shave his beard or cut his hair until the ship came home.

Many, many others who are too numerous to mention, but who form the nucleus of support necessary to sustain and promote this remarkable ship in her resurrected state.

Bibliography

"The Iron Ship." E.C.B. Corlett, MA, PhD, FEng, MIMarE. Moonraker Press, 26 St Margaret's Street, Bradford on Avon, Wilts. SBN 239 00112 5. (Available at SSGB Project, Great Western Dock, Gas Ferry Road, Bristol BS1 6TY.)
"The Return of the Great Britain." Richard Goold Adams, Chairman of the S.S. *Great Britain* Project. Published by Weidenfeld and Nicholson, 11 St John's Hill, London SW11.
"The Great Britain." K.T. Rowland. Published by David and Charles (Publishers) Ltd., South Devon House, Newton Abbott, Devon.
"The Saga of the S.S. Great Britain." John O'Callaghan. Published by Rupert Hart Davis Ltd., 3 Upper James Street, London W1R 4BP.
"The Sway of The Grand Saloon." Prof John Malcolm Brinnin. Published by Macmillan, London Ltd., SBN 333 13612 8.
"Isambard Kingdom Brunel." L.T.C. Rolt. Published by the Longman Group Ltd. 1957.
"The S.S. Great Britain." Booklet published by Illustrated London News with the co-operation of the S.S. *Great Britain* Project, written and researched by Victoria Wegg-Prosser.
"Merchant Steamers and Motor Ships." H.P. Spratt, BSc, ASME. Science Museum Descriptive Cat. Pt. II.
"The History of Ships." Peter Kemp. Published by Orbis Publishing Ltd., 20–22 Bedfordbury, London WC2.
"The Oxford Companion to Ships & The Sea." Ed. by Peter Kemp. Published by Oxford University Press, Ely House, London W1.
"American Notes and Reprinted Pieces." Charles Dickens. Originally published by Chapman and Hall Ltd., 11 Henrietta Street, Covent Garden, London WC.
"Ships of the High Seas." Erik Abranson. Published by Peter Lowe, 2–4 Queen's Drive, London W3 0HA.
"Square Rigged Sailing Ships." David R. MacGregor. M.A.P. Published by Argus Books Ltd., 14 St James Road, Watford, Herts.
"Victorian and Edwardian Merchant Steamships." Basil Greenhill and Ann Giffard. B.T. Batsford Ltd, 4 Fitzhardinge Street, London W1H 0AH.
"The Blue Riband of The Atlantic." Tom Hughes. Published by Patrick Stephens Ltd., Bar Hill, Cambridge CB3 8EL.
"Ships for All." Frank C. Bowen. 1923. Published by Ward Lock and Co Ltd.
"The Liners." A History of the North Atlantic Crossing. Terry Coleman. Published by Penguin Books Ltd., Harmondsworth, Middlesex, England.
"Powered Ships. The Beginnings." Richard Armstrong. Published by Ernest Benn Ltd., 25 New Street Square, Fleet Street, London EC4A 3JA.
"The Illustrated Marine Encyclopedia." Capt H. Paasch 1890. Facsimile copy published by M.A.P. Argus Books Ltd., 14 St James Road, Watford Herts.
"Nare's Seamanship." 1862. Facsimile copy published by Unwin Bros Ltd., The Gresham Press, Old Woking, Surrey.
"The Techniques of Ship Modelling." Gerald Wingrove. Published by M.A.P. Argus Books Ltd., 14 St James Road, Watford, Herts.
"The World of Model Ships and Boats." Guy R. Williams. Published by Andre Deutsch Ltd., 105 Great Russel Street, London WC1.
"Ships in Miniature" Donald McNarry. Published by David and Charles, Newton Abbott, Devon.
"The New Larousse Encyclopedia of Mythology." Hamlyn, Astronaut House, Feltham, Middx.
"The S.S. Great Britain Project." Macmillan, London, Ltd. ISBN 0333 128079. Official Guide issued by S.S.G.B. Trading Ltd, Great Western Dock, Gas Ferry Road, Bristol BS1 6TY. Tel 0272 20680.
"The S.S. Great Britain." The Macmillan Press Ltd. SBN 128060.
"Brunel's Three Ships." R.J. Lumsden, in "Ships Monthly".

"The Victorian Scene." 1837–1901. Nicholas Bentley. Published by Weidenfeld & Nicholson, 5 Wimsley Street, London W1.

"Victorian Engineering." L.T.C. Rolt. Pelican.

"Model Boilers and Boilermaking." K.N. Harris. Argus Books Ltd., 14 St James Road, Watford, Herts.

"Machinery for Model Steamers." Ed. Percival Marshall, M.A.P. Technical Publication, Argus Books.

"Rope, Twine and Net Making." Anthony Sanctuary. Shire Publications Ltd., Album 51. Cromwell House, Church Street, Princes Risborough, Aylesbury, Bucks.

"The Anatomy of Nelson's Ships." C Nepean Longridge, MAP, Argus Books, 14 St. James Rd., Watford, Herts.

Specialist Suppliers

Allcraft Ltd, 11 Market Street, Watford, Herts. Tel. Watford 38131. Suppliers of 'Foundry Craft' sand casting kits.

Art Veneers Co. Ltd, Industrial Estate, Mildenhall, Suffolk. Mail order service for wood craftsmen.

Bassett Lowke (SM), Kingswell Street, Northampton.

Causer & Co, 216 Goldhawk Road, London W12. Tel. 01 749 3441. Plans enlarged or reduced by photography.

Cintride, range of abrasives, hand sanders.

Euro-Models, PO Box TK6, Twickenham TW1 2JD. Tel. 01 891 0342. Aeropiccola Vibro-saw; many specialist ship fittings.

Expo Drills Ltd, Unit 10, Sustanum Works, Titchfield, Hants. Tel. 03294 41752.

Fyne Fort Fittings, Golden Hill Fort, Freshwater, IOW PO Box 409TF. Steam fittings specialists.

The Guild of Master Craftsmen, Lewes.

H.G.H. Models Ltd, 6 Westminster House, Kew Road, Richmond, Surrey. Tel. 01 940 7489. Boat fittings, especially period.

Humbrol Ltd, Marfleet, Hull HU9 5NE. Tel. 0482 701191; Telex 52534.

Linden Lea Sails, 33 Bembridge Place, Leavesden, Watford, Herts.

Model & Allied Publications Ltd, 35 Bridge Street, Hemel Hempstead, Herts. Tel. 0442 41221. Publishers, 'Model Boats' etc.

Modelcraft, 5 Cross Street, Blaby, Leics. Tel. 0553 771397. Stuart Turner Suppliers.

Model Maker, 11 Poet's Walk, Penrith, Cumbria CA11 7HJ. Tel. 0768 65378. Timbers, fittings, full range Stuart Turner etc.

Myford Ltd, Beeston, Nottingham. Tel. 254222; Telex 37100. Lathes, millers etc.

Parry & Sons (Tools) Ltd, 325–333 Old Street, London EC1. Tel. 01 739 9422/3/4. Radial arm saw etc.

Parson's Controls Ltd, Worcester Road, Stourport, Worcs. Tel. Stourport 2551.

'Pressletta', Rufford Road, Southport, Merseyside PR9 8LE. Tel. 0704 27577.

P.T. Coatings Ltd, Four Pools Industrial Estate, Evesham, Worcs.

A. J. Reeves & Co, Holly Lane, Marston Green, Birmingham B37 7AW. Tel. 021 779 6831-2-3. Steam engines and equipment.

H. Richards & Son, Upton Snodsbury, Worcs. Automobile Engineers.

Stuart Turner Ltd, Henley-on-Thames, Oxon. Tel. 04912 2655. Manufacturers and suppliers of model steam engines and equipment.

Treetower Ltd, Boilermaker, G. Sheppard, 10 Teewell Hill, Staple Hill, Bristol BS16 5PA. Tel. 0272 560 869. Boilers, burners etc.

Whitemans Bookshop, 7 Orange Grove, Bath BA1, 1LP. Tim Graham.

INDEX